PHILOSOPHICAL ANTHROPOLOGY:
AN INTRODUCTION

D1608118

PHILOSOPHICAL ANTHROPOLOGY:
AN INTRODUCTION

Midwest Theological Forum
Downers Grove, Illinois

Midwest Theological Forum
4340 Cross Street, Suite 1 • Downers Grove, Illinois 60515 USA
Phone: (630) 541-8519 • Fax: (331) 777-5819
mail@mwtf.org • www.theologicalforum.org

Philosophical Anthropology, An Introduction
Original Title: *Antropologia Filosofica, Una introduzione*
Second Revised and Corrected Edition
Copyright © 2007 – Edusc srl
Via Sant'Agostino, 7/A – 00186 Roma

This English edition copyright © 2014, 2015, 2017, Rev. James Socias
Third Printing, 2017
ISBN 978-1-936045-76-1

Authors: José Angel Lombo and Francesco Russo
Translator: Piers Amodia
Publisher: Rev. James Socias
Editor in Chief: Jeffrey Cole
Design and Production: Stephen J. Chojnicki

ACKNOWLEDGEMENTS

The editor would like to thank EDUSC for giving permission to translate *Antroplogia Filosofica, Una introduzione*, Seconda edizione riveduta e corretta (Rome, 2007). He also extends thanks to all who have collaborated on the edition of this book.

Disclaimer: The editor of this book has attempted to give proper credit to all sources used in the text. Any miscredit or lack of credit is unintended and will be corrected in the next edition.

Library of Congress Cataloging-in-Publication Data

Lombo, José Angel.
  [Antropologia filosofica. English]
  Philosophical anthropology : an introduction / José Angel Lombo, Francesco Russo. -- English edition.
    pages cm
  Includes bibliographical references and index.
  ISBN 978-1-936045-76-1
1. Philosophical anthropology. I. Russo, Francesco. II. Title.
  BD450.L574413 2014
  128--dc23

2014004112

Table of Contents

PART TWO: PERSONAL SELF-FULFILLMENT, BETWEEN RELATIONALITY AND HISTORICITY

Foreword

Mihi quæstio factus sum.[1] If there is one subject we should know well, that subject is the human person because it is what we are and what those with whom we are in continual contact are. Why, then, is it important to reflect upon this subject? Precisely because it directly concerns us and our own lives. Thus, as Plato wrote, a philosopher, even at the cost of becoming an object of derision, never ceases "to account" for his existence. "What a human being is and what is proper for such a nature to do or bear different from any other, this he inquires and exerts himself to find out."[2]

It is not always easy to enter into this field because one may come up against very different ways of dealing with the question; indeed, we believe it is possible to agree, at least to some extent, with the following affirmation of Heidegger:

> No other age has had so many and varied conceptions about man as the present. Never before as today has knowledge about man been presented so insistently and fascinatingly. Yet it is also true that no age has known less than ours about what man is. Never has man assumed such a problematic aspect as in our own time.[3]

That this observation is not unjustified is shown by the fact that, especially during the 1950s and 1960s, there was a recurring tendency to speak about the "problem of man" as may be seen in the titles of works by, among others, M. Buber and by G. Marcel, which used that literal expression.[4]

Aware of this difficulty, the purpose of the book we are presenting here (in which, with respect to the earlier editions, various modifications and corrections have been introduced) is to guide readers to

---

1. "I have become a question to myself." Augustine, *Confessions*, 10, 33, 50.
2. Plato, *Theaetetus*, 174 B; in the dialogue these words are attributed to Socrates.
3. M. Heidegger, *Kant und das Problem der Metaphysik*, in *Gesamtausgabe. I. Abteilung: Veröffentlichte Schriften 1910–1976*, Band 3 [Klostermann: Frankfurt am Main 1991, p. 209]. In this context, Heidegger refers in a footnote to the work of Max Scheler, *Die Stellung des Menschen im Kosmos*.
4. Cf. M. Buber, *Between Man and Man*, translated by Ronald Gregor Smith. [London—New York: Routledge, 2002] (the book was published for the first time in German in 1954); G. Marcel, *L'homme problématique*. Paris: Aubier-Montaigne 1955. Apart from these two famous texts, other books of philosophical anthropology have used the same expression in the title. A brief analysis of man's current cultural disintegration is to be found in S. Palumbieri, *L'uomo, questa meraviglia. Antropología filosófica I. Trattato sulla costituzione antropologica* [Rome: Urbaniana University Press, 1999, pp. 27–36].

reflect upon the human person. It does not intend to be a treatise upon philosophical anthropology in the strict sense but an introduction to the study of that subject — an introduction that seeks to offer the fundamental elements for such study yet without delving exhaustively into the details of each subject and without dwelling on more specialized questions or on all ongoing debates.

In order to keep to our purpose, we have chosen to adopt a concise style and to divide the work into relatively short chapters. This latter characteristic inevitably brings the risk of an apparent fragmentation, yet it should make the work easier to read and to consult. The book is divided into two distinct and separate parts: the first (entitled "The Human Person: A Corporeal-spiritual Living Being") uses an analytical method to reflect upon the human person as a living being in the world, possessing his own fundamental properties; the second (entitled "Personal Self-fulfillment: Between Relationality and Historicity") adopts a synthetical and dynamic perspective to demonstrate the particularity of human existence as characterized by freedom.

Philosophical anthropology cannot but be metaphysical anthropology in the Aristotelian sense, in other words, a philosophical reflection that extends to the ultimate, the radical, causes and principles of human reality. For this reason, the book, and the first half in particular, draws from classical thought, especially Aristotelian-Thomistic thought, in order to analyze man in metaphysical terms. Following a brief explanation of the role of philosophical anthropology (Chapter 1), we begin by explaining the notion of life and the various levels of life before then examining the vital principle, i.e., the soul (Chapters 2 and 3), which pervades the body of the living being and makes it an organism (Chapter 4). The activity of the living being is accomplished through operational faculties, or principles (Chapter 5), which enable vegetative and sense functions, both external and internal, to be performed (Chapters 6 and 7). In the human person cognitive activity reveals its highest grade of immanence in intellective knowledge (Chapter 8), the role of which helps bring us to understand the particularity of the dynamism of human beings and especially the nature of their freedom (Chapter 9). Having reflected upon affectivity and sexuality (Chapters 10 and 11), Part One concludes with Chapter 12, dedicated to the spirituality and immortality of the person.

Chapter 13, on the notion of the human person, acts as a foundation for the entire second part of the book. It is the comprehension of personal identity, ontological and existential, that enables us to understand why the human being is called to fulfill himself in a manner that conforms to the dignity of the person (Chapter 14). This self-fulfillment comes about constitutively in relations with others (Chapter 15) and within a culture (Chapter 16), which is a vehicle of the values to which the behavior of an individual refers (Chapter 17). Self-fulfillment as relational individuals requires our involvement in work, the idea of which is better understood with reference to celebration and play (Chapter 18), yet it is above all evident that human beings achieve self-fulfillment in time and history, projecting themselves towards the future and towards eternity (Chapter 19).

In concluding this brief presentation, the words of St. Augustine come to mind: "What each man is today, man himself has difficulty in knowing. Yet to some extent he knows what he is today, but he does not know what he will be tomorrow."[5] This highlights, among other things, the importance of uniting theoretical reflection to concrete reality through a constant effort of application and verification. Our duty to understand is never ending, and this is particularly true for self-understanding because the human person is not a static object and can understand himself only with reference to that which surpasses and transcends him. As Plato says, only in comparison with that which is "utterly and perfectly righteous… the true cleverness of a man is found, and also his worthlessness and cowardice."[6]

5. Augustine, *Sermo* 46, 27.

6. Plato, *Theaetetus*, 176 C. In the text, Socrates is speaking of God, who is always "supremely just."

CHAPTER 1

PHILOSOPHICAL ANTHROPOLOGY, OR THE PHILOSOPHY OF MAN

1. PHILOSOPHICAL REFLECTION ON THE HUMAN PERSON

Many areas of knowledge concern the human person or identify their objective as being able to elaborate an *anthropology*, that is, in etymological terms, a discourse or a treatise about man. But in each of these areas a "sectorial" approach is used, in that one or another aspect of human existence is examined, and hence the noun "anthropology" is accompanied by an adjective circumscribing the scope of the investigation.

Thus, although the terminology used is not always the same, we have *cultural anthropology*, which studies the usages and customs of human societies as they are structured over time as expressions of specific relationships with others and with the environment, and *psychological anthropology*, which studies human behavior from the point of view of mental dynamics in order to understand how psychological identity is constituted and how personality disorders and disturbances arise. To cite another example, *social anthropology* analyzes the dynamics of relations between individuals in order to highlight the elements common to the various forms of society. Finally there is *ethnological anthropology*, which studies human groups, describing and comparing their shared traits in association with the geographical, historical, and climactic conditions in which they live.[1]

As may be seen, each of these scientific disciplines concerns itself with just a single aspect, important though it may be, of the human person; but each cannot, in itself, comprehend man in all his rich-

---

1. There is also *physiological*, or *physical*, *anthropology*, which deals with the somatic traits of individuals, and *paleoanthropology*, which studies fossilized human remains. In an even more specialized perspective, there is also *criminal anthropology*.

ness and complexity. What they are, in fact, are scientific-experimental analyses (i.e., based on observation, on empirical verification), which cannot account for the person in himself; that is, seen globally and not from a particular point of view.

Philosophical anthropology, on the other hand, reflects upon man in order to understand him in his entirety, grasping the fundamental principles of his existence in the world and his behavior. Hence, it could be said that, whereas science investigates *how* the human individual manifests himself toward his environment and his fellow man, philosophy asks itself about the *why* of human beings, about the ultimate principles of their existence and activity.[2] The difference between the scientific and the philosophical approaches to the human person can also be expressed by saying that philosophy seeks to answer the question, *Who is the human person?* while the aforementioned scientific disciplines are more concerned with, *How does he act? How does he evolve?* and, *How does he interact with others?* This does not mean that the two sectors cannot communicate with one another; quite the opposite: Philosophy must take the results of science into account, for they will often stimulate further study or the reformulation of certain theses, and scientists, in their methodological autonomy, must seek not to lose sight of this area of knowledge, which constitutes the *source of meaning*.

The expression *"philosophical anthropology"* is a relatively recent one in philosophy. Though it has remote roots in I. Kant, the term became consolidated in the twentieth century thanks particularly to the works of M. Scheler, H. Plessner, and A. Gehlen. And although these authors give the discipline a precise connotation (that of reflecting upon man above all on the basis of biological data and of comparison with animals), this book aims to present a philosophical anthropology beyond that thematic limitation, reflecting on the human person in the more general sense indicated above.[3]

---

2. Cf. S. Palumbieri, *L'uomo, questa meraviglia: Antropología filosófica I: Trattato sulla costituzione antropologica* (Rome: Urbaniana University Press, 1999), 51–52.

3. The expression *philosophical anthropology* is used to designate philosophical currents very different from one another. An interesting overview is found in E. Conti, *"Antropologia filosofica in Italia," "La Scuola Cattolica,"* 31–74 (2004).

2. THE METHOD OF PHILOSOPHICAL ANTHROPOLOGY

We must now consider what methodology to adopt in our philosophical reflections upon the human person. The *analytical method* alone, with which the individual phenomena or each aspect of the person is examined, is inadequate, for if indeed, on the one hand, it would have the advantage of yielding precise results and definitions, on the other we would achieve the effect of dismantling the individual into an agglomerate difficult to reassemble into a unitary whole. Yet the *synthetical method* alone, which studies the individual as an already extant totality, is also inadequate, for if, in one way, it would make it possible to gain some understanding of the whole, in another it would ignore the particularity of the various human dimensions and neglect the dynamism of the individual, i.e., the fact that he is an open, not closed or static, being.

We must, then, adopt a different approach, one that may be defined as *systemic*, which is to say that we approach the human person as a "system," the elements of which are in close coordination with one another. These elements are understood with reference to the whole, and the whole requires the interaction of the individual elements. Thus, for example, human speech cannot be fully understood if it is considered only as an isolated faculty, but it can be understood with reference to the existence of a rational, relational, and cultural individual; at the same time, linguistic communication (which may be nonverbal) is fundamental for the development of the whole individual.

In order to follow this *systemic approach* in the philosophical study of the human person, two aspects come together: an *analytical-inductive* aspect, which seeks to work back from the observable phenomena to the principles, and a *synthetical-deductive* aspect, which seeks to apply the principles to the phenomena and gathers the information emerging therefrom. As will be seen, in the following chapters we will seek to take both these aspects into consideration without, however, forgetting an important peculiarity of this particular philosophical discipline: Let us see what it is.

Philosophical anthropology reflects upon the human person, but human beings are not objects of study in the same way as, say, a fragment of bauxite, a rhododendron, or a beetle. First of all, as is also the case with the objects just mentioned, there is a degree of *pre-comprehension*; in other words, of prior knowledge of what they are and what man is. They are not entirely unfamiliar, and it is not possible to neglect completely what we already know; at most we can rectify our opinion if we discover it to be incorrect. But the difference lies mainly in the fact that reflection upon the human being is linked to *self-comprehension*, in other words, to the knowledge I have of myself as a human being and to comparison with my fellows. This primal and fundamental experience cannot be eliminated; indeed, on more than one occasion it will serve as a solid starting point for philosophical analysis.[4]

3. Philosophical Anthropology as It Relates to Other Fields of Philosophy and Theology

We have mentioned the relationship between philosophical anthropology and other areas of knowledge about man, but we must say also something about its relationship with other areas of philosophy. The two subjects with which its connection is more obvious are ethics and metaphysics. Anthropology acts as a foundation for the former, while the latter acts as a foundation for anthropology.

All ethics presuppose some form of philosophical anthropology, a precise conception of the human being. Firstly, because to speak of ethics means to hold that man is free; otherwise, it would make no sense to worry about duty, norms, responsibility, and so on. Secondly, because whatever the orientation of philosophical ethics, it accentuates a particular aspect of the human person; for example, the ethics of virtue hold that the individual is oriented toward a happy life in the sense of a life that fully conforms to the good of man, while hedonistic ethics hold that morality consists in the search for pleasure and hence emphasize the affective and sensory sphere of human life.

Philosophical anthropology's relationship with metaphysics is already implicit in what we explained above. When we reflect profoundly upon man we seek to understand his being as the radical

---

4. Mounier makes a useful observation on the subject: "It is not the case, then, that stones exist, trees exist, animals exist, and human persons exist, being nothing other than self-propelling trees or animals more astute than others. The person is not an object (even the most marvelous object in the world) that we understand as we do other objects, from the outside. It is the only reality we are able to know and, at the same time, to construct from within" (E. Mounier, *Personalism* [New York: Routledge & Paul, 1970], 11).

foundation of human expressions. Since metaphysics is the part of philosophy that concerns itself with the ultimate principles of reality, it follows that philosophical anthropology cannot but be metaphysical anthropology (implicitly if not explicitly) because it will have to utilize metaphysical concepts such as power, action, matter, nature, and person. For example, in order not to limit himself to merely describing free will, the philosopher must ask himself about the basis of freedom, about its relation with truth and values, about the problem of the relationship between freedom and human nature, and so on. Although the historiographical references in coming chapters will be fairly limited, it can be said that, for many modern and contemporary philosophers who dedicate serious study to the human person, the bond between anthropology and metaphysics is implicitly present, despite certain critical observations they may make about a particular way of understanding the role of metaphysics.[5]

Apart from ethics and metaphysics, there is also a very evident link between philosophical anthropology and other philosophical disciplines that deal with the behavior of man, his organization of society, and his openness to transcendence; for example, political philosophy, sociological philosophy, the philosophy of culture and art, and the philosophy of religion. In these cases, too, the slant given to the subject matter is determined by a specific view of the human being.

Finally we would like to mention philosophical anthropology's relationship with theology and in particular with deliberations on the content of Christian Revelation. The study of the human being leads us to ask, among other things, whether the individual is entirely circumscribable to the material universe or if there is something incorporeal in him, whether his longing for happiness is destined to remain forever unsatisfied or if it is oriented toward a transcendent dimension, whether his demise marks the irrevocable end of everything or if the self survives death. These are questions that the philosophy of man cannot elude *a priori* because to do so would not only limit its area of analysis but also risk giving a partial interpretation to certain fundamental questions. In asking itself these and similar questions, reason can supply a number of precise answers, but it finds itself also facing problems the solution to which is partly beyond its reach — such as questions about man's ultimate destiny

---

5. This is evident, among other places, in the aforementioned book by E. Mounier, *Personalism*.

after death—or the drama of evil, which always contains an unfathomable nucleus. Christian Revelation throws a light on these subjects thanks to which reason can extend its area of investigation even beyond its own limitations.[6]

Furthermore, even with explicitly philosophical questions, Revelation can offer a valid aid to speculation. Think of the important role that the biblical notion of man created in the image and likeness of God has played in the elaboration of the philosophical notion of the person and the understanding of his universal dignity. We cannot forget that our culture is so steeped in the contribution of Christianity that to seek to exclude it from reflections on the human being would be practically impossible. In conclusion, therefore, philosophical anthropology, on the one hand, makes a necessary contribution to the theological task of understanding revealed truth, while on the other the philosophy of man is challenged by the contents of the Revelation, which stimulate and enhance the work of reason.

SUMMARY OF CHAPTER 1

Many sciences deal with the human person, but each tends to concentrate on one single aspect. Philosophical anthropology, on the other hand, reflects upon man in his entirety, seeking to understand his ultimate principles, in other words, the "ultimate why" man exists and acts as he does. Philosophical anthropology seeks to respond to the question, "Who is the human person?"; to reach an answer, it must also take account of the contributions made by the other human sciences. The methodology of philosophical anthropology has to be both analytical-inductive (working back from lived experience to ultimate principles) and synthetical-deductive (applying the principles to observable phenomena in order to gather new data).

Philosophical anthropology is the foundation of ethics and is, in its turn, founded on metaphysics. Since the human person is oriented toward transcendence, philosophical anthropology remains open to theology and is receptive to the light coming from divine Revelation.

---

6. A recent brief exposition of the relationship between faith and reason is to be found in John Paul II, encyclical letter *Fides et Ratio* (September 14, 1998).

CHAPTER 2

LIFE AND THE DEGREES OF LIFE

1. THE NOTION OF LIFE

When we talk about life or describe a particular being as "alive," we are referring to a certain kind of activity. In fact, we distinguish a living from a nonliving being because the former moves "alone" or "by itself." But if we observe reality more carefully, we discover a movement that is not just movement in space: Some living beings, such as the plants and certain animals, do not travel from one place to another, yet they are nonetheless described as "living." With the word "life," then, we refer to an activity and, more precisely, to the activity that a being undertakes on the basis of itself and affecting itself, through growth, nutrition, and reproduction.

Thus, even if something lifeless is not entirely static — it may undergo a certain movement — we recognize that such movement is nothing more than inertia and thus that the thing is, in fact, inert. Hence, one proof indicating the presence of life is the capacity to "react" to stimuli, for, while an inert being has, of itself, no spontaneity or movement, a living being "reacts" to external factors and makes a movement of its own.[1]

For a living being life is not an extrinsic or accessory factor. Life cannot be reduced to some particular action even though particular actions are evidence of life: An individual can perform certain actions precisely *because* it is alive, not vice versa. Observing this fact, Aristotle affirmed, "In the case of living things, their being is to live."[2] Indeed, for living beings there is not only continuity but also identity between being and living. For example, it would make no sense to affirm, "This thing exists; it is large and it is *also* alive." For living beings, life is not some accidental factor that is added to

---

1. Cf. S. Palumbieri, *L'uomo, questa meraviglia: Antropología filosófica I: Trattato sulla costituzione antropologica* (Rome: Urbaniana University Press, 1999), 149.
2. Aristotle, *De Anima*, II 4, 415 b 13.

being but something essential so that, for them, not living would simply mean ceasing to exist.

2. LIFE AS IMMANENCE AND TRANSCENDENCE

Thus, we come to understand that living beings have a more perfect degree of existence than do nonliving beings: To live is to exist in a superior way. But in what does this greater perfection consist? Briefly, we may say that life can be interpreted in terms of two fundamental aspects: as a capacity for immanence and as a capacity for transcendence.

2.1. Immanence

Generally speaking, the actions of a living being are distinguished by the fact that they remain within the agent that accomplishes them. This means that they are not merely an effect of external reality, and that they do not modify only that reality. Rather, they are undertaken by the living being principally on the basis of itself and acting on itself. Food, information, and memories, for example, remain within the living being and, indeed, make it what it is. Thus we see a correlation between the "remaining" of the activity and the "self" of the living being. This characteristic is given the name of "immanence" and may be defined as a kind of "interiority" of activity.[3]

In any case, it is clear that immanence is present in varying degrees and that a greater capacity for immanence reveals a greater perfection of life. As St. Thomas says, "The more sublime a nature is, the more that which emanates from it will be intimately part of it."[4] Broadly speaking, any action by a living being is immanent because it always involves some form of self-movement, in other words, of activity upon the self. Thus we describe as immanent such actions as feeding, growing, and reproducing, which are also to be seen in plants. However, these activities remain in the agent only very imperfectly because they are limited to their external effects and denote a very low degree of "interiority."

Some living beings, however, have capacities superior to those we have just mentioned, as is the case with animals that are able to recognize reality and to tend toward it. A sensation or a desire remains

---

3. Cf. J. Vicente Arregui and J. Choza, *Filosofía del hombre: Una antropología de la intimidad* (Madrid: Rialp, 1991), 59–60.

4. Thomas Aquinas, *Summa Contra Gentiles*, l. IV, c. 11, n. 1: "*Quanto aliqua natura est altior, tanto id quod ex ea emanat, magis ei est intimum.*"

in the living being not only more stably but also more profoundly and more internally than, say, food. Even so, such actions have their origin in an external stimulus and thus their immanence depends to a large extent on the surroundings.

Finally, there are certain activities that not only remain within the living being and at a deeper level but also have their origins in the being itself. These are the actions of the intellect and the will, which are specific to man. Indeed, intellectual and voluntary actions — which we will consider later — are much more stable than any other activity, and thus they remain within the being with the highest degree of immanence.

2.2. Transcendence

Immanence, then, is an unmistakeable characteristic of life, but it should not be mistaken for a kind of closure or self-sufficiency. Immanence contrasts with dispersion, or what may be called "transitivity." Such dispersion would cause the living being no longer really to be "itself"; in other words, it would cause it to fragment into its various activities without preserving an overall unity. Thus, immanence does not oppose the relationship of the living being with others; rather, it is complementary to the capacity for transcendence.[5]

In very general terms, transcendence means openness and breadth as opposed to the closure and limitedness of nonliving beings. St. Thomas mentions this expressly: "The action of the living being transcends the action of nature which operates in inanimate things."[6] This openness implies overcoming the limits of existence through action. A living being is always able to produce an effect superior to the starting conditions of its action; for example, in nutrition certain external elements are integrated in order to maintain and develop a being's physical structure; in perception the influence of external reality is assimilated as information useful for a being's activity.

As with immanence, the capacity for transcendence is also present in living beings in differing degrees, which reveals differing levels of perfection of life. The most elementary level is to be found in the

---

5. We can say that immanence and transcendence are correlative in the sense that a higher capacity for immanence corresponds to a higher capacity for transcendence. On this subject, see Thomas Aquinas, *Quæstio Disputata De Anima*, a. 13, c. We will return to the subject from an existential viewpoint in Chapter 14.

6. *Ibid*: "*Actio enim animæ transcendit actionem naturæ in rebus inanimatis operantis.*"

plants, which interact with their surroundings through the activities of nutrition, growth, and, in particular, procreation.[7] Yet their openness to reality through such actions is very limited. Plants do not, indeed, "have" experience of reality, rather they merely "undergo" phenomena that affect their physical structure.[8]

Transcendence is present in a higher degree when there is an "experience" of reality, and this is possible only through knowledge and inclination, something we will discuss in coming chapters. Through these activities, which are specific to animals, living beings are open to *any corporeal reality*.[9] In this context, St. Thomas wrote some significant remarks: "In material existence—which is circumscribed by matter—each thing is only what it is; hence, this stone is only this stone. On the other hand, in immaterial existence—which is broad and in some way infinite, not being circumscribed by matter—a reality is not only what it is but also, in some way, all other realities."[10]

Beyond the transcendence of sensory knowledge and inclination is the transcendence of the intellect and the will. Through these activities the rational being—man—is open to the experience of *all reality*, not just corporeal reality. Thus, Aristotle said that a being endowed with intellect and will "is, in a certain way, all things."[11] In some sense, the human capacity for transcendence can be described as unlimited, and this links back, as we will see, to the natural desire for God and to happiness.

---

7. Thomas Aquinas states that procreation is the most perfect of the vegetative operations and that it is close to sensitive life because it opens the living being to external reality: cf. *Summa Theologiæ*, I, q. 78, a. 2, c.

8. In plants, openness is very similar to exteriority (i.e., simple external contact) precisely because of their low level of immanence. Only openness "from within" can be called "transcendence," and not mere "transitivity" in the definition given above. Once again, the close link between immanence and transcendence is evident.

9. Corporeal reality is physical reality, in other words, the reality located within a specific time and space.

10. Thomas Aquinas, *In De Anima*, l. 2, lec. 5, n. 5: "*Secundum esse materiale, quod est per materiam contractum, unaquæque res est hoc solum quod est, sicut hic lapis, non est aliud quam hic lapis: secundum vero esse immateriale, quod est amplum, et quodammodo infinitum, inquantum non est per materiam terminatum, res non solum est id quod est, sed etiam est quodammodo alia.*"

11. Cf. Aristotle, *De Anima*, III 8, 431 b 21.

3. GENERAL CHARACTERISTICS OF LIVING BEINGS

Having seen in what, in its fundamental aspects, the perfection of life consists, we must now analyze the characteristics that are generally to be found in all living beings. It is necessary, first of all, to make an important distinction. We have said that living beings have the capacity to move themselves, but we must also note that, depending upon their activity, they are also endowed with a particular structure. Indeed, without an appropriate arrangement of its parts, a living being would not be able to carry out its activities. In nature there is a reciprocal correspondence between structure and dynamism.[12] For this reason, we will consider the characteristics of living beings on the basis of these two viewpoints: their *structure* and their *dynamism.*

3.1. Constituent, or Structural, Characteristics

From the point of view of its structure, a living being is characterized by its *unity* and its *organicity.*

3.1.1. Unity

A living being possesses a specific form of cohesion among its component parts, which renders it physically stable. The being is not disjointed but a totality of conjoined parts. Unity means stability but not rigidity, and hence cohesion is not incompatible with the power to change; on the contrary, it is the condition that makes change possible. If the living being did not have sufficient stability, any change would cause its destruction.

All living beings maintain their unity through their own operations, and that unity is so fundamental that, if it is lost, death, or the end of life, is the result. It is true that in some living things division does not necessarily mean cessation of life, but in these cases partition is their way of reproduction (a process known as "binary fission"), and anyway it is clear that the result of such division is not one divided being but a number of different beings. Life, then, implies unity, and division is incompatible with the life of the same individual.

---

12. Cf. M. Artigas and J.J. Sanguineti, *Filosofía della natura* (Florence: Le Monnier, 1989), 217–236.

3.1.2. Organicity

The aforementioned unity does not signify the uniformity of a living being's component parts; these parts do not form a homogeneous whole but an organized system. The term "organism" expresses precisely the internal order of the parts, and this means that the relationship between them is not extrinsic but intrinsic within the constituted whole. In fact, each part has a different function, but the relationship among them all has its direction, or goal, in the conservation or enhancement of the entire individual. By contrast, in inert things we see that the parts are barely differentiated; clearly an order does exist — think, for example, of the crystallization of minerals — but it is a uniform and, so to say, monolithic order. This implies that the division of these realities is not significant for their nature; for example, a fragment of rock is still a rock, not dissimilar from other fragments of rock.

A monolithic being is by definition static and passive,[13] whereas a living being can move itself, inasmuch as some of its parts act upon the others.[14] Thus we come to understand that the organic consistency of the living being — the differentiation and order of its component parts — is what enables it to act by itself and upon itself. It is precisely because they constitute an organic whole that the parts of the living being are called "organs." The greater the order between the organs, the greater the capacity to act and the more perfect life is.

3.2. Dynamic, or Operational, Characteristics

As regards its activity, or dynamism, a living being is characterized by its *self-movement* and its *adaptation*.

3.2.1. Self-movement

From the point of view of its dynamism, the living being's most obvious and testable ability is to move itself. We have already seen that such movement must not be understood exclusively as the power to move from one place to another but, more generally, as the ability to

---

13. Nondistinction among the parts must not be mistaken for simplicity. God is simple but not inert or uniform; he lives in the most exalted way. On the other hand, all created things are composite, and their simplicity is therefore always relative. Generally speaking, what determines the perfection of life is not the multiplicity of parts but the intrinsic order among them.

14. Cf. Thomas Aquinas, *Quæstio Disputata De Veritate*, q. 22, a. 3, c; *Summa Contra Gentiles*, II, 48, n. 3.

undertake an activity starting from itself and acting on itself. In this context, it is important to distinguish the self-movement of living beings from that of machines. In fact, certain machines ("robots") are designed in such a way as to be able to accomplish actions without the apparent intervention of external factors, i.e., "alone." Nonetheless, the origin of their movement is not intrinsic because it does not lie in the machine itself but in its constructor. In the natural world, on the other hand, the origin of operations is intrinsic to each being and is called the "nature" of that being.[15] Hence, the movement of living beings is distinct from that of machines as the natural is distinct from the artificial.[16]

Self-movement may be considered at numerous levels, as numerous as are the activities of living beings themselves. Self-movement as self-construction is particularly interesting: The living being is at one and the same time, in differing degrees, the architect and the result of its own activity. This is observable in all its actions (nutrition, growth, procreation, etc.) but particularly in knowledge and inclination. Through these activities, in fact, living beings acquire the experience necessary for their own conservation and enhancement. Self-construction can, then, be extremely complex: The experience acquired and conserved by an animal is already a form of self-construction and becomes even more perfect in intelligent beings capable of acquiring habits—think, for example, of the process of education—and creating a culture.

3.2.2. Adaptation

Closely associated with its self-movement, the living being also has the capacity to adapt to its surroundings and to react to the stimuli emerging therefrom. This means, on the one hand, that a being's relationship with things is not merely passive and, on the other, that this relationship is in some way conserved and elaborated inside the being itself. It is highly significant that all living beings (plants, animals, and man) undergo or develop certain mutations depending upon climate, geography, or other external factors. In plants,

---

15. In the light of Christian Revelation we know that the entire universe was created by God and, consequently, has its origin in him. God could be described as an Artist, the "Constructor" of the world, but he is so at a level infinitely superior to that of created beings because *everything* and *all things* come from him.

16. It must, however, be reiterated that externally, at the phenomenological level, there may be no discernable difference. Only by transcending the phenomena in search of their foundation, or origin, does the effective difference between artificial and natural things become evident.

the relationship with the environment is purely physical; in other words, it consists in an exchange of material elements. In animals, this relationship also takes place through knowledge and inclination and, hence, is much more complex than in plants. Thus, animals can develop strategies for attack and defense, modify the environment to make it more agreeable (nests, dens, etc.), and organize themselves into forms of group life. For his part, man is capable of developing much more complex forms of adaptation through his reason and will such as cultivating the earth, raising animals, building, cultural achievements (science, art, technology, games), forms of social life (institutions, laws), and so on.

4. Degrees of Life and Operations of Life

Now that we have an adequate idea of the general characteristics of living beings, we must seek to identify, still at a very general level, the differences among those beings. In the course of our explanations, we have made repeated reference to the differing degrees of perfection of life. The fundamental aspects of life — immanence and transcendence — and the general characteristics of living beings — structural and dynamic — are both present in varying degrees, and this enables us to establish different levels among living beings.

On the basis of what we have thus far explained, we may briefly say that the degree of life is determined by the degree of immanence and of the transcendence of its operations. Thus we can establish three fundamental levels: the life of plants, the life of irrational animals, and the life of man. These levels are called, respectively, *vegetative life, sensitive life,* and *intellective life.*[17]

4.1. Vegetative Life

Plants are distinguished by the fact that they perform three kinds of operations: nutrition, growth, and procreation. Through growth the living being acquires its appropriate quantities and proportions. It could be said that this is the most basic of life's operations because it is the essential expression of the idea of self-movement which, as we have seen, is a characteristic peculiar to life. Through nutrition the being assimilates (correctly speaking, it metabolizes) external reality and uses it to maintain its own physical structure. Finally, through procreation, the being produces another being similar to

17. Cf. Aristotle, *De Anima*, II, 3, 414a 29–415a 13; Thomas Aquinas, *Summa Theologiæ*, I, q. 78, a. 1.

itself and thus acquires a certain perpetuity, although this quality is more correctly to be attributed to the species as a whole.

In plants these functions are associated with certain fixed move-ments—natural proclivities—over which the being has no control, for example, the movement toward water, toward light, etc. Gener-ally speaking, we can say that vegetative operations have as their object the body of the living being itself,[18] its survival, its develop-ment, and the propagation of the species to which it belongs.

4.2. Sensitive Life

Animals' relationship with the environment is different from that of plants thanks to the system of perception that characterizes sensi-tive life. Sensitive life manifests itself, in the first place, in the ability to recognize material reality and, in a certain way, appropriate it. It is for this reason that, although the goal to which an individual being's aim is determined by its nature, the origin of the movements depends on the living being itself, which recognizes the sense quali-ties of surrounding objects. This ability enables it to have a certain measure of control over its actions. Animals thus have an inclination (or, to use classical terminology, an appetite) associated with their sense perception: The awareness of what is perceived as pleasurable or as harmful necessarily provokes a reaction.

In the second place, and as a consequence of what has just been said, sensitive life manifests itself in the capacity for locomotion, which is more elementary in the lower animals and more complex in the higher animals.

4.3. Intellective Life

The most exalted degree of life in corporeal beings is that of intellec-tive life in which, as we have noted, the capacity for immanence and transcendence is at its most perfect. As has been said, intellective knowledge has greater openness than sensory knowledge because it addresses both corporeal and incorporeal reality and comprehends the relationship between the end and the means to achieve that end. This capacity lies at the root of technical progress and the con-struction of tools. Man has an intellective tendency thanks to which the individual tends toward that which he has known intellectively, i.e., in its universal aspect.

---

18. Cf. Thomas Aquinas, *Summa Theologiæ*, I, q. 78, a. 2, c.

Hence, rational beings are, in a more fitting sense, "masters" of their own actions because they tend toward ends that they themselves have decided, though within the limits of their nature. Of course, rational beings also have natural impulses, but the response to these impulses does not come about "automatically"; it requires the mediation of reason and the acquisition of habits, as we will see when we come to speak of freedom and culture in Chapters 9, 14, and 16.

4.4. Conclusion: The Degrees of Life Are Characterized by "Cumulativeness," Depending on the Operations of Life

This brief explanation about the degrees of life will be developed over coming chapters, especially in Chapter 3, which will focus specifically on the vital origin of living beings. At this point, however, we must add that the higher degree of life presupposes the lower degree or degrees, and hence we can speak of a "cumulativeness" of the degrees of life, in other words, of a sequential relationship between them.

This means that sensory operations can only be accomplished on the basis of vegetative operations and that, in their turn, intellective operations can only be accomplished on the basis of sensory and vegetative operations. Thus, the presence of the lower operations is a condition for the fulfillment of the higher: There are living beings that perform only vegetative operations (plants), but the sensitive life of animals requires a vegetative life and, in man, intellective life requires both sensory and vegetative life.[19]

SUMMARY OF CHAPTER 2

Life is self-movement, and a living creature is a being that can influence itself and act by itself; this means that all living beings have a capacity for immanence and a capacity for transcendence, but each possesses this capacity to a differing degree. From the point of view of its structure, the living being is distinguished by unity and organic consistency; as regards its activity or dynamism, it is characterized

---

19. As Movia observes with reference to the philosophy of Aristotle, "The lower soul is a condition for the existence of the higher, and the latter potentially contains the former, that is, it is also capable of performing its functions" (G. Movia, "Introduction" to Aristotle, *L'anima*, 21 [Milan: Bompiani, 2001])."Thence derive two very important consequences: the first is that man does not have three souls but a single and unique soul. The second is that the intellective soul diffuses, so to speak, its spiritual tenor also onto the sensory and corporeal dimension of man" (*ibid*, 45).

by self-movement and adaptation. There are three degrees of life: vegetative life (the activities of nutrition, growth, and reproduction), sensitive life (characterized by a cognitive relationship with the surrounding environment), and rational or intellective life (characterized by the rational capacity to know the universal aspects of reality). In order to be able to carry out the operations of the higher degree of life, the operations of the lower degrees must be present; sense perception is not possible without vegetative activity, and abstract concepts cannot be formed without sense knowledge and vegetative activity.

CHAPTER 3

THE SOUL, OR
THE VITAL PRINCIPLE

1. PREMISE: FORM AND MATTER,
SUBSTANCE AND ACCIDENTS

We have seen how life may be considered as a certain kind of activity and, more precisely speaking, the activity that is carried out from the self and upon the self, i.e., "self-movement." Nonetheless, if we give careful consideration to any process of change, we discover that, in fact, there is a variable aspect and a constant aspect; in other words, there are various states that change on a certain stable base. On the basis of this experience, Aristotle[1] came to recognize two principles present in all realities. On the one hand, there is a subject, or the permanent base of the process, which he called "matter"; on the other, there is some property that is acquired or lost, called "form."[2] According to Aristotle each material thing is a "being that changes" in which there is something that remains and something that changes: matter and form.

Of the various changes, however, some concern only partial aspects of a thing—such as its color, weight, position, etc.—while others involve the thing radically and totally as is the case with procreation and decay. Aristotle thus established distinctions between, respectively, "accidental changes" and "substantial changes." The first kind of change enables us to distinguish the partial aspects of a thing (its "accidents" or "accidental forms") from the thing itself, which is the subject of that change. By contrast, with the second kind of change, substantial change, we do not have a new state of the same reality but a completely different reality. Thus, even more radical principles of things emerge: on the one hand, the principle by which a reality is of a certain kind or species (the "substantial form") and, on the other, the basic subject of that specification (the "prime matter").

---

1. He discusses this, above all, in the seventh and eighth books of his *Metaphysics*.
2. Aristotle denied that reality was pure random movement, as Heraclitus asserted it was, or mere rigid stability, which was Parmenides's view.

Let us consider an example: A horse can undergo various changes such as the growth of its mane or movement from one place to another. These are accidental changes that highlight the distinction between the horse itself (the "substance") and its variable aspects (the "accidents"). But it is also true that the horse was at some point born and that it must, some day, die. Concerning birth and death, we must talk about substantial changes. In these cases, the property that is acquired with birth and lost with death is not some specific individual aspect but precisely the horse's "being a horse," in other words, its "substantial form." And yet this property does not simply appear and disappear without undergoing any process; rather, there is something that "before" existed in a certain way and "afterward" exists in a different way. This base, or subject, of the radical change (in this case, of being born or dying) is what is called "prime matter."

Briefly, then, we can say that all material reality is composed of "substance" and "accidents" and that "substance" is in turn composed of "substantial form" and "prime matter."[3] *Substantial form* is the primary specification for any form of reality, in other words, its most radical way of being, that which causes it to belong to a certain species and to carry out the activities specific to that species. *Prime matter* is that which is determined by the substantial form and hence — the latter being the most basic form of existence — is not *per se* determined. It is simply the fundamental principle of any possible determination. Finally, *substance*, composed of substantial form and prime matter, is in its turn the base, or subject, of various partial determinations, the accidents.

2. THE SOUL AS SUBSTANTIAL FORM OF LIVING BEINGS: TWO DEFINITIONS OF SOUL

Ever since antiquity (in the West, since at least the sixth century BC), the name "soul" has been given to the most radical principle of human life. Over history, however, the meaning of the term has been presented in different ways, especially as regards its relationship with the body and with man as a whole.

In order to understand what the soul is, the first point to consider is that man is a living being; that is, he is capable of acting from himself and upon himself as we saw in Chapter 1. We recognize

---

3. We are speaking here of material things, things subject to change; hence, we do not include the angels or, even less so, God.

that there is life in him, even if we do not always see it at work and there must, then, be something that keeps him alive even when he is not undertaking any kind of operation, at least perceptibly. It is to this vital principle that the name of soul (*anima* in Latin) was given; hence, we say that living beings are "animate," while those without life are "inanimate," or "inert." The peculiarity of living bodies with respect to nonliving bodies does not derive from any corporeal factor but from a different principle: the soul.

Furthermore, we must consider that man is a being who belongs to the natural order[4] and hence, like all natural realities, is composed of form and matter. By virtue of his substantial form, each man is an individual of the human species possessing a particular constitution, disposition of component parts, and so on, which enable him to carry out the operations characteristic of his species. Therefore, substantial form must be considered from two viewpoints: First of all, we must consider the fact that it confers a certain structure upon substance, and then we must examine the fact that it makes this substance capable of carrying out certain operations.[5] For this reason, Aristotle considered the soul as the first and radical principle of living beings and defined it in two complementary ways: one relating to the structure of living beings, and the other to their dynamism.[6]

2.1. The Structural, or Constituent, Viewpoint: The Soul as Form of the Body

From the point of view of the constitution of a living being, substantial form is what gives it life, makes it an organized whole, and causes it to belong to a certain species. Hence, Aristotle defined the soul as "the first actuality of a natural body having life potentially in it."[7] In this definition, the expression "first actuality" indicates that which most fundamentally constitutes reality, i.e., what we have called substantial form, while "natural body" indicates the matter adequate to be constituted as a living body.

The soul, then, actualizes or enhances matter in such a way as to constitute, with that matter, a unitary and ordered whole, in other

---

4. However, as we will see, he is not "merely" natural.

5. Bear in mind the explanations we gave in section 3 of the last chapter.

6. A clear summary of Aristotelian thought on this subject is found in C. Fabro, *L'Anima: Introduzione al problema dell'uomo* (Segni: Edivi, 2005), 114–115.

7. Aristotle, *De Anima* II, 1, BK 412, a 27; cf. *ibid*, 412, b 5.

words, an "organic or animate body." This does not mean, however, that the soul is reduced to merely organizing the body, to oversee-ing the order between its various parts. The soul is the principle — not the result — of that order. To put it briefly, we can say that the soul is the act or "form of the body" (*forma corporis*), and the body is the material principle of the living substance.[8] As Vanni Rovighi said, "Affirming that the human soul is the form of the body means affirming that that which makes man alive and aware is the same principle, the same reality, as that by which he has a specific body."[9]

2.2. The Dynamic, or Functional, Viewpoint: The Soul as First Principle of Operations

If, on the other hand, we examine the living being from the view-point of its activities, we see that substantial form is what enables it to perform various operations — operations that, indeed, are the expression of life: local motion, nutrition, perception, etc. Aristotle thus offered a second definition of soul, complementary to the first: The soul is "the primary cause by virtue of which we live, perceive, and think."[10] With this formulation, the philosopher's aim was not to cover all of a living being's activities rather than to underline the fact that the soul is their "first" principle.

In a substance endowed with life, operations have many immediate principles: eyes for sight, legs for movement, etc. These organs are not, however, the "first" principle of such activities because they are in turn moved by another principle that activates them in order to see, to walk, etc. It follows that in each living being there must be a first principle for all its activities, and this is given the name of "soul."

3. CHARACTERISTICS OF THE SOUL

The soul, then, is the form of the body and the first principle of the operations performed by a living being. We must now consider what

---

8. Commenting on these notions, Basti emphasizes that matter and form must not be understood as two irreducible terms in apparent contrast with the uniqueness of existing things; they designate the "constituent relations" of existing things in the sense that, due to their causal relationship, an existing thing has a specific nature; cf. G. Basti, "*Dall'informazione allo spirito: abbozzo di una nuova antropologia,*" in *L'anima*, 48 (Milan: Mondadori, 2004).

9. S. Vanni Rovighi, *Uomo e natura: Appunti per una antropología filosófica* (Milan: Vita e Pensiero, 1980), 176.

10. Aristotle, *De Anima* II, 2, BK 414, a 12–13; cf. *ibid*, 413, b 11.

it is like in itself, what are its fundamental characteristics. Generally speaking, whatever the species of living being, each soul is characterized by the fact of being *simple, incorporeal, inextensive,* and *unique.*

In the first place the soul is *simple;* i.e., it has no parts. What *can* be divided into parts is the substance as a whole because it is composed of substantial form and matter, but, for its part, the soul — as substantial form — designates the living being only partially and not in its entirety. From this simplicity derive the other characteristics that we will consider below.

The soul is *incorporeal;* i.e., it is not a body. It translates the potency of the matter into action and makes it an organized whole, but of itself it is not identified with the body nor with a part of the body (the brain, the heart, etc.), for otherwise it would be unable to configure action out of matter.

The soul is *inextensive;* i.e., it is without extension. Being extended means having *partes extra partes;* that is, parts separate from one another, something that would be incompatible with the soul's simplicity. Extension is a property of matter — and of substance composed of matter — but not of form *per se.* Hence, the soul cannot be measured or weighed nor have its location in a specific organ of the body.

The soul is *unique,* a uniqueness that has given rise to considerable discussion throughout history. This characteristic derives from the fact that the soul is the substantial form of the living being. Thanks to its substantial form, in fact, each thing is what it is and acts according to its nature. To affirm that in one reality there are various substantial forms would be a contradiction because, in such a case, the reality in question would not be one substance but various substances juxtaposed, and it would be necessary to find the principle that holds them together. Therefore, for the same reason for which there is only one substantial form in each substance, there is only one soul in each living being.

The soul and the body together constitute a single substance: the living being. One proof of this is to be found in the fact that death is followed almost immediately by absence of movement and decomposition. Consequently, the fact that man has capacities that are not only intellectual but also sensory and vegetative cannot be explained by postulating the coexistence in him of various souls but by recognizing different operations of the same soul.

We have said that the soul is not confused with the body, that between the two there exists a relationship that unites form to matter, i.e., a "substantial" relationship. It is evident that such a relationship implies mutual dependency, but this does not mean that the dependency is the same for both parties. The body depends on the soul completely and receives therefrom all its perfection, but the soul's relationship to the body is different. In many living things the soul cannot exist independently of the body because its perfection is limited to conferring a certain structure on the body and to making it capable of action. However, there are beings in which the soul is more perfect than is necessary merely to activate the body. This is the soul of man, which for this reason is defined as spiritual. Later we will see how this greater degree of perfection is justified. For now we will limit ourselves to the following statement: Even if the human soul is the form of the body and, with the body, constitutes a single substance, at the same time it has a "relative" independence of being and action that clearly distinguishes it from the soul of nonrational beings.

4. The Global Perspective

Thus far we have sought to present the idea of the soul as the vital principle of living beings using an analytical perspective that is part and parcel of the systematic approach we are using. With this analytical method it is inevitable that we should proceed by dissecting the object of study, that is, in our case, isolating the vital principle from the totality of the individual being or, as we will see in the next chapter, isolating the body from its vital principle. If to this we add the natural tendency to imagine our subject matter in material terms, it is easy to run the risk of considering the soul as one more thing among other things, as an element that is added to another and that may be removed at will.

Although we will return to this subject in section 4 of the next chapter, and in Chapter 12, it is worthwhile reiterating that, when reflecting on the human person, we must never lose sight of the global perspective, in other words, the perspective that considers the individual in all aspects (somatic, mental, and spiritual). The soul, as form, is not a "part unto itself" of the living being but, as we explained above, it is the principle that organizes the being, giving it structure and keeping it alive. For this reason the soul is sometimes compared to the rhythm of a symphony or to the conductor of an orchestra: Without rhythm there would be no symphonic music, but this nonetheless requires sounds, and without the conductor a piece of music could not be properly played, although this still needs musicians and their instruments.[11]

SUMMARY OF CHAPTER 3

Aristotelian-Thomistic philosophy offers two definitions of the soul. According to the first of these, the soul is the *substantial form of the living being*; the second defines the soul as the *first principle of the operations of the living being*. When we speak of *substantial form* we mean the metaphysical principle by which a living being belongs to a particular species. The soul is simple, incorporeal, inextensive, and unique. Philosophical reflection must never lose sight of the global perspective; therefore, we must not forget that the soul is one of the two coprinciples of the living being, the other coprinciple being the body.

---

11. See J. Villanueva, *Intorno al* body-mind problem, *"Acta Philosophica,"* 1/3 (1994), 135–143; for further useful clarification, cf. L. Borghi, *L'antropología tomista e il* body-mind problem *(alla ricerca di un contributo mancante)*, *"Acta Philosophica,"* II/1 (1992), 1279–292; J.J. Sanguineti, *Filosofía della mente: Una prospettiva ontologica e antropologica* (Rome: Edizioni Università della Santa Croce, 2007), chapter 3.

CHAPTER 4

THE LIVING BODY

1. INERT MATTER AND LIVING BODY

In the preceding chapter we reached the conclusion that the soul is the substantial form of the body. Yet to make this affirmation is, in some way, to presuppose the very idea of what the living body is. We must, then, seek to understand corporeity because such an understanding can bring great clarity — or lead to many errors — about man.

The fact that man is a material being is evident from everyday life: Our movement from one place to another and our inevitable limitations such as tiredness, vulnerability, sickness, and even death are the immediate experiences we have of our material condition. Nevertheless, we also have an awareness of not being exclusively material, a fact evinced by "awareness" itself, for it is thought that makes this detachment, or surmounting of matter, possible. Through reflection we understand that the body is part of ourselves and come to discover its importance for the totality of our being. Since we have defined the soul as substantial form and as first principle of a living being's activities, this means that the body receives life and movement from the soul, but it is at this point that we must introduce some important elucidations.

In the first place, the term "body" is not used only to apply to living beings but also, more generally, to realities that have a certain extension in space and that undergo changes over time. This, for example, is the meaning with which the word is used in formulating physical laws such as Archimedes's famous principle: "A body immersed in a liquid receives a buoyancy equal to the weight of the displaced liquid." Thus, in general terms, "body" is used to refer to a reality possessing certain physical-chemical properties, which may be of many kinds; for example, a body is touchable, visible, and audible, subject to certain dynamic factors and possessing measurable properties such as weight, temperature, or electrical charge.

When Aristotle affirms that the soul is "the first actuality of the natural body," he is considering the body as a material reality that "precedes" substantial form and is capable of receiving it. This should be understood in the sense that, since the soul is the principle of all the perfection and activity of the living being, the body "without" the soul lacks structure and cannot carry out its vital activities, and even if it does have some kind of structure and dynamism, they are certainly not those of living beings.

Thus, when we speak of "body" with reference to living beings, we are referring to something very different from inert matter. We are talking about an assembly of material elements regulated by the vital principle, or soul and, therefore, structured and prepared for vital activities. It is in this case that we can speak of "living body," i.e., a body possessing the structure and dynamism that character-izes beings endowed with life. Precisely in order to underline the difference between inanimate and living matter, Aristotle observed that it is wrong to say a corpse is "human" just as it would be wrong to say as much of a painting or sculpture.[1]

This is an important premise because it helps us to understand that the human body — or the body of a living being in general — is not to be identified as prime matter infused with activity by the soul. The body we can see and touch is itself the living being made up of form and matter. Obviously, form and matter are two metaphysical principles of reality that we can neither see nor touch; we can under-stand them only by reflection.[2] And yet, as we said in the preceding chapter, we are aware that the reality present in our experience is a composite reality possessing, precisely by virtue of matter, certain physical-chemical properties. Consequently, the specific living sub-stance is, at one and the same time, a living body and a corporeal being.

2. THE BODY AS SYSTEM: THE IDEA OF ORGANISM

The living body, then, is distinct from inert matter. But how do we become aware of this? Fundamentally, we can do so in two ways: firstly, by recognizing the ordered structure of the body; secondly, by reflecting upon its autonomous dynamism. The living body is, in fact, first and foremost a unitary and organized assembly of parts capable of performing certain activities independently of other bod-

---

1. Cf. Aristotle, *De Anima*, II 1, 412 b 21–22.
2. Form and matter are not the object of our senses but only of our intellect.

ies. This is why it is called an "organism," i.e., a system in which the internal parts are ordered and directed toward the perfection of the whole. Unlike inert matter, the living body has these characteristics by virtue of the perfection conferred upon it by the soul, in other words, precisely because it is an animate body. We must, then, now seek to understand in what this perfection consists at the structural level and at the dynamic level.

2.1. The Animate Body at the Structural Level: "Organicity"

Firstly, the living body is composed of heterogeneous parts. We have already seen how the diversity and order among these parts is what enables the living being's actions and how a simple material being—structurally undifferentiated—is a passive being. The living being, then, has multiple parts that are closely related to one another,[3] but theirs is not a homogeneous relationship because the distinction between them is not just quantitative but qualitative. Each part is distinct from the others both because it occupies a different space and because it has its own specific function within the whole. Thus we may see that the internal order of the living being is hierarchical, each part contributing in its own way to the overall perfection.[4] For example, in the case of the human body, it is clear that the correct functioning of certain parts is absolutely necessary for survival (heart, brain, lungs), others are less indispensable (hands, feet, eyes, ears), and still others are not indispensable at all (hair, nails, teeth). All this goes to show that some of these parts have a principal role, others a secondary role, and this overall structure is what allows us to speak of "system": The animate body is not a mere grouping of elements, an aggregation of fragments of matter, but a totality of parts hierarchically ordered on the basis of their multiple functions.

It is worth noting that the complexity and internal hierarchy of the parts differ depending upon the degrees of life. The more perfect a living being is, the more complex its body structure.[5] Thus, a plant is relatively simple even though it has a very clear structure—root, stem, leaves, and flowers—with its own system for absorbing and assimilating chemical substances. The bodies of animals are much more complex, with a marked differentiation of tissues and organs;

---

3. This relationship is so close that the modification of one part entails a change in the others.

4. For this reason physical ailments in certain parts can cause more or less serious dysfunctions and even the death of the individual.

5. Cf. Thomas Aquinas, *Quæstio Disputata De Anima*, q. un., a. 7, c.

this differentiation differs in degree, ranging from bodies that are, in a certain sense, similar to those of plants—think, for example, of sponges and jellyfish—to others that are highly differentiated—as is the case with the higher mammals—in which there is also a differentiation of internal systems: nervous, digestive, reproductive, respiratory, and so on.

Finally, the human body stands out for its structure and complexity, perhaps the most exalted in the natural world. Although it is difficult to establish a precise and linear hierarchy among the animals, man's preeminence seems clear from the intricacy of all his internal systems—respiratory, circulatory, immune, etc.—but especially the nervous system. At this point we must make it clear that the greater perfection of the human body is evident not only in the great complexity of its parts but above all in the very close relationships among them. In the case of the nervous system in particular, contact between neurons can come about in so many different ways as to constitute the foundation for an immense range of experiences.

2.2. The Animate Body at the Dynamic Level: "Intentionality"

Nonetheless, the perfection of the body is not only manifest in the complexity of its parts and their hierarchical arrangement. Such a structure implies that each part is preordained for the perfection of the whole, as it is for its own specific goal. To say that the body is an organic system, then, means that each individual part is not closed in on itself but open to the others with which it is in more or less immediate contact. This dynamic aspect is evident in the fact that there is no part of the body that does not have a precise function or finality. Indeed, in order to carry out complex activities, it is necessary for the parts of the body not to be rigidly determined and independent—"crystallized," so to say, as in minerals—but for them to connect to the others with which they carry out those activities. Such a characteristic may be called the "openness" or "intentionality" of the body and its parts.

All the elements in a living body are interdependent, even if their relationship is not always equally direct. This is already evident in plants, the roots of which transmit nutritional substances to the stem, and the stem to the leaves and fruit. The correlation among the parts of animals' bodies is even closer, firstly among the internal organs (nervous system, digestive tract, and respiratory and reproductive systems) but also among the external members (paws, spinal column, skull, and so on). Nevertheless, it is in the human body that we see the greatest degree of openness.

Since ancient times attempts have been made to understand the relationship that exists between the morphology of the human body and the functions it is capable of performing. The first philosopher to establish a link between intellectual capacity and the use of the hands seems to have been Anaxagoras, to whom the following words are attributed: "The possession of these hands is the cause of man being of all animals the most intelligent."[6] Aristotle takes up this idea but maintains rather the opposite view: Man has hands because he is the most intelligent. Thus he emphasizes the correlation between the intellect and the hand, affirming that the latter is "the tool of tools."[7] For his part, Thomas Aquinas observed that nature, "although it has not provided [man] with weapons and clothing as it provided other animals, it gave him reason and hands, with which he is able to get these things."[8] The hand, in fact, is not a specialized instrument; on the contrary, it is highly versatile and can be put to many different uses. This operational flexibility allows man not only to accomplish certain actions that are necessary for life — support, defense, handling food — but also to create complex and precise tools for activities that accord with his intelligence such as technology and the arts.

At the same time, man's "bipedalism"—i.e., the ability to walk constantly on two feet — is an indispensable condition for the use of the hands which, indeed, would not be free or endowed with such a high degree of mobility if they had to bear the weight of the body, as do the paws or hooves of animals. Bipedalism, in its turn, obviously depends on the erect posture of the spinal column, which enables a balanced attitude of the head. This position permits, on the one hand, greater cranial capacity, while, on the other, it ensures that the

---

6. This assertion has come to us through Aristotle, *De Partibus Animalium*, IV 10, 687 a 7. Cf. G.S. Kirk, J.E. Raven, and M. Schofield, *The Presocratic Philosophers: A Critical History with a Selection of Texts* (Cambridge, MA: Harvard University Press, 1983), 383, fragment 508.

7. Aristotle, *De Anima*, III 8, 432 a 1–2: "The soul is analogous to the hand; for as the hand is a tool of tools, so the mind is the form of forms." See also Thomas Aquinas, *In De Anima*, l. 3, lectio 13, n. 4.

8. Thomas Aquinas, *Summa Theologiæ*, I-II, q. 5, a. 5, ad 1; cf. *ibid*, I, q. 76, a. 5, ad 4. A more developed form of the same idea crops up again many centuries later in Arnold Gehlen, who accentuates the initial "precariousness" or "incompleteness" of man with respect to the other animals in order to highlight the unique position the human individual has in the world (cf. A. Gehlen, *Man, His Nature and Place in the World* [New York: Columbia University Press, 1988], 194).

head does not have to lean forwards (for attack, defense, or feeding). And the mouth does not have to have the form of a snout; rather, it can have thin lips, an extremely mobile tongue, and set-back teeth that enable — together with the rest of the vocal apparatus — the emission of highly variegated sounds, the physiological foundation for articulated language.[9]

The intentionality of the body also differs in degree depending on the perfection of the living being's activities. A distinction must then be made between the intentionality of the body as regards vegetative operations and its intentionality as regards operations of knowledge and inclination. In fact, the parts of the body that concern themselves with nutrition, growth, and procreation are structured in such a way as to undertake functions that surpass the mere physical-chemical properties of matter.[10] These activities require a certain morphological and functional specialization at various levels. Thus, the organs of nutrition are regulated and adapted for food; those of the motor system are adapted for a certain physical environment; those of the reproductive system are open to complementarity with the other sex, to the feeding and protection of offspring, and so on.

An analogous state of affairs, but at a much higher level, is to be found in the parts of the body that act as the foundation for knowledge and inclination. In this case, the body itself, in a certain sense, surpasses the limitations of matter and enables the individual to perform operations that are not exclusively material.[11] The "immateriality" of activities of knowledge and inclination requires an appropriate disposition of the body, a disposition that may be described as a greater "openness," or "nondetermination," of the parts that carry out these functions. Clearly, all parts of the body are related to the others and are "structured" to carry out certain "functions," yet in the case of the human body such functions do not correspond to merely material needs but go beyond them. Thus we see a rela-

---

9. Cf. Thomas Aquinas, *Summa Theologiæ*, I, q. 91, a. 3, ad 3; J.C. Eccles, *Evolution of the Brain: Creation of the Self* (London and New York: Routledge, 1989), 73–99.

10. This demonstrates the specific nature of biology as an autonomous discipline and its irreducibility to physics or to chemistry.

11. At this point, the distinction between natural bodies and artificial things becomes more evident: The operations of a machine cannot be compared with the cognitive or voluntary acts of a person. Even recent prototypes of robots are mere automatons that reproduce only the characteristics of human activity. Thus, for example, the calculations that may be performed by a computer cannot be called "knowledge" in the strict sense, nor can its movements be called "inclinations." We will examine the immateriality of these operations more closely in Chapters 8 and 9.

tionship between intelligence — the spirit — and the morphology of the body, which is reflected in its greater "openness," or "non-specialization."

3. THE NOTION OF ORGAN:
ANATOMY AND PHYSIOLOGY

In speaking about the parts of the living body we have highlighted how the diversity of operations depends upon the structure of those parts. The various parts of the organism, by virtue of their structure and function, are called "organs." This concept is of great importance because it enables us to understand the relationship between the morphology of the body and its dynamism, i.e., the correlation that exists between anatomy and physiology. In fact, each of the living being's functions takes place by means of a separate and suitably predisposed part.

The relationship between the physical constitution and the specific activity of a part of the body is a measure of its specialization. The more perfect the operation, the more specialized the organ. If, for example, we consider the eye, we discover that it is in fact an extremely complex organ: Apart from having its own muscles and tissues, which require a particular form of blood supply, we discover that the retina has special cells (called "rods" and "cones") which make it possible to perceive colors and light within a defined spectrum. It is precisely this structure as a whole that enables us to see; it would be no use for hearing, tasting, or any other operation, and without it the specifically human form of sight would not be possible.[12]

The specialization of organs should be seen not as a form of limitation or closure but as their being preordained for a certain kind of activity. The operation of an organ requires, in fact, a specific complexity and proportion among its material elements and, in their turn, the operations of the various organs enable the development and equilibrium of the entire being. This is the reason for the existence, within the body, of different tissues and systems.

---

12. We know that other animals can perceive sense data that man cannot. Some, indeed, can "see" body heat, others hear very high frequency sounds, etc. However, the world in which man lives would be completely different — perhaps it would not even be "human"—if his sensory capacities were different than the ones he has.

Vital functions, which depend on the organs as their material foundation, require a greater degree of specialization depending on their degree of perfection. Thus, the plants have relatively simple and unspecialized organs, though highly complex if compared with the matter of inert things. The roots, for example, serve to gather water and other substances, but this function can be carried out at a secondary level by other parts, such as the leaves or stem. In other words, even though the parts of plants are specialized, they are nonetheless "relatively" interchangeable.[13]

In animals organic specialization is much greater and enables more specific activities to be carried out. Even the vegetative functions — nutrition, growth, and reproduction — require, in animals, a greater complexity of organs and a more specific combination of their material elements. This characteristic becomes much more evident in the case of the functions of knowledge and inclination and, indeed, the organs necessary for such functions have to have a highly specific and particular structure. In this context Aristotle spoke of the "mean," indicating an appropriate equilibrium in the composition of the organ that enables it to react to certain stimuli and not to others.[14] The parts of the body preordained for knowledge — and the same holds true, as we will see, for inclination — must have a very precisely balanced composition in order to be stimulated by very differing qualities. This is the reason why plants cannot have sensitivity, not even the sense of touch. Although they may be subject to the action of external objects, they do not have the necessary organic properties to be able to perceive the qualities they receive as being distinct; rather, they undergo them passively as a simple physical change to their bodies.[15]

We see, then, that there is a relationship between bodily structure and the object capable of stimulating an organ: The former conditions the intensity and type of action which the latter is capable of performing, and hence "mean" may be understood as a kind of "organic openness." This characteristic, however, does not run counter to specialization; rather, it is the specific way in which the organs of sense are specialized. They would be no use in carrying

---

13. Obviously, this is not true in the same way for all plants: Some have a greater degree of specialization, others a lesser.

14. Cf. Aristotle, *De Anima*, II 12, 424 a 16–424 b 21.

15. For example, they do not "perceive" hot or cold but "become" hot or cold. Cf. Thomas Aquinas, *Sententia Super De Anima*, lib. 2, l. 24, n. 7.

out their functions if they did not have such a "mean." Thus we can say that the more perfect the life operations, the greater "openness," or "mean," the respective organs must have.

4. THE CAUSAL RELATIONSHIP BETWEEN SOUL AND BODY

Having examined the nature and the characteristics of the living body, we can now briefly return to the relationship between soul and body. Later on we will dedicate a specific section to studying the unity of the individual human being; for now we must reiterate what we said at the end of the last chapter concerning the global perspective: Human nature is neither purely material nor purely spiritual; rather, it is a reality made up of a material principle (i.e., the body) and a spiritual principle (i.e., the rational soul).[16] Thus, soul and body are united as integral parts of one single substance — man — and constitute a "substantial" unity.[17]

In order to understand better what we are saying, it is helpful to recall that Aristotle distinguished four kinds of cause: material, formal, efficient, and final.[18] Given that the reality made up of the soul and the body is the total man, the causal influence of these two coprinciples refers principally to the individual; in other words, between the soul and the body there exists a causal relationship that first and foremost concerns the substance that is the human individual. At the same time, however, they are also causes, the one with respect to the other: The soul is the cause of the body, and the body is the cause — in a limited sense, as we will see — of the soul.

Matter and form have an influence on the structure, or constitution, of reality. The formal cause is that which determines something as being a particular type of reality, while the material cause is that of which something is made or in which it exists. We can, then, say that the soul is the formal cause of the human composite in that it makes

---

16. Here it is worth quoting this effective passage from Sciacca: "Man is a light of intelligence and reason, of intuition and discourse and will, but also of blood, muscles, nerves, and bones. A gesture of the hand, a flash of the pupils, a grimace or a smile, tears or indifference, a look, a shrug of the shoulders, any movement expresses a thought, a feeling, a repulsion, a pain, a pleasure, always something from his emotional or volitive life" (M.F. Sciacca, *L'uomo questo "squilibrato,"* [Palermo: L'Epos, 2000], 78).

17. As we will see in Chapter 12, it would be wrong to consider their relationship as something "accidental" because this would imply a form of dualism (spiritual or material).

18. The various causes are explained in Aristotle, *Metaphysics,* V 2, 1013 a 24–1014 a 25.

it of a certain species. For the same reason, it is also the formal cause of the body because it makes it of a certain type (living body, sensitive body, and so on). For its part, the body is the material cause of the living being because it is that of which it is made (the wood of trees, the muscles and bones of animals and man, etc.). But the body is also the material cause with respect to the soul not because the soul is made of matter but because it exists "in" the body and the body is pervaded by it.[19] As we will see, however, the human soul can subsist after death.

By contrast, the efficient and final causes concern the dynamism, or activity, of things. The efficient cause is that from which the action comes, and the final cause is that to which the action tends, that which attracts it. The soul is the efficient cause of the body and of all the living being because it is the first principle of all its activities. This does not mean, however, that the soul is the only principle of activities nor that it is their immediate principle. As we will see, it acts through specific faculties that are the direct or immediate principles of actions. Finally, the soul is also the final cause of the body, in the sense that the body's purpose is to carry out activities that have the soul as their principle.[20]

5. THE BODY AND CORPOREITY

The explanations contained in the preceding section are important because they help us not to lose sight of the unitary nature of the person. In fact, by following the analytical method used thus far, we have studied the soul and the body in two separate chapters, but it must not be forgotten that the soul always remains the vital principle of a body and that the body, in our field of study, is always an animate or living body. It is worth reiterating once again, then, that there is no body (human or animal) into which a soul is subsequently infused nor a preexisting soul which is assigned to a body.

In the context of modern culture, it is important not to lose sight of the global perspective about which we spoke in the last section of

---

19. One question that has given rise to much speculation is that of the "location" of the soul. Obviously, it is not "located" in the body like a physical object occupying a certain space. Rather, it is "located" in the body by virtue of its causality: The body receives all its perfection from the soul and the soul acts and shows itself through the body. In this sense, it must be affirmed that the soul is located in all of the body and in every part thereof. Cf. Thomas Aquinas, *Summa Theologiæ*, I, q. 76, a. 8.

20. Cf. *ibid*, I, q. 91 a. 3 c.

the preceding chapter. It is evident that the scientific study of the body involves an attitude of detachment toward the object being examined, considering it almost as a self-contained unit to be found in all living beings and possessing measurable properties. But it is not possible to consider the human body only from the biological or physiological viewpoint, ignoring entirely the ethical, cultural, and existential dimensions that are specific to the human person. According to some commentators, this reduction of the body to a self-contained object of examination is also to be found in the philosophical and, in particular, metaphysical study of the body.

In order to avoid the risk of studying the body only from the standpoint of the detached and neutral observer, modern philosophy often makes use of the distinction between *body* and *corporeity*.[21] To speak of *corporeity* is to refer to the experience each human individual has of his own existential situation (i.e., of his own condition as a living corporeal-spiritual being); it is to highlight the fact that the human body is already *per se* different from that of other living beings because it is the fitting correlative of a spiritual soul. Each individual experiences, in himself and in others, how a reality inseparable from the totality of the individual (the body, with its spatiality, temporality, sexuality) manifests and expresses the self. Only in extreme situations can there be a disassociation between the corporeal and mental-spiritual dimensions.

This distinction partly reflects that made in German between *Körper* and *Leib,* as developed by E. Husserl[22] and M. Scheler.[23] *Körper* is the body considered objectively in its physicality, while *Leib* is one's own body as perceived by the individual in his subjectivity. Reflection on corporeity is, in fact, an important element in the work of phenomenological philosophers.

---

21. Cf. S. Palumbieri, *L'uomo, questa meraviglia: Antropología filosófica I: Trattato sulla costituzione antropologica* (Rome: Urbaniana University Press, 1999), 103–105. The various perspectives in the study of the body are well presented in M.T. Russo, *Corpo, salute, cura: Linee di antropologia biomedica* (Soveria Mannelli: Rubbettino, 2004), 75–131.
22. Cf. E. Husserl, *Cartesian Meditations: An Introduction to Phenomenology* (New York: Springer, 1977), 120 ff; *id., Ideas Pertaining to a Pure Phenomenology and to a Phenomenological Philosophy* (The Hague and Boston: Kluwer Academic Publishers, 1989), book II, section I, chapter III; section II, chapter III; book III, chapter I §§ 2–3.
23. Cf. M. Scheler, *Formalism in Ethics and Nonformal Ethics of Values: A New Attempt Toward the Foundation of an Ethical Personalism* (Evanston, IL: Northwestern University Press, 1985), 398–424.

6. ORIGINS AND EVOLUTIONISM

Behind the explanations given in this chapter and the last lies the question concerning the origins of life, of the world, and of man. This in turn calls into question the debate about evolutionism, to which much attention was given last century and at the beginning of this one.[24] We cannot offer a complete picture of the problem and will seek only to define in what way it affects the study of philosophical anthropology and, more specifically, the philosophical study of the human body.

It must not be forgotten that evolutionism cannot present itself as a response to the question about the ultimate origin of reality because in order to evolve something must first exist. Of itself, therefore, evolutionary theory does not oppose the Jewish-Christian doctrine of creation. The conflict arises when we forget that the Bible is not there to supply the answers to scientific research about the world or when it is felt necessary to make the unwarranted passage from the scientific theory of evolution to an atheist and materialist vision of the world and mankind.[25]

Above all, it must be borne in mind that there is not one single evolutionary theory but various theories often significantly at odds with one another.[26] Thus it is appropriate to distinguish, as some scholars do, between evolution and evolutionism: The former is observable (although some of its details are still the subject of discussion), while the latter is frequently a doctrine that includes a very precise concept

---

24. In this section and the next, we will make reference to the following texts, which it is advisable to read: M. Artigas, *Le frontiere dell'evoluzionismo* (Milan: Ares, 1993); J.C. Eccles, *Evolution of the Brain: Creation of the Self*, cit.; F. Facchini, "*Uomo, identità biologica e culturale*," in *Dizionario interdisciplinare di scienza e fede*, Vol. 2, 1462–1483 (Rome: Città Nuova and Urbaniana University Press, 2002). The bibliographical information found at the *Portale di Documentazione Interdisciplinare di Scienza e Fede* (*www.disf.org*) is also very useful.

25. On April 26, 1985, at the end of a symposium on "Christian faith and the theory of evolution," St. John Paul II explained: "There is no obstacle in a correctly understood faith in creation or a correctly understood teaching of evolution. Indeed, evolution presupposes creation. Creation stands in the light of evolution as an event extended over time — like a continuous *creatio* — in which God becomes visible to the eyes of the believer as 'Creator of heaven and earth'" (John Paul II, *Insegnamenti*, Vol. VIII, 1 [1985] [Vatican City: Libreria Editrice Vaticana, 1986], 1132).

26. A brief overview of the situation is to be found in J. Villanueva, *Le spiegazioni scientifiche dell'evoluzione*, "*Acta Philosophica*," 1/8 (1999), 135–149. On the theoretical limits of certain evolutionary doctrines, see R. Spaemann, "*Essere ed essere divenuto: che cosa spiega la teoría dell'evoluzione?*" in *Natura e ragione: Saggi di antropología* (Rome: Edizioni Università della Santa Croce, 2006), 41–65.

of the human person and of the world. When evolutionism presents itself as an attempt to respond to the question concerning the origin of man, in the radical sense, this necessarily involves a certain degree of a reductionism; i.e., it becomes an attempt to explain everything about man on the basis of certain of his characteristics that are susceptible to calculation and measurement.

7. COSMOGENESIS, BIOGENESIS, AND ANTHROPOGENESIS

The question about the origin of man (*anthropogenesis*) is linked to that about the origin of the universe (*cosmogenesis*) and about the origin of life (*biogenesis*). Since no one has had direct experience of the origin of the cosmos or of life, any scientific explanation is extremely indirect — focusing on effects far removed from their cause — and so only very hypothetical theories can be formulated.

As regards the origin of the universe, the most widely accepted theory today is that of the great primordial explosion (the Big Bang), which took place some 15 billion years ago and since which the universe began its expansion and became progressively colder. It is presumed that the earth was formed 4.5 billion years ago, while the oldest fossils of living beings date back to some 3.5 billion years ago. These, however, were extremely simple organisms, and this makes it difficult to explain the arrival of complex organisms, which can only be dated to much later, around one billion years ago. Another question yet to be clarified is the passage from inert elements (chemistry) to living beings (biology) because there is an enormous qualitative leap from the cell to the chemical elements involved in the vital functions.

In considering the origin of man, a distinction must be made between two aspects: Indeed, although they are intimately linked, we cannot identify the question about the origin of man with that about the origin of the human body. The former topic is of a strictly philosophical nature and has theological implications, while the latter belongs both to philosophy and to the other academic disciplines. Evolutionism, basing itself on the positive sciences, should seek a response to the second of these two questions and not directly to the first. It is for this reason that, in the study of anthropogenesis, we usually speak of two distinct processes: the *process of hominization* and the *process of humanization*.

Hominization concerns the "preparation of the human body," in other words, the nonhuman stages of development of the living beings that preceded mankind's appearance on earth. Thus, it relates to man's so-called "ancestors." Humanization, on the other hand, concerns the "development of the human body," that is, the stages over which the already extant man, using his intelligence and freedom, perfected the characteristic elements of a specifically human form of life. By studying these two processes, it is possible to highlight certain significant stages, but it is not empirically possible to demonstrate the passage from one process to the other. In other words, paleoanthropology has to admit a break in continuity between the hominids and the appearance of the human being. This is why the expression "man's ancestors" can be used only to refer to the living beings that preceded the appearance of the human species and not to take for granted some supposed relationship of direct descent between hominids and human beings.

Furthermore, what we have called hominization is not a linear process but developed following a series of crisscrossing evolutionary lines, of which some intertwined and others became extinct. Moreover, genetic changes interacted with environmental factors in such a way that the human species came to find itself at the confluence of a series of changes that make it entirely unique.[27]

Let us briefly consider some of the stages of the process that led to the formation of the species *homo sapiens sapiens*, which is that of modern man. The first primates appeared around 65 million years ago, while the appearance of the hominids may be dated to around 10 million years ago. Thanks to fossil remains it is possible to date (with greater precision, though still with a variable of a few million years) the appearance of the australopiths on the African savannah to between 4 and 5 million years ago. These hominids,

---

27. As Facchini observes, the understanding of the process of hominization must be associated with the question of animation, to which we will return in Chapter 12: "In the case of animation, there is an intervention by God the creator at the moment in which the organization of a living form is achieved in such a way as to have the characteristics of human life" (F. Facchini, *Origini dell'uomo ed evoluzione culturale: Profili scientifici, filosofici, religiosi* [Milan: Jaca Book, 2002], 266). Thus, "the true alternative is not between evolution and creation. Rather, between a vision of an evolving world, dependent upon the transcendent creator God, in accordance with his plan, and a vision of an evolving world, self-sufficient and capable of creating and transforming itself by a kind of immanent power and intelligence" (*ibid*, 267). The book is a competent and serious work, although the understanding of some of the ideas it contains may require a certain degree of theological formation.

though accustomed to living in trees (as evinced by the length of their upper limbs) walked erect (that is, they were bipeds) and had an average cranial capacity of 400–500 cc. One famous specimen is known by the name of "Lucy," classified as *australopithecus afarensis*, discovered at Afar in Ethiopia and dating to 3.2 million years ago.

The various forms of australopiths became extinct about 2 million years ago. Also around this period *homo habilis* appeared, whose remains have been found in eastern and southern Africa. The name is due to the fact that these hominids in some way organized their own territory, used primitive stone tools, and had a developed cranial capacity of some 700 cc. Beginning around 1.6 million years ago, various parts of Africa became inhabited by *homo erectus*, so called even though the erect posture had not yet been definitively acquired. *Homo erectus* remains dating back to more recent periods have also been found in Europe. His cranial capacity was about 950 cc., and he was capable of working stone, using fire, and organizing his living space.

A gradual process of coexistence between the two species led to archaic forms of the species *homo sapiens*, which appeared around 100,000 years ago; these include the European and Middle Eastern Neanderthals, although recent studies show that Neanderthal man was already present in Europe (for example, in Spain) some 400,000 years ago. Neanderthal man was succeeded by the modern human species, *homo sapiens sapiens* (who appears around 35,000 years ago), although there is only proof for a relationship of contiguousness between the two, not for one of continuity. The *sapiens* have been shown to have had a highly evolved culture: There are traces of artistic representations, of work in stone and bone, and of funerary practices.

This, in very few words, is the body of data known to paleoanthropology, which must be integrated with that of biochemistry and molecular genetics. The understanding of the passage from one species to another is often the work of hypothesis, although, over recent years, research on the genome of the various species has provided some very useful indications. In any case, from what we have summarized in this section, it follows that the process that led to the appearance of human beings incorporates (apart from the attendant and necessary influence of environmental changes) diverse mechanisms or evolutionary lines, the action of which does not *per se* prevent us from recognizing a finalism that interconnects the development of the various forms of life.

SUMMARY OF CHAPTER 4

The body is one of the two coprinciples of the living being. The bodies of all living beings are already pervaded by a soul; indeed, a body without a soul would be mere organic matter, not the body of a living being. In living beings the body is an *organism* because its parts are structured and synchronized with one another. Each part, or organ, has a precise function or finality, and thus we can speak of the *intentionality* of the parts of the body in the sense that each is preordained for its own specific goal and for the goal of the living being as a whole. In humans, as in all living beings, the soul and body constitute a substantial unity, and the relationship between them is like that between the formal and the material cause of the being. Modern philosophy, in particular phenomenology, makes a distinction between the body (*Körper* in German) and corporeity (*Leib*) in order to underline the difference between the objective study of the body and the subjective perception of one's own body. Evolutionary theories seek to explain the changes that species undergo over the centuries, including those of the human species. Such theories aim to explain *cosmogenesis* (the origin of the universe), *biogenesis* (the emergence of life), and *anthropogenesis* (the appearance and development of the human being), but the specific nature of humans, who are corporeal-spiritual beings, cannot be explained merely in terms of organic and genetic changes.

CHAPTER 5

THE FACULTIES, OR
OPERATIVE PRINCIPLES:
ACT AND OPERATION

1. ACT AND POTENCY, OPERATION
AND FACULTY

In Chapter 3 we saw how the soul is the substantial form of the living being, and we examined this from two different perspectives: that of the being's structure and that of its dynamism. The soul is the first principle of vital activities, but this does not exclude the role of other intermediate principles that cause the activities in a more direct way. The truth is that corporeal living beings are complex organisms in which the operations arise through the interaction of different causes. These intermediate principles are the faculties and the organs.

In the last chapter we discussed the notion of organ. Now we must turn our attention to the *faculties*. We can define faculties in general terms as the stable capacities of the soul to act in a certain way, but in order to achieve a full understanding of the notion of faculty, we must consider the relationship between the notions of act, potency, and operation. The distinction between act and potency has already arisen on a number of occasions in the course of this work, mainly in the explanation of the fundamental structure of reality, which is made up of "substantial form" and "prime matter." The notions of act and potency, however, cannot be defined because they are the basis for all the others notions; i.e., it is not possible to explain them using more simple elements but only to describe them and to seek to "recognize" them in things.

By way of a preliminary approximation we can say that the *act* is the perfection of a thing, at any level, while the *potency* is the disposition or capacity to reach that perfection. Thus, we say that something "has potency" in that it has the capacity to arrive at a certain act; the reference, then, is not to a mere absence of a certain perfection, but to a real operational capacity. Thus, potency always refers to an act and is always "potency for" a certain act.

Nonetheless, an act is not necessarily a stable perfection because there are acts—such as movement and actions—that signify a perfection "underway," or "in progress." In order to distinguish these two kinds of acts, the stable act and the act "in progress," classical philosophy coined the terms, respectively, "first act" (*actus primus*) and "second act" (*actus secundus*) or, more simply, "act" and "operation."[1] An example of "first act" is the form (substantial or accidental) of a thing, while its actions are "second acts."

Now, if potency, as we have seen, always refers to an act and is understood on the basis of the act, it follows that we must distinguish between two kinds of potency: a potency referring to the first act and another referring to the second act. The first is called "passive potency" and consists in the ability to receive a perfection; the second is called "operative potency" and consists in the capacity to undertake an operation. When we speak of the faculties, or powers, of the soul, we mean precisely the operative potencies of the living being, in other words, the direct or immediate principle—not the first principle, which is the soul itself—of its actions.

2. FACULTY OF THE INDIVIDUAL OR FACULTY OF THE SOUL?

Faculties are distinct from both the soul and from the individual operations. The soul is the first substantial act of the living being, while the faculties are its powers, or operative capacities. And why is it important to distinguish between the soul and its faculties? Because the living being's operations are not continuous but discontinuous, for, while the being always remains alive, it does not always act in accordance with all its capacities;[2] i.e., it is not always moving or always perceiving sounds or smells. If the soul were not just the first principle of activity but also the only and immediate principle, the living being would have to be using all of its capacities all of the time.

---

1. Cf. Aristotle, *De Anima*, II 1, 412 a 20 ff; Thomas Aquinas, *Summa Theologiæ*, I, q. 48, a. 5, c.
2. In general, no distinction is made between "faculties of the being" and "faculties of the soul." The soul is the first principle of operations, but, as we will see below, the final subject of the actions is the living being itself, not its parts; i.e., what acts is the living being and not one of its faculties or its soul.

And we know that living beings do not, in fact, do so: The individual being acts through the operative potencies, or faculties, of the soul in such a way that the latter is (to use the terminology we have just outlined) a first act ordered to a second act.[3] Now, if the soul is the substantial form of the being, this means that, on the one hand, it confers the species on the individual and, on the other, that it is the first principle of its activities. Hence, the relationship between the soul and the faculties may be considered from the point of view of the being's constitution and from that of its dynamism.

2.1. Structural Viewpoint:
The Faculties as Accidental Properties of the Soul

Substantial form, as we have emphasized on various occasions, is the most radical act of substance (that is, of the individual being), by virtue of which it belongs to a certain species and can have other perfections.[4] The subject of the substantial form is not an already formed reality but something that exists only in potency. On the other hand, an already-in-act reality can have various partial perfections, which are accidental forms; for example, a person can be taller or shorter, in one place or in another, with light or dark hair. Thus, we can say that, in the living being, the soul is the first substantial act, while the faculties are kinds of accidental properties (or accidents), though of a very special nature. In fact, in each substance there are some perfections, which, though remaining distinct from the substantial form, necessarily arise therefrom and are called "proper accidents": The faculties are accidents of this kind and, to be more precise, are a certain kind of quality.[5]

Being accidental properties, the faculties are acts, perfections of the individual; yet the various faculties do not all inhere in the living being in the same way.[6] Some faculties such as the intellect and the will do not have their own organ, while others such as vegetative and sense faculties act on a specific organic base. Thus, the first two perfections (the intellectual and the elective) inhere directly in the

---

3. Cf. Thomas Aquinas, *Summa Theologiæ*, I, q. 77, a. 1, c; see also Aristotle, *De Anima*, II 1, 413 a 1–10.

4. Here we are not considering the act of being that, though it is not a second act, neither can be said to be a form, either substantial or accidental.

5. Quality, one of the accidents about which Aristotle speaks, can in turn be of three kinds: operative potencies (which we are discussing here), affective qualities, and habits. Since the accident of quality perfects the substance through its form, the faculties may be called "accidents of the soul," or "accidents of the being."

6. Cf. Thomas Aquinas, *Summa Theologiæ*, I, q. 77, a. 5, c.

spiritual soul, while the others are perfections that have as their subject the living organism as a whole.

Moreover, in a way analogous to that in which the soul determines and specifies the human body, the faculties determine and specify the organs; i.e., they make them suitable for certain operations.[7] Faculties, in their turn, are specified by their operations and objects. We can, then, affirm that the diversity of organs arises from the diversity of faculties, and that the diversity of faculties arises from the diversity of operations and objects.[8]

2.2. Dynamic Viewpoint:
The Faculties and the Activity of the Individual

We have already explained that, in the course of activity, the soul moves the various faculties to accomplish the single operations. We must, however, again make mention of another aspect and never lose sight of it although the analysis of the faculties itself may cause us to forget it: An individual with operative structures that are sepa-rate and independent from one another is unthinkable.[9] We have said, and will say it again, that the analytical perspective must not make us lose sight of the global perspective.

Thus, to affirm that the soul is the subject of all the activities (both spiritual and corporeal) of a living being does not mean that these activities can be attributed only to the soul or to its faculties, and even less so to the organs. Actions are to be attributed to the living being as a whole, which acts thanks to its soul and its faculties.[10] We do not normally say, "My eye sees," or, "My intelligence under-stands," but, "I see," or, "I understand." Correctly speaking, then,

---

7. Cf. *id*, *In De Anima*, l. 2, lec. 2, n. 8; lec. 24, n. 5.

8. Cf. *ibid*, l. 1, lec. 8, n. 5.

9. Sciacca observes: "Sense, intelligence, reason, will, etc., are undoubtedly distinct forms of activity, each having its own object, but sense does not, as such, exclude the presence of the other forms, so that one who senses (or reasons, or wants, etc.) senses with all of his self. Only abstract intellectualism can consider the 'faculties' not only as distinct from one another but as acting individually as if the rest did not intervene; thus, truth would be the object of reason *alone*, beauty of sense *alone*, etc.... All life, even purely biological life, proceeds by inclusion, and each of its acts is a synthesis; abstractions are for philosophers, not for concrete existence" (M.F. Sciacca, *L'uomo questo "squilibrato"* [Palermo: L'Epos, 2000], 22).

10. Cf. Aristotle, *De Anima*, I 4, 408 b 14–15.

acts belong to the living individual and not to its individual parts.[11] Thus, it must be concluded that the soul, as the substantial form of the living being, communicates its own act to the faculties, and these produce the individual operations which refer to various objects.

3. TYPOLOGY AND INTERACTION OF THE HUMAN FACULTIES

We must now turn to consider the diversity of the human faculties. Bearing in mind the fact that these faculties are operative potencies, their distinction depends on the acts for which they are ordained, in other words, on the operations they are capable of carrying out. The operations, in their turn, are distinguished on the basis of the object to which they relate. We can say, then, that the faculties are distinguished by their operations and the operations by their objects.[12]

This does not mean the faculties and their operations are to be identified with one another. The former are always distinguished from the latter as the (operative) potency from the (second) act. Having a stable capacity to act in a certain way is not the same thing as the effective accomplishment of certain operations. This is evident from our personal experience: We have the capacity to act even when we do not, in fact, do so; for example, we possess the faculty of sight even when our eyes are closed or the faculty of touch even when we are not touching anything.

It must be made clear that not all operations require a different potency to accomplish them; rather, the faculties are specified and distinguished by operations of different "types." For example, seeing the color black or the color blue — both are qualities — does not require different faculties but different operations of the same faculty, whereas seeing a color, hearing a sound, or tasting a flavor are operations that require different faculties.

---

11. The case of the human soul is, however, very special because, being spiritual, it can subsist without the body after death (we will return to this in Chapter 12). Yet not even when it is in this state can the soul alone be considered a perfect man. Cf. Thomas Aquinas, *Quæstio De Potentia*, q. 9, a. 2, ad 14: "The soul separated by death from the body is not … a person." See also S.L. Brock, "*Tommaso d'Aquino e lo statuto fisico dell'anima spirituale*," in *L'anima* (Milan: Mondadori, 2004), 69–72.
12. Cf. Aristotle, *De Anima*, II 4, 415 a 14–22; Thomas Aquinas, *Summa Theologiæ*, I, q. 77, a. 3, c.

3.1. Distinctions Among the Faculties

Later we will consider the nature and acts of the various operative potencies in greater detail; for now we will seek only to provide a general outline. Firstly, there are three sizeable groups of faculties in living beings: vegetative, sense, and intellectual faculties.

The *vegetative faculties* are so called because they are the only ones that plants have. The vegetative powers have the characteristic of being indispensable for life and, in fact, they belong to all living beings. They are nutrition, growth, and reproduction.

The *sense faculties* are possessed by the animals and by man along with the vegetative functions. Through them the living being is open to any form of corporeal or material reality. They are the knowledge and inclinations that come from the senses.

The *intellectual faculties* are possessed exclusively by rational beings.[13] Through the intellect and the will, which he possesses together with the vegetative and sense functions, the human person is open to all reality, both material and immaterial. One important characteristic of the intellectual faculties is their immateriality, in other words, the fact that they do not have their own specific organ.

3.2. The Interaction of Man's Faculties

In order to understand the dynamic interaction that exists between the various faculties, we must examine the question at two levels: that of the nature of the faculties (which, in the final analysis, is determined by the object to which they refer) and that of the chronological sequence of the operations. If we consider the nature of the faculties, the "first" potencies are the intellectual faculties, followed by the sense faculties and, lastly, the vegetative faculties. To say that a faculty is "first" by its nature means that it has the primacy or priority and, hence, that the others are subordinate to it.

If, on the other hand, we consider the chronological order of the operations, then the "first" are the vegetative faculties, followed by the sense faculties and, lastly, the intellectual faculties. The higher faculties, by their nature, need the inferior ones in order to be able to carry out their actions. This means that man's first contact with reality—and, in general, that of any living being—is through his body and its vegetative potencies. Experience comes about when

---

13. Obviously, consideration will only be given here to man and not to the angels or God.

this initial contact at the vegetative level is then elaborated by the senses and the intellect.

To conclude this chapter we will mention two important aspects related to the interaction of the faculties. The first is that the potencies, like the degrees of life, implicate one another; i.e., the higher faculties depend on the operation of the lower. Thus, the intellectual potencies imply the prior activity of the sense potencies, which, in their turn, require the operation of the vegetative potencies. The second aspect is that, while for the preservation and development of life many of the lower faculties must intervene, at the intellectual plane few faculties are involved: only the intellect and the will, which act at various levels. In other words, complexity is a sign of perfection in the material world just as simplicity is in the spiritual world.[14] Yet man participates in both these worlds, and this is reflected in the complex interaction of his organs and in the simplicity of his intellectual operations. Obviously, this means that human faculties have greater perfection and operative capacity.

SUMMARY OF CHAPTER 5

The soul is the first principle of the living being's activities. Yet each being, while alive, is not always undertaking the operations it is capable of performing; for example, it is not always moving or always knowing. Thus, we speak of faculties, that is, of those immediate principles of action which are the operative potencies of the living being. They are operative potencies because they consist in the capacity to undertake a particular operation. In human beings, some faculties have a specific organic base (vegetative and sense faculties), while others (intellective faculties, i.e., intellect and will) do not have their own organ even though their operations extrinsically depend on the organic base.

---

14. Cf. Thomas Aquinas, *Quæstio De Anima*, q. un., a. 7, c.

CHAPTER 6
HUMAN KNOWLEDGE: THE EXTERNAL SENSES

1. COGNITIVE LIFE

In Chapter 2 we quoted Aristotle to the effect that "in the case of living things, their being is to live." Indeed, developing the ideas we have already explained, we may assert that to live means to exist reflexively (immanence) and in development (transcendence): to be "from the self and toward the self." Thus, we see that there is a continuity and a discontinuity between being and living: To live is to be, but in a more perfect way than inert or inanimate objects. On the basis of this conclusion, we indicated that the degrees of life are also degrees of being and that between them there is continuity (the higher degrees include the lower) and discontinuity (the higher degrees surpass the lower). Consequently, to live is to be, but life also implies a novelty in being: Each grade of life is in continuity with the preceding grades but also introduces something new. It is in this chapter that we must speak about the novelties that cognitive life introduces with respect to vegetative life.

To know is a way to live and a way to be. If it is true that living can be described (in broad terms) as a reflexive or immanent way of being, we must now add that to know is to live reflexively, with an undisputedly higher degree of immanence and transcendence with respect to vegetative life. Indeed, as we will seek to show later, immanence and transcendence only really occur in cognitive life.

1.1. To Be and to Know

Cognitive life, then, is characterized by its greater immanence and transcendence. Yet how should this perfection with respect to living beings without knowledge be understood? We may encounter this perfection at two levels: that of the existence of living beings and that of their activity.

Substantial form is, as by now we know, the principle of the existence and activity of all living beings. In substances endowed with life, the soul (their substantial form) organizes the body and makes it capable of carrying out operations from itself and upon itself. In the case of plants, the activity of the soul consists only in perfecting their own bodies; thus, they can possess only their own forms and perfections, the substantial and the accidental. A plant can of course absorb other substances—water and various chemical elements—but it does not "have" them as distinct from itself; it merely transforms them into itself. If those substances have certain qualities of temperature or color, etc., the plant cannot have these qualities in their alterity but is passive toward them, i.e., it does not feel cold but becomes cold.[1] We can conclude, then, that its having is not distinguished from its being in the sense that it does not acquire other perfections.

Living beings with the capacity for knowledge go a step further. They can "have" not only their own forms but also those of other realities and can direct their activities on the basis of this experience.[2] The cognitive soul does not limit its activities to the formation of its own body; it is endowed with what may be called "formal overflow," in other words, the capacity to surpass materiality in some way. Thanks to this, the living being can not only "be" in one way or in another but also "have," or possess, other realities as distinct from itself. Knowledge, then, cannot be compared with nutrition: In cognitive activity the forms "had" do not passively modify the living being, nor does the being modify those forms.

Thomas Aquinas thus spoke about two ways of being: natural being and intentional being.[3] Natural being is that which things have in nature, outside the mind; for example, the existence of the apple lying before me, the green color of its skin, the chemical composition of its flesh. In the case of corporeal things, their natural being includes matter. Intentional being, on the other hand, is the existence things have in the soul: the apple perceived, the color seen, or the sweetness tasted. Unlike natural being, intentional being is always immaterial. It is not, in fact, possible for things to exist materially in the soul because the soul itself is immaterial. Moreover, if things were in the mind materially they would be modified at the moment they were known because matter cannot be located in different places at the same time (it always has specific dimensions).

1. Cf. Thomas Aquinas, *In De Anima*, l. 2, lec. 24, n. 7.
2. Cf. *id, Summa Theologiæ*, I, q. 14, a. 1, c.
3. Cf. *ibid*, I, q. 56, a. 2, ad 3.

This is why we said that the activity, or perfection, of the cognitive soul is not limited to organizing and structuring the body of the living being because it is capable of possessing other things depending upon their intentional being. Thus, Aristotle repeatedly states that the cognitive soul "is in a certain way all existing things."[4] In speaking of "being in a certain way" he is referring not to natural but to intentional being, in other words, to the being which respects the alterity of things. In this context, the following words of St. Thomas are very significant: "According to material being, which is restricted by matter, each thing is only what it is, e.g., this stone is nothing else but this stone; whilst according to immaterial being, which is broad and in some way infinite, in so far as it is not circumscribed by matter, a reality is not only what it is but also, in some way, other realities."[5]

1.2. Transitive Action and Immanent Action

At this point we may ask ourselves: In what sense does the cognitive being, intentionally and immaterially, "have" other realities? Why can knowledge not be compared with nutrition? To answer this we must study the activity of cognitive beings, and to do so it is necessary to examine the distinction, already made by Aristotle, between two kinds of activity: immanent activity and transitive activity.

Aristotle distinguished two kinds of actions, which he called *póiesis* and *praxis*.[6] These notions passed into classical philosophy with the terms of "transitive actions" and "immanent actions," respectively. If we consider any kind of activity, we see that it is always oriented to some end: "Every agent acts for an end," as St. Thomas would say.[7] That end is sometimes something external to the action; in other words, an exterior result or product such as, for example, building a house. At other times, however, the end is not external to the action but consists in the accomplishment of the action itself.[8] This

---

4. Aristotle, *De Anima*, III, 8, 431 b 21.

5. Thomas Aquinas, *In De Anima*, l. 2, lec. 5, n. 5. See Chapter 2, note 10.

6. Cf. Aristotle, *Nicomachean Ethics*, VI, 4, 1140 a. For an explanation and evaluation of the Aristotelian conception, consult A. Malo, *Il senso antropologico dell'azione: Paradigmi e prospettive* (Rome: Armando, 2004), 22–51.

7. Thomas Aquinas, *Summa Theologiæ*, I, q. 44, a. 4, c: "*Omne agens agit propter finem.*" A profound study of the Thomistic conception is to be found in S. L. Brock, *Action and Conduct: Thomas Aquinas and the Theory of Action* (Edinburgh: T & T Clark, 1998).

8. St. Thomas gives the example of the distinction between "to illuminate" something and "to shine." Cf. *Quæstio De Veritate*, q. 8, a. 6, c.

happens in actions that do not yield a tangible, external, product or result such as observing a painting or listening to music. The first of these two actions, the one that produces an external effect, is called *póiesis*, or "transitive action"; the second, which leaves an effect only in the agent of the action, is given the name of *praxis*, or "immanent action." Let us now consider these two forms of activity in greater detail.

1.2.1. Transitive Actions

Actions such as building a house, preparing a meal, or driving a car are directed toward an object other than the agent that accomplishes them. Thus, their outcome is distinguishable from the action itself, and, to speak correctly, we could say they have a "goal" rather than an "end." This distinction is clear in many modern languages,[9] but the Greeks already distinguished between *peras* ("goal")[10] and *telos* ("end").[11] Transitive actions, then, have a *peras* (goal) rather than a *telos* (end).[12] It follows that such actions are not instantaneous but protracted over time. The ultimate reason for this lies in the fact that transitive activity concerns the natural being in its materiality, and since matter always has certain dimensions, this necessarily implies that the action has a spatiotemporal goal.

1.2.2. Immanent Actions

Immanent actions enhance the agent that accomplishes them. Into this category fall such operations as, for example, seeing, hearing, wanting, or thinking. Their end consists in the action itself: The end of observing a painting is not to modify it or to produce any other external material effect but simply to see the painting. They are, then, instantaneous actions that do not take place via a process. We may use Aristotle's words to describe them: "At the same time we are seeing and have seen, are understanding and have understood, are thinking and have thought."[13]

A further point must also be made clear. In Chapter 2 we explained how life is distinguished by immanence, but we were then speak-

---

9. Italian distinguishes between *fine* and *termine*; German between *Ende* and *Ziel*. In English it is possible to make a distinction between "goal," as purpose, and "end," as the conclusion of something.

10. Whence the word "perimeter," the external limit of a surface or volume.

11. Whence the word "teleology," the doctrine of evidence of purpose.

12. Cf. Aristotle, *Metaphysics*, IX 6, 1048 b 18ss.

13. *Ibid.*, IX 6, 1048 b 23–24.

ing of immanence in the broad sense to distinguish the existence and activity of the living being from the pure exteriority of inert objects. Now we can say that immanence is to be found—correctly speaking, or at least to a more obvious degree—in cognitive life. In fact, we speak of immanence only when activity surpasses the exteriority of matter and its effect remains within the agent, and this is possible only if the action is immaterial, i.e., if it concerns forms and not matter.

1.3. Cognitive Activity

It should now be clear that knowledge is an immanent, not a transitive, activity. Among the immanent actions, cognitive activity has a "possessive," or "apprehensive," character. This distinguishes it from appetitive-type activities (about which we speak later), which depend upon inclination. Indeed, while in knowledge the cognitive being assimilates reality to itself, in inclination the subject is oriented, or tends, toward reality. As we have seen, immanent action relates to intentional existence, which is immaterial. Knowledge can be defined, then, as "the immaterial or intentional possession of a form."[14] This means that the form possessed through knowledge exists in the soul in a way different from that in which it exists in reality, i.e., intentionally and not naturally. In this definition, however, the terms "immaterial" and "intentional" are not completely synonymous.

"Immaterial" means "not formed of matter." The substantial or accidental forms of things exist united to matter,[15] whereas the form as it is known is called "immaterial" because it is conserved in the soul, separate from matter. For example, the perception of an apple has no flavor, but it is the real apple that has flavor; the thought of fire does not burn, but real fire does burn. Thus, it is said that the "known" form is a "likeness" of the real form that exists united to matter.

"Intentional" means "existing in the soul." The forms of extramental reality give things their specific existence, while the form possessed cognitively brings no reality into existence but itself exists only in the soul. Its existence is intentional; in other words, its activity consists in referring to the form of extramental reality that gives the substance its natural existence.

---

14. Cf. Aristotle, *De Anima*, II 12, 424 a 18–19.

15. Here we take no account of subsistent forms (i.e., the angels) since their existence is a matter of faith and, hence, their study is the province of theology.

Intentionality is an important characteristic of forms in the mind, and it presupposes immateriality. In the context of cognitive activity, "intentionality" does not mean something voluntary or desired; rather, it indicates that the knower, through the form possessed, is "turned," or "referred," toward the reality known. The cognitive form or species (the apple eaten, the flavor tasted) is in the mind, but it refers to the reality that it represents (the real apple, the real properties of its flesh) and that is known. In an etymological sense, we could say that we are "informed" by what we know and about what we know.[16]

2. Sense Knowledge

2.1. Sense Faculties and Intellectual Knowledge

Cognitive activity has two degrees: that of the senses and that of the intellect.[17] Sense knowledge belongs to the animals and to man. Its fundamental characteristic is the fact that it comes about through an organ of the body.[18] We have seen how the relationship between the faculty and the organ of sense is "hylomorphic" (of form and matter): Each faculty organizes and moves its organ in a way analogous to that in which the soul organizes and moves the body. The organs of sense are body parts specialized in the functions necessary for knowledge. Hence, their material constitution always implies some kind of limitation in the activity that they are capable of performing; i.e., the eye serves only to see and not to hear, and it cannot support an excessively bright stimulus; the ear serves only to hear and not to see, and it cannot support an excessive acoustic stimulus, and so on.

What we have just said concerning the limits of sense knowledge may be better understood if we compare it to intellectual knowledge. As we will see later, the intellectual faculties do not have a specific

---

16. Cf. S.L. Brock, *Tommaso d'Aquino e lo statuto fisico dell'anima spirituale*, cit., 71.

17. Keeping to the analytical approach being used in these early chapters, here we will examine sense knowledge in the specific aspects that distinguish it from intellectual knowledge. However, as we have already repeatedly observed, man's life experience is one of profound unity. Sciacca says: "The body moves the spirit, and the spirit the body. There is no spiritual movement that is not communicated to the body, which immediately feels and expresses it through internal feelings and external signs. There is no conscious sensation that does not also involve the spirit and cause it to move. Sensation is corporeal-spiritual; to feel is 'to think feeling' and to think is 'to feel thinking,' as Plotinus said" (M.F. Sciacca, *L'uomo questo "squilibrato"* [Palermo: L'Epos, 2000], 82).

18. On the subject of sense knowledge, a very clear explanation is to be found in J.J. Sanguineti, *Introduzione alla gnoseologia* (Florence: Le Monnier, 2003), 45–82.

organ, and they are not designated by matter to apprehend certain objects or undertake certain operations. The sense faculties, on the other hand, receive forms through the physical alteration of their specific organs so that those forms, though not material themselves, are determined by certain material conditions. These material conditions consist in the individuality and accidentality of the sense form, and this means that the sense faculty (or more simply the "sense") always knows an individual (i.e., not universal) and an accidental (i.e., not substantial) form: My sight sees *this* blue of *this* sea that I am contemplating but not *the* blue of *the* sea in a general or abstract sense. Moreover, a sense faculty can know only those objects capable of altering its organ within certain limits.[19]

2.2. The Organs and Faculties of Sense

How does sense knowledge, or more simply the action of "feeling," come about? In the first place, the organ is stimulated by something physical or corporeal. This alteration involves the reception of a specific extramental form such as the green of an olive tree or the perfume of a jasmine plant. However, it must be, as we have already explained, a form quantitatively and qualitatively "proportional" to the material capabilities of the organ, in other words, within its performance thresholds. In general, the eye can see colors and the ear hear sounds, but the human eye cannot see the chromatic range of infrared or that of ultraviolet, and the ear cannot hear very high- or very low-frequency sounds.

When the organ is physically stimulated, it receives a specific form in a material and purely passive way; i.e., it is "modified" by the act of a reality. For its part the sense faculty—which, together with the organ, forms a single unit[20]—receives the same form but in a formal, or intentional, way. In fact, the cognitive faculty is an operative, not a passive, potency, so its reception of a form cannot be material nor merely passive; quite the contrary, the faculty itself actualizes the form received and makes it known. It must also be made clear that the extramental form would not be known without the activity of the cognitive faculty; for example, a specific chemical quality of

---

19. The top and bottom limits within which sense phenomena can stimulate an organ are called the "threshold" capacity of each organ.

20. Cf. Thomas Aquinas, *In De Anima*, l. 2, lec. 24, n. 5.

the apple would not be a "flavor" if the apple was not tasted.[21] Thus, the "passage" from the specific natural form to the intentional sense form comes about by virtue of three factors: (1) the physical altera-tion or stimulation of the organ; (2) the unity between the organ and the faculty; and (3) the reception of the form in the faculty, which actualizes it. Bearing these three factors in mind, three important observations must be made.

1. Sense knowledge cannot be reduced to a physiological process even though it requires such a process in order to come about. The physical alteration of the organ, with the consequent reac-tion of the nervous system, does not constitute knowledge *per se* but is a prior transitive activity. The immanent activity of knowing occurs only in the act in which the form is received by the faculty, which actualizes it and makes it known. There is no process (i.e., an initial moment, a development, and an end) between the reception of the form and its becoming actu-alized: Knowledge is an immanent, and hence instantaneous, activity.

This specification is important because it might be thought that philosophical discourse on sense knowledge introduces excessive complication with respect to the (apparently sim-pler) explanations that a neurologist could give concerning the working of the organs of sight or hearing and their rela-tionship with the various areas of the brain. But the neurolo-gist only explains the mechanisms of the organ and, being a scientist, does not dwell on the ultimate principles of cognitive sense activity. We could say that, while the scientist exam-ines the physical changes and reactions that take place in the sense process, the philosopher reflects on the spiritual and intentional change associated with the physical change of the organ. Returning to the distinction made in Chapter 1, it could be added that the neurologist or physiologist explains how the sense perception of a stimulus (for example, something hot) occurs, while the scholar of philosophical anthropology asks himself what is this heat that I feel. These are two different, though interconnected, levels.

---

21. It is not enough for there to be a chemical exchange between material reality and the organ. This happens in plants, but their behavior does not show that they have what could properly be called knowledge.

2. The immanence and immateriality of sense knowledge are not complete. This is because of the organic foundation of such knowledge, i.e., its need for the physical alteration of an organ in order to come about. As we have noted, this incompleteness of immanence and immateriality is principally evident in the conditions of individuality and accidentality of sense forms. Later, we will see how complete immanence and intentionality belong only to intellectual activity.

3. The form received by the faculty has the "same" form as what is perceived, which exists, as we have reiterated on a number of occasions, naturally outside the mind and intentionally in the soul. From this derives a fundamental observation of Aristotle: "The activity of the sensible object and that of the percipient sense is one and the same activity."[22] This means, on the one hand, that no act of knowledge exists without an object—a kind of "pure thought"—because some *thing* is always known, and, on the other hand, that the known form is a single act in which the act of the knower (the faculty) and the act of the known (the real form) come together. Without these two acts, there is no knowledge.

Finally, we must make it clear that when we speak of *sense organs* we are referring to a complex structure that includes a peripheral part and a central part. The former gathers the sense stimuli that then, via the nervous system, reach specific areas of the brain where they are processed. The correct working of the sense faculties requires that all these structures should remain intact and, vice versa, if the peripheral or central parts were damaged, sense perception can be affected. Thus, for example, following the amputation of a limb, some sense of touch may persist at a neurological level, or a trauma in a specific area of the brain can prevent an individual from recognizing the stimuli from a peripheral organ.

3. EXTERNAL SENSES

Sense knowledge has various levels, depending upon the degree of immanence of the form known. The fundamental difference is the one that exists between the external senses and the so-called

---

22. Aristotle, *De Anima*, III 2, 425 b 26. Elsewhere Aristotle is even more terse: "Actual knowledge is identical with its object" (*ibid*, III 7, 431 a 1); "The mind that is actively thinking is the objects which it thinks" (*ibid*, III 8, 431 b 23).

internal senses, but even within these two categories it is possible
to establish a hierarchy on the basis of the degree of immanence, as
we will see shortly. The external sense faculties are in more direct
contact with reality, of which they distinguish more specific but, at
the same time, more superficial aspects. For their part, the internal
sense faculties process the external experience, distinguishing more
profound and more general aspects. In this chapter, we will consider
the external senses, leaving the study of the internal senses for the
next chapter.

We have said that sense knowledge distinguishes individual forms,
which are accidents of the substance, in other words, accidental
aspects of that which exists.[23] Yet not all accidents (quantity, relationship, or place, for example) are capable of directly stimulating
a sense organ; only the sense qualities can do so.[24] The external
senses, then, may be divided according to the various ways in which
real qualities stimulate their respective organs. Since Aristotle's time
it has been traditional to enumerate five senses: sight, hearing, smell,
taste, and touch. As we have said, among these we can establish a
hierarchy depending upon their degree of immateriality and immanence. This depends on two factors: the physical alteration of the
organ and the alteration of the means by which the qualities enter
into contact with the organ.[25]

Some senses such as touch and taste require direct contact with the
object and even material absorption of the qualities in order to perceive them (one cannot feel heat without to some extent warming
oneself, although warming oneself is not the same as feeling heat).
By contrast, other senses such as smell, hearing, and sight can work
at a distance from the object without having materially to acquire
the qualities sensed (the ear does not have to ring in order to hear,
nor the eye to change color in order to see).

Scientists still discuss the number of the external senses, and there
is some tendency to consider that there are more than five. It is a
problem that, for a number of centuries, has also aroused considerable interest among philosophers. Nonetheless, it seems probable
that certain sense activities, other than those listed above, are merely

23. Remember the explanations given in Chapter 3.
24. It must be further specified that not all qualities (for example, the figure something
   has, an operative potency, a habit, etc.) can alter the sense organ but only the so-
   called "affective qualities"; cf. Thomas Aquinas, *Summa Theologiæ*, I, q. 77, a. 3.
25. Cf. *ibid*, I, q. 78, a. 3, c.

joint operations of more than one sense or different modalities of the sense of touch.[26]

3.1. Touch

Touch is the most basic of the senses. Although other senses may be lacking in certain animal species, the tactile faculties are present in all living beings endowed with feeling. All the external senses are based on this sense and could, in some way, be considered as more- or less-developed configurations thereof.[27] In the case of man, a baby in the first months of life is principally dependent upon touch both for nutrition and for obtaining the information about its surroundings that it needs for development. Nevertheless, this is the most "material" and least immanent of all the senses because it requires not only direct physical contact with the object but also a certain material participation in its qualities; i.e., we cannot feel heat or cold without heating or cooling ourselves.[28]

In higher cognitive beings, the sense of touch is more developed (more "sensitive," we could say) in relation to the more balanced constitution of their bodies. Thus, Thomas Aquinas held that man is the creature that possesses this faculty in the most perfect degree. The animals may have other natural gifts that are more developed (as is the case, for example, with the senses of smell and sight of many animals), but only in man is touch open to such subtle and

---

26. For example, some hold that *proprioception* (the perception, through specific receptors, of the movements of one's own body) constitutes another sense. Others speak of "cutaneous senses" and distinguish the sense of touch from the sense of pain and the sense of temperature: cf. W. Arnold, H.J. Eysenck, and R. Meili, *Encyclopedia of Psychology* (New York: The Seabury Press, 1972), 688. For his part Peter Gray holds that a sense of pain does exist but then goes on to reach a somewhat perplexing conclusion: "Any attempt to define an exact number is entirely arbitrary because that which for one person is a single sense for another may consist of two or more senses" (P. Gray, *Psicología* [Bologna: Zanichelli, 1997], 299). Here, we feel, it would clearly be useful to unite the conceptual precision of philosophy with the experimental foundations of science.

27. Cf. Thomas Aquinas, *Summa Theologiæ*, I, q. 76, a. 5, c; *ibid*, I, q. 91, a. 3, ad 1. In fact, today we know that not only qualities of taste and smell but also of sound and light are actually particular states of matter (undulatory or corpuscular). We could, then, think in terms of a kind of "impact" of these qualities with the sense organ and hence the assimilation of all the senses with the sense of touch.

28. However, it must also be said that the immediacy of the contact does have degrees: We can feel the temperature of an object without having to touch it, but we cannot tell whether it is wet or dry without touching it.

diverse qualities.[29] As for the organic basis of this sense, it covers
the entire body of the living being, although some areas are better
predisposed than others. The fingers are particularly well adapted,
and so are the skin in general and even the internal tissues. The
activation of this organic base requires, as is the case for all organs
of sense, the concentration of specific nerve endings, and the sense
of touch is completely lacking, or much reduced, in those parts of
the body where such endings are absent or scarce, such as the hair
or nails.

3.2. Taste

With its higher degree of immateriality and immanence, the sense
of taste comes after that of touch. With the preceding sense it shares
the need for immediate contact with the object, and for a certain
material acquisition of the taste quality perceived. Despite this, it can
be maintained that taste is more immaterial than touch because it
has a more localized peripheral organ (the taste buds on the tongue)
and because taste qualities are more specific than tactile qualities. It
is also very interesting to note how the tongue can clearly differenti-
ate between tactile sensations and taste sensations. This underlines
the definite distinction between the two faculties.

Another specific characteristic of the organ of taste is its dampness:
Flavors are always perceived intermingled with a liquid such that
the complete absence of moisture would prevent the sensation and,
perhaps, even damage the organ. Even the driest of foods are dis-
solved or mixed with liquids secreted by the tongue itself (saliva) in
order to be tasted (this is what happens, for example, with salt and
with sugar). Conversely, an excess of liquid would make the flavors
imperceptible, as happens when many flavors are superimposed and
we find it difficult to recognize new ones.[30]

From the point of view of a living being's survival, taste may seem
like a superfluous faculty, yet it does provide vital information concerning the suitability of what an individual knows. Certainly, a reality is not suitable or unsuitable by the simple fact of being "tasty,"

29. Cf. Thomas Aquinas, *Summa Theologiæ*, I, q. 76, a. 5, c; *Sententia De Anima*, lib. 2,
l. 19, nn. 4–5. For example, the sense of touch is little developed in animals with an
external skeleton (insects and arachnids), and those whose skin is covered in scales
or notably thick (such as the great reptiles, hippopotamuses, and rhinoceroses, in
many fish, and in crustaceans). Referring back to Aristotle, St. Thomas relates the
development of the sense of touch to intelligence.
30. Cf. Aristotle, *De Anima*, II 10, 422 a 8–422 b 16.

but there is certainly a close relationship between the two aspects. For example, an animal tends to eat what it finds pleasurable, which is, at the same time, the food most suitable for it. Obviously, man's case is much more complex, fundamentally because the suitability of reality is understood at a much more profound level than that of the instinct or the senses; i.e., it is understood at the level of reason.

3.3. Smell

A great affinity with the sense of taste is to be found in the sense of smell, which has, however, a higher degree of immateriality and immanence because its organ does not have to be in direct contact with the object, nor does it have to acquire real qualities materially. With smell, sense forms can be perceived at a distance from the thing that possesses them. The greater immanence of the known object is also evident in the vast diversity of olfactory qualities and in the facility with which they can be linked to experience.

For example, it is a very common experience to associate a smell with a person, a house, a specific event of the past, and so on; something that may be called the "evocative capacity" of smells. This has great importance for animals in their search for food, reproduction, and defense. In man, on the other hand, the sense of smell is not particularly precise or well developed and is inferior to that of many animals. Nonetheless, the olfactory capacity of human beings is able to distinguish many qualities, which can be grouped into precise categories.[31]

As regards the peripheral organ of smell, it lies in a compact surface area located in the upper region of the nasal cavity (the "olfactory mucosa") and, partially, in certain zones near the sides of the nasal septum (the "olfactory epithelium"). From here the nerve stimulus reaches a center very near the brain. This center is one of the first parts of the nervous system to develop in the initial phases of the organism and, together with sight, is the first sense organ to become differentiated in the formation of the brain.[32] This shows the fundamental importance of the sense of smell in the life experience of a living being, at least as regards the elemental cognitive functions that control nutrition and reproduction.

---

31. Cf. J. Jiménez Vargas and A. Polaino-Llorente, *Neurofisiología psicológica fundamental* (Barcelona: Editorial Científico-Médica, 1983), 147.
32. Cf. *ibid*, 146–147.

3.4. Hearing

The sense of hearing has an even higher level of immateriality and immanence. With the sense of smell it shares the characteristic of functioning at a distance from its object and of not having to acquire materially the qualities perceived.[33] But in the case of smell, the air inhaled has to be heated in the nasal cavity in order for the chemical elements it contains to activate the organ, while for hearing the sound qualities require only a spatial and local alteration of reality.[34] Furthermore, hearing shares with sight the fact that the material agency that interacts with the organ is not chemical, as in the case of taste and smell, but physical, as in the case of touch — sound waves for hearing and light waves for sight.

Together with the faculty of sight, then, hearing is considered to be one of the higher external senses because of its greater degree of immateriality and immanence. However, unlike sight, the sense of hearing requires a certain change in reality in order to perceive sound qualities. These qualities are produced by the movement of bodies and, therefore, necessarily take place over time. In other words, even if the action of hearing, being immanent, does not follow a process, the real qualities must manifest themselves sequentially in order to be "heard."[35] The importance of this sense for human life is evident both in the diversity of sound qualities — tone, timbre, intensity, rhythm, duration, etc. — and in the fact that sound provides a special form of knowledge concerning the succession of phenomena. Hearing, then, can be considered as the sense *par excellence* of time and duration.

As regards the peripheral organ of hearing, it lies in the three parts of the ear: outer, middle, and inner. Air is of vital importance in the reception of sound because sound waves cannot pass through a vacuum. They can, however, pass though a solid body and even through water, although the ear of land animals is less well adapted to perceive sounds in a liquid.[36]

---

33. Cf. Aristotle, *De Anima*, II 8, 419 b 4 ss.
34. Cf. Thomas Aquinas, *Summa Theologiæ*, I, q. 78, a. 3, c.
35. The idea of "duration" is more relevant for a sound than for an image. It could be said that an instantaneous sound would be imperceptible as would a movement without time.
36. Cf. Aristotle, *De Anima*, II 8, 419 b 18.

3.5. Sight

The sense of sight is the most immaterial and immanent of the external faculties. Unlike touch and taste, and in common with smell and hearing, its organ — the eye — does not have to materially acquire the qualities perceived, e.g., it does not have to become colored or luminous in order to see. However, unlike smell and hearing, the organ of sight does not require a significant alteration in reality in order to be stimulated. The fact that the thing seen has to be illuminated is an irrelevant change compared with other changes in reality.[37]

Today we know that light is a physical medium and that its waves are transmitted over time, but such is their speed that they come close (at least as far as everyday experience is concerned) to being simultaneous. Thus we can say that sight requires the simultaneity of phenomena just as hearing requires their sequentiality. And it is certain that a sense, the organ of which can interact with real qualities almost simultaneously, is a sense very near those faculties that enjoy complete immanence and immateriality; hence the fact that the words "vision" and "illumination" have often been used to describe the activity of the mind.[38]

4. PROPER, COMMON, AND PER ACCIDENS SENSIBLES

Thus far we have dwelt, in general terms, on the external senses of sight, hearing, smell, taste, and touch, which have as their objects, respectively, colors, sounds, smells, tastes, and tactile qualities. These are called *proper*, or "primary," sense objects (or sensibles) both because each is perceived by just one sense and cannot be perceived by another and because in distinguishing them the sense with a correctly functioning organic base cannot mistake them.[39]

Yet, as we have already suggested, there also exist articulated and complex sense aspects that cannot be reduced to a single sense. These do not require the existence of different external senses but

---

37. St. Thomas, to whom we have made repeated reference, believed that light did not bring any form of material change (cf. Thomas Aquinas, *Summa Theologiæ*, I, q. 78, a. 3 c). Science in the last century proved that light, though a form of wave, is made up of particles called "photons," and so we must recognize that illumination always involves a modification, minimal though it may be, in the thing illuminated.

38. Cf. Thomas Aquinas, *Sententia De Anima*, lib. 2, l. 14, nn. 19–20.

39. Cf. *ibid*, lib. 2, l. 13, n. 2.

the interaction of the existing ones to give a more complex experience. These complex aspects have traditionally been given the name of *common*, or "secondary," sensibles, and they are the following: movement, rest, unity, number, figure, and magnitude.[40] In fact, with our senses we can apprehend whether something is moving or is still, whether it is one or many, that it has a certain external figure, whether it is large or small. It must not, however, be thought that these aspects are objects of all the senses at the same time. On the one hand, it is true that movement, rest, and number can be perceived by all the senses at once, whereas this does not hold true for figure or magnitude; on the other hand, touch and sight can distinguish all the common sensibles, whereas taste, smell, and hearing cannot.

Proper and common sensibles are called "sensibles *per se*" because they are the accidental, or individual, aspects of reality, which the external senses can apprehend for themselves. There are, however, other aspects of reality which are improperly said to be the object of the sense faculties. These are called "sensibles *per accidens*." Let us, for example, imagine that we are looking at a white horse: The object of our sight is actually the color, but, since the color white always belongs to a subject, we say that "we see" the horse; in other words, we attribute an accident to a corporeal substance. Yet, when we say this, we are not referring to the substantiality of the horse because substantiality is not something capable of stimulating a sense organ: It is not an accident or a set of accidents. Correctly speaking, then, "the individual existing horse" is not an object of sense knowledge but of intellectual understanding.[41] Something similar could be said about causality: To see something white born of a mare — the colt — is not to witness causality, even though that reality is the effect of a cause. Causality, like substance, is the object only of the intellect.[42]

SUMMARY OF CHAPTER 6

In Chapter 2 we spoke of the living being's capacity for immanence and transcendence. These two capacities are the basis of the dis-

---

40. Cf. Aristotle, *De Anima*, III 1, 425 a 15–17.

41. Cf. Thomas Aquinas, *Sententia De Anima*, lib. 2, l. 13, n. 5.

42. Precisely because substance and causality are the object of the intellect, certain theories that sought to reduce human knowledge to sense experience such as British empiricism of the seventeenth and eighteenth centuries (Berkeley, Locke, and Hume) have criticized these notions.

tinction between two kinds of action the being performs: transitive actions and immanent actions. Transitive actions are those which produce an external result distinct from the action itself, e.g., building, painting, cooking, etc. Immanent actions are those which do not produce a result distinct from the action itself because their outcome remains within the agent that performed them. Both sense knowledge and intellective knowledge are immanent actions. Cognitive activity may be defined as the immaterial or intentional possession of a form. In knowing, an individual intentionally assimilates reality.

Sense knowledge, which is specific to animals and human beings (plants do not, in the strict sense, possess it), comes about through particular organs of the body. These organs are the seat of the sensory faculties, which perceive cognitive forms in accordance with certain material conditions. This means that the cognitive sense form is always individual and accidental, i.e., it refers to the accidental aspects of reality.

Aristotelian-Thomistic philosophy distinguishes between the external and the internal senses. There are traditionally five external senses: touch, taste, smell, hearing, and sight, each with its own sense object (respectively, tactile qualities, tastes, smells, sounds, and colors). Through the interaction of the various senses, the common sensibles—including size, rest, and movement—are perceived.

CHAPTER 7

HUMAN KNOWLEDGE: INTERNAL SENSE EXPERIENCE

1. EXTERNAL SENSES AND INTERNAL SENSES

Sense experience is not limited to the external knowledge described in the last chapter but is processed at a more profound level by the so-called "internal senses."[1] Such processing is indispensable for the lives of cognizant beings because, as Thomas Aquinas explains, "We must observe that for the life of a perfect animal, the animal should apprehend a thing not only at the actual time of sensation, but also when it is absent. Otherwise... an animal would not be moved to seek something absent: the contrary of which we may observe specially in perfect animals, which are moved by progression."[2]

In external sense experience, many limits have to be overcome in order to be able to act on the basis of knowledge: No sense can perceive the object of the other senses, and hence it cannot unify or distinguish the phenomena; no sense conserves its sensations, and hence it does not enable the living being to act in the absence of the perceived reality; no sense is capable of evaluating the reality it apprehends, and hence it does not provide knowledge sufficient for action. However, observation shows that living beings endowed with knowledge overcome these limits in their behavior. We must, then, seek to understand what faculties "organize" sense experience and enable living beings to act on the basis thereof.

Firstly, a living being must be able to receive data from the external senses in a unitary but differentiated way; this comes about through the *common sense* (*sensus communis*). Secondly, it is necessary for this knowledge to be conserved in order for it to be used in various circumstances; this is the role of the *imagination*. Thirdly, the

---

1. The classical terminology of "external senses" and "internal senses" does not refer to the fact that the organs of the external senses are on the outside of the body, while those of the internal senses are inside. Rather, it suggests that the former are directly activated by a physical, chemical, or mechanical stimulus, while the latter come into play following the reception of external sense data: cf. C. Valverde, *Antropología filosófica* (Valencia: Edicep C.B., 2000), 149.

2. Thomas Aquinas, *Summa Theologiæ*, I, q. 78, a. 4, c.

living being must be able to apprehend the suitability or harmfulness of sensory reality in order to be able to act on the basis of its
knowledge; this task falls to the *estimative power* of animals and the
cogitative power of man. Finally, the living being must be capable
of conserving its evaluations in order to act at various moments in
time; this is the function of *memory*.[3]

As we explained in the last chapter, the sense faculties may be categorized according to the degree of immanence of the perceived
form. Now, having considered the various levels of immateriality
and immanence in external sense experience, we must do the same
for the internal senses, and to this end we may divide them into two
groups. On the one hand, certain senses receive or conserve sense
forms and are called the *formal senses*; these are the common sense
and the imagination. On the other hand, certain senses receive or
conserve sense values of suitability and are called the *intentional
senses*; these are the estimative powers (in man, cogitative powers)
and memory.[4] Each of the two groups has a hierarchy depending
upon their degree of immanence: The imagination is more immanent than the common sense, and the memory is more immanent
than estimative power (in man, cogitative power).

Lastly, as regards the organs of the internal senses (let us not forget
that we are talking about organic faculties), these are much less
clearly demarcated than is the case for the external senses. They are
located in various parts of the nervous system, particularly in the

---

3. This is the list given by Aristotle (*De Anima*, III, 1–3) and subsequently developed
   by Thomas Aquinas (cf. *Summa Theologiæ*, I, q. 78, a. 4, c). Scholars today use varied
   terminology; for example, some talk of "perception" to refer to the common sense
   or include cogitative powers in the study of learning; others diversify these senses
   or consider them all together in their joint activity (cf. J. L. Pinillos, *Principios de
   psicología* [Madrid: Alianza, 1988], 217–404). Aristotle's analysis still retains great
   value in the study of internal sense experience and helps us to understand the unity
   of man in his actions.

4. Cf. Thomas Aquinas, *Summa Theologiæ*, I, q. 78, a. 4, c. The aspects apprehended
   by these two senses are called "intentions" (*intentiones*) by St. Thomas: cf. Thomas
   Aquinas, *Summa Contra Gentiles*, l. II, c. 60, n. 1. This is why cogitative powers and
   memory are called the *intentional senses*, while the common sense and imagination
   are called *formal senses* because they refer directly to sense forms: cf. C. Fabro,
   Percezione e pensiero (Brescia: Morcelliana, 1962), 193–195.

so-called *areas* of the brain.[5] However, two clarifications must be made. Firstly, there is no unambiguous correspondence between the internal senses and these areas; in other words, a single sense may act on the basis of the stimulus—simultaneous or successive—of different areas. Secondly, the stimulus that triggers the operation is not an external stimulus but the action of the external senses themselves, which is processed by the brain at various levels. Let us now move on to give closer consideration to the internal senses.

2. THE COMMON SENSE

As we have seen, each of the external senses apprehends its particular object, but it has neither the ability to perceive its own operations nor that of distinguishing its own objects from those of the other senses. For example, sight apprehends the red color of an apple and, in normal conditions, distinguishes it from the green of the leaves, but it does not perceive the action of seeing, nor does it distinguish the redness of the skin from the sweetness of the flesh. These operations that are not performed by the external senses are, nonetheless, fundamental for the living being, which must be capable of absorbing sense aspects in a unitary and ordered fashion. What we perceive is not, in fact, a mishmash of phenomena presenting itself to our senses; rather, sense data has an order that reveals the unity of what we perceive outside the mind. Moreover, the living being is aware it is sensing, even without reflecting on its own acts, and this enables it to unify its own experience.

It follows, then, that there must be a faculty that unites the operations and objects of the external senses. This faculty is called the "common sense." Its object is no different from that of the individual external senses; rather, it is constituted of those same objects together with the operations of the senses themselves, apprehended

---

5. This is the conclusion that emerges from experimentations on animals and medical studies on man. It may be observed, in fact, that an injury to a specific area of the brain can lead to loss of memory, of imagination, of evaluation, or of the ability to give unity to sensations or distinguish them. These things, however, do not exclusively involve one single area. Today, in fact, neurophysiology tends to view the brain as a kind of "network" rather than as a grouping of "regions," or "areas," because there is almost complete interaction both among the parts of the brain and between them and the nervous system.

in a unitary fashion.[6] For this reason, the common sense has been called "perceptive synthesis" and "sense awareness," and it may be considered as the first level of the being's self-knowledge.[7] Its action is, then, a unification of sensations, or a grouping of unified sensations, and is given the name of "perception."

Hence, we can say that the common sense is the formal sense of the unity of sense experience, i.e., the faculty that unifies, in perception, the plurality of external sensations. It follows that it is the faculty responsible for the perception of the objects we have called "sensibles *per accidens.*" In fact, as we suggested in the previous chapter, a first approximation[8] of substance and causality (though not in the proper sense, i.e., not the nature of the reality perceived, nor the causal link in itself) is apprehended precisely in the sensorial unification of perception. For example, in knowing an apple the common sense attributes the sensation of red and that of sweetness to the same reality, linking them both to nutrition. It must, however, be clear that the common sense unifies but does not conserve the forms perceived by the external senses. This, as we will see, is the task of the imagination. Thus, the common sense is activated only in the presence of the reality concerned.

As for the organic foundation of this sense, neurophysiology holds that it is not highly localized but is to be found throughout the cerebral cortex.[9] By way of summary, we can here recapitulate the functions of the common sense as (a) apprehending the objects of all the external senses, (b) distinguishing those objects, (c) unifying them in perception, and(d) apprehending the acts of the external senses in a kind of "sense awareness."

---

6. Cf. Thomas Aquinas, *Sententia De Anima,* lib. 2, l. 13, n. 8. In this passage, St. Thomas also attributes to common sense the task of "perceiving that we live." Sanguineti, quite rightly, rather than talking of "common sense," uses the term *percezione integrale* (integral perception), which may appear less ambiguous today: cf. J.J. Sanguineti, *Introduzione alla gnoseologia* (Florence: Le Monnier, 2003), 57.

7. It is not a reflection in the true sense because the common sense does not know its own operation but that of other lower faculties.

8. We speak here of "first approximation" to underline the fact that substance and causality are apprehended in a way that is still vague and imprecise. For this reason, in psychology, this operation is sometimes called "primary organization of sensorial data," to distinguish it from the more perfect knowledge of the cogitative powers, which is given the name of "secondary organization of perception": cf. C. Fabro, *Percezione e pensiero,* cit., 108 ff., 193 ff.

9. Cf. H. Brown, *Brain and Behavior: A Textbook of Physiological Psychology* (Oxford: Oxford University Press, 1976), 149–274.

3. IMAGINATION

The unification of the external senses, performed by the common sense, is not momentary or transitory but is conserved at a sensory level. If this did not happen, knowledge would be interrupted in the absence of the reality that caused it and there would be a discontinuity among the various perceptions, which would make sensory life impossible. In order to conserve the perceptions, then, a faculty other than the common sense is necessary, and this faculty is *imagination*. Here, we find ourselves with a greater degree of immanence than that of perception because what is known "remains" in the cognizant being; i.e., it is conserved by the faculty. Consequently, imagination is not linked to the physical presence of reality but works independently.

It is evident that imagination is of great importance for living beings because conserving perceptions enables them to give continuity to their life experience and to unify it more completely. Such unification takes place as a kind of "generalization," i.e., an integration and extension of the known forms.[10] This faculty's capacity to "conserve while unifying" makes it particularly akin to the intellect and, we could say, it prepares the way for the latter's activity, for, as we will see, it is on the basis of images that intellectual abstraction can take place. Indeed, without imagination there can be no thought because something cannot be understood without some prior imaginative representation.[11] Yet it is equally important not to confuse imagination with thought because it is possible to imagine things that are false, while the comprehension of something cannot be false.[12]

Nor must we confuse imagination with the perception that belongs to the common sense. For example, we can exercise our imagination while we are asleep, but we cannot do the same with our perception; moreover, some form of reality may arouse a sensation in us and be

---

10. The processing of these forms is, in fact, called "image" or, to use classical terminology, "phantasy." Later, we will see that the unification performed by the intellect is of a higher level, not being a simple generalization but a "universalization," in other words, a knowledge that is superior not so much in the breadth of what is known but in its in-depth "comprehension."

11. Cf. Aristotle, *De Anima*, III, 3, 427 b 14–16.

12. In the sense that we either understand or do not understand, that which has been understood cannot be false. We must not confuse the understanding of a thing with the judgment or evaluation of what has been understood. Later, we will see the distinction between these two operations of the intellect.

perceived without being represented in the imagination.[13] Nonethe-less, it remains true that the activity of this faculty follows the action of the common sense (that is, of perception); i.e., we cannot imagine without having sensed and perceived.[14] Based on a number of stud-ies, Jolivet observes that people are able to create images only on the basis of the senses they have or have had. For example, those born blind and deaf can use tactile, olfactory, and taste images with great precision but not other images,[15] while the loss of a sense function through the damage of a periphery organ does not involve the loss of images relating to objects specific to that sense.[16]

Imagination performs the first integration of space and time into knowledge.[17] Indeed, this faculty is able to bring together the com-mon sensibles — previously acquired by the external senses and partially unified in the perception[18] — into a single complex form.

We spoke above of a continuity between human imagination and intellect. The truth is that such continuity is to be found in all man's sense faculties, and this makes them more perfect than those of the animals. Such perfection is evident at a lower level in the external senses and the common sense, but it is more obvious in the imagi-nation, for, while in animals this faculty is a simple "archive" of perceptions, in human beings it supplies the intellect with "material" on the basis of which to extract universal concepts.

In other words, human imagination is the faculty that establishes the link between sensory life and intellectual life. And human imagina-tion has a greater operative range and more complex objects than does animal imagination, which is simpler and more rigid.[19] Indeed, it is precisely because human imagination establishes continuity

---

13. Cf. Aristotle, *De Anima*, III, 3, 428 a 6–10.

14. Cf. *ibid*, III 3, 429 a 1.

15. Cf. R. Jolivet, *Trattato di filosofia*, Vol. II: *Psicologia* (Brescia: Morcelliana, 1958), 213.

16. Cf. *ibid*, 234, which cites the example of Beethoven who continued to compose music even after becoming deaf.

17. Cf. J. Vicente Arregui and J. Choza, *Filosofía del hombre: Una antropología de la intimidad* (Madrid: Rialp, 1991), 185.

18. Let us again say that the incompleteness of the unification is due to the fact that the common sense unifies sensations but does not conserve the perceptions. This conservation is the task of the imagination.

19. This is why we sometimes use "imagination" to refer only to the human faculty while the analogous faculty in animals is referred to with the term "fantasy."

between sense experience and the higher faculties that it is at the disposal of those faculties, i.e., of the intellect and the will.[20]

Imagination is of particular importance when it comes to invention and artistic creation. Of course, some discoveries are strictly rational and not merely sensory (a mathematical theorem, for example, or a chemical formula), but we speak of "inventions" to refer specifically to imaginative processes which may concern the field of art, the sciences, or technology. In fact, any work, technical or artistic as it may be, requires design and planning and, in this, imagination plays an important role.[21] Later, we will see that creative capacity would serve little purpose if it were not guided by intelligence, and, hence, when we speak of "creative imagination," we are really referring to the imagination as guided by practical intelligence, which is the faculty (the nonsensory faculty) capable of organizing the means with a view to an end.[22] It is clear from what we have said that it is important to educate the imagination in order to contribute to the formation of the personality.

Identifying the organ of imagination is a complicated question, even more so than it is for perception. We have seen how, unlike the external senses, the organic basis for the internal senses is not clearly demarcated. In the case of the imagination, however, it is not even fixed or determined, although it is localized. It could be said that the organic basis of the imagination is made up of certain neuronal circuits that change over the course of an individual's life. In other words, the brain and the nervous system progressively adapt in keeping with the activity of the imagination.[23] This is a

20. It could be argued that a large part of mental disturbances are due to a lack of harmonization of the imagination with the will and the intellect, in other words, to a kind of "independent" functioning. This partly explains why drawings and the recounting of dreams are used in clinical tests: cf. J. Vicente Arregui and J. Choza, *Filosofía del hombre: Una antropología de la intimidad*, cit., 187. Later, we will see that the relationship between the sensory imagination and the volitive-rational sphere is not one of dependency or of absolute dominance but of relative control.

21. The importance of a design, or a sketch, in the arts and sciences is evident from the fact that often it is necessary to produce a model of a work before realizing it. In this field, for example, science and technology currently make great use of computer simulations.

22. Cf. R. Jolivet, *Trattato di filosofia: Vol. II: Psicología* (Brescia: Morcelliana, 1958), 261–262.

23. This theory accords with a fact of neurophysiology: Although the cells of the nervous system—the neurons—do not significantly increase in number after birth (around 100 billion, with a certain progressive loss), encephalic mass increases fourfold before reaching adulthood. This is due to the growth of the dendrites and axons, which are the parts of the neuron responsible for receiving and transmitting information (i.e., the biological material of neuronal circuits).

very important observation because only an organ that is not rigidly determined (unlike the organs of the external senses) is capable of conserving forms in the absence of the physical presence of the reality from which those forms came.

By way of summary, we can say that imagination is the faculty that conserves perceptions and causes them to be present once again. It can be defined, then, as the formal sense of the continuity of external sense experience. If, as we have already observed, perception is a unification of sensations, we can now add that imagination is an archive of perceptions.[24] The functions of the imagination can, then, be recapitulated as follows: (a) conserving the perceptions of the common sense, (b) completing them by adding other previously conserved perceptions, (c) combining various perceptions to obtain more general images, and (d) supplying the intellect with general images in order for it to be able to extract universal concepts.

4. COGITATIVE POWER

Let us now move on to consider other internal senses, those we have called "intentional." These apprehend and conserve the particular sensory aspects that concern the suitability or harmfulness of things. These aspects (called, indeed, *intentiones*, i.e., intentions) provoke a certain movement of the will in living beings, for the truth is that known realities do not attract or repel if they are not considered as being either suitable or harmful.[25] As Aristotle observes, we can imagine the most terrible things yet remain calm, as happens when we see some horrific scene depicted in a painting, yet this does not happen if we consider those realities to be dangerous or harmful.[26] A sheep, for example, does not flee the wolf because it is black and ugly but because the sheep recognizes it as something that may harm her.

The faculty that apprehends the suitability or harmfulness of an individual sensory reality is called *cogitative power* in man and *estimative power* in animals. The action of cogitative and estimative power contains some degree of anticipation of the future because it implicitly distinguishes the end to which the individual is oriented.

---

24. The idea of "archive" implies not only the unification of forms but also their conservation, which is the specific function of the imagination.

25. Cf. C. Fabro, *Percezione e pensiero*, cit., 196–201.

26. Aristotle, *De Anima*, III, 3, 427 b 21–25.

On the basis of various evaluative perceptions, this faculty can orient activity and enable the acquisition of experience. Hence, cogitative or estimative power may also be called the "intentional sense of the future."[27]

The functions of cogitative and estimative power may be summarized as follows: (a) appraising the individual aspects of the sensory reality, (b) directing activity on the basis of that evaluative perception, and (c) acquiring experience both of the individual aspects themselves and of the practical action that concerns them. This is the basis of the ability to learn and be trained.

From what we have just said, it is evident that cogitative and estimative power are closely related to natural instinct, about which we will speak more fully in Chapter 9. Here, we will limit ourselves to observing that all instincts contain an aspect of inclination and an aspect of knowledge. Think, for example, how a swallow recognizes the material appropriate for building its nest. Nonetheless, estimative power in animals is guided by natural instinct and, hence, offers rigidly defined information concerning the suitability or harmfulness of a particular reality. On the other hand, cogitative power in man is guided by reason and, hence, is capable of considering various motives for the suitability or harmfulness of things, applying the judgment of reason to concrete reality. This is why cogitative power is also called "particular reason" (*ratio particularis*)[28] because in some way it participates in intellectual knowledge and acts by gathering the various elements of sense knowledge.

5. MEMORY

Memory has the task of conserving and re-presenting the evaluative perceptions of the cogitative power. Hence, it may be called the "intentional sense of the past" just as the cogitative or evaluative power is of the future, as we said above. The relationship between these two intentional senses is analogous to that which exists between the formal senses, i.e., the common sense (which apprehends forms unitarily) and the imagination (which conserves the forms and re-presents them).

---

27. Cf. J. Vicente Arregui and J. Choza, *Filosofía del hombre: Una antropología de la intimidad* (Madrid: Rialp, 1991), 189.
28. Cf. Thomas Aquinas, *Summa Theologiæ*, I, q. 78, a. 4, c.

The function of memory is, then, similar to that of imagination, although it concerns evaluations and not forms. Yet, precisely because it deals with evaluations, there is another important difference between the two: Memory in some way distinguishes time, while imagination is unable to do so. Indeed, evaluations do not merely correspond to the qualities of the external realities that are the object of our senses but also refer to our own subjective dispositions. Thus, that which is conserved in the memory — having first been apprehended by the cogitative or estimative power — is the interior activity of the living being itself, in other words its own "life experience."[29] From this description, it is evident that memory is vital for the consolidation of acquired experience. In the immediate, it is the estimative or cogitative power that makes such experience possible, but it is in the memory that it is conserved and consolidated.

Bearing in mind the fact that memory is a sense faculty (and hence an organic faculty),[30] it may be understood why certain brain injuries can result in a loss of the perception of subjective identity. This fact, however, does not mean we can affirm, as some authors have, that the self is located in the brain.[31] The human "I" is not reducible to the experience of self, nor to the soul or body separately; rather, it implies the totality of spiritual and corporeal substance.[32] Nonetheless, sense memory — by the conservation of its own experience — does involve a kind of "awareness of one's own identity," though very limited; yet this awareness is not exclusive to the internal sense of memory because the human self is not merely corporeal and thus cannot be fully apprehended by the senses. The area of the brain responsible for memory is sometimes inappropriately called "localization of awareness of self." As we will see, such awareness only really exists at the intellectual level because the intellect is capable of apprehending and conserving both the material and spiritual aspects of experience.

The functions of memory may be summarized in the following three points: (a) conserving evaluative perceptions, (b) articulating sensa-

---

29. We will return to this subject in Chapter 19, when we discuss human temporality.

30. There are various kinds of memory involving different areas of the brain and the limbic system: the sensory memory (the short-lived trace of the sensory stimulus in the ear or eye, for example), a short-term memory, and a long-term memory (cf. P. Gray, *Psicología* [Bologna: Zanichelli, 1997], 399–436).

31. Cf. K.R. Popper and J.C. Eccles, *The Self and Its Brain* (New York: Routledge, 1984), chapters P4, E7.

32. We will return to this subject in Chapter 13.

tions over time, and (c) giving continuity to internal experience. In this faculty, too, there is a notable difference between human beings and animals, for, while animals remember things instinctively, in human beings memories can be controlled and arranged[33] thanks to the fact that memory also participates at the level of the intellect and the will.

Cogitative power and memory have their organic basis in certain highly localized areas of the brain. Injury to these areas can cause a partial or total loss in the ability to recall.

SUMMARY OF CHAPTER 7

In the preceding chapter, we explained how Aristotelian-Thomistic philosophy distinguishes between the external and the internal senses. While the external senses are directly activated by a stimulus, the internal senses are activated subsequent to the reception of the external sensory data. Indeed the internal senses can be activated even in the absence of an external stimulus.

Although today some scholars use partly differing terminology, there are traditionally four internal senses: firstly, the common sense, which brings together and distinguishes between the perceptions of the external senses. Secondly, the imagination, which conserves and unifies the sense perceptions; sense images are the basis for the intellective activity of human beings. Thirdly, cogitative power (called estimative power in animals), which apprehends sensory aspects regarding the suitability or harmfulness of things. Fourthly, the memory, which conserves and re-presents the evaluative percep-tions of the cogitative power; in this way memory articulates sensa-tions over time and gives continuity to internal sense experience.

---

33. To underline this distinction St. Thomas speaks of memory in animals and of reminiscence in man: cf. Thomas Aquinas, *Summa Theologiæ*, I, q. 78, a. 4 c.

CHAPTER 8

HUMAN KNOWLEDGE: THE INTELLECT

1. INTELLECTUAL KNOWLEDGE

In Chapter 6 we gave a general presentation of cognitive life, affirming that it is distinguished by its immanence and immateriality. However, we also explained that in sensory knowledge these two characteristics are always limited by the material condition of sense forms and that only intellectual knowledge is fully immanent and immaterial. The previously quoted Aristotelian phrase to the effect that the cognizant soul "is in a certain way all existing things" finds its full confirmation at this level, for the intellect can know everything that is and hence "conform itself" thereto (although each sense can only apprehend its own objects with the specific characteristics with which they present themselves).

This is why we can speak of a potentially unlimited openness of the intellect—a consequence of its immateriality. Yet, what do we mean when we say that intellectual knowledge is immaterial? We have already partly answered this question in the last two chapters when we explained that sense faculties are limited by their organic base; i.e., they can only distinguish certain stimuli within certain thresholds. An overly strong stimulus might harm the organ, at least temporarily, while too weak a stimulus would not be perceived as in the case of an explosion that may damage the hearing or a sound so low as not to be heard. This is due precisely to the materiality of sensory knowledge. Intelligence, on the other hand, does not have a threshold below which it cannot work since no reality is too small to be understood; nor is there a threshold above which the intellectual faculties would be damaged. Quite the contrary, a higher level of intellectual knowledge enables a better understanding of other areas of reality. Of course, this does not mean that we know everything that exists, but it does mean that if, at the present time, we do not know some specific aspect of the world (for example, a new animal species or one of the genes of the human genome), this does not depend upon structural limitations of the intellect.

Based on an idea of Aristotle's, Thomas Aquinas formulated the following conclusion: "It is clear that by means of the intellect man can have knowledge of all corporeal things. Now whatever knows certain things cannot have any of them in its own nature because that which is in it naturally would impede the knowledge of anything else…. Therefore, if the intellectual principle contained the nature of a body, it would be unable to know all bodies…. It is likewise impossible for it to understand by means of a bodily organ since the determinate nature of that organ would impede knowledge of all bodies."[1]

To argue that intelligence is immaterial does not, of course, mean to forget that the person is a corporeal-spiritual being. On the contrary, it must be recognized that the role of the senses is indispensable to the intellect because, in order to be able to achieve a knowledge of the "nature of bodies" (i.e., the essence of things), we need the sense forms apprehended by the external and internal senses. Thus, we can say that "the phantasm [i.e., the image supplied by the imagination] is to the intellect what color is to the sight."[2] For example, we can know the essence of a cat, understand what a cat is, and provide a definition of cat only on the basis of earlier sense perceptions of individual cats. Here, once again, we see the importance of not introducing a fracture (body / soul, senses / intellect) into the unity of the person.

2. WHAT WE KNOW WITH THE INTELLECT, AND HOW WE KNOW IT

At this point, we must explain, at least in general terms, what it means "to know the nature of bodies," leaving the task of more profound definitions to the philosophy of knowledge. This expression means that, while the senses apprehend individual aspects of the things we have before us (their color, size, smell, and so on), the intellectual faculty knows what each thing is; in other words, its essence (not the individual trees that I can see and touch in this garden but what each tree is in itself). Thus, while the sense faculties

---

1. Thomas Aquinas, *Summa Theologiæ*, I, q. 75, a. 2, c. Cf. Aristotle, *De Anima*, III, 4, 429 a 13–429 b 6.

2. Thomas Aquinas, *Summa Theologiæ*, I, q. 75, a. 2, ad 3. As Brock explains, "Although the operation of the intellect in man is *per se* incorporeal, it does nonetheless possess a natural link with the body because of the fact that it takes place in conjunction with the operation of the senses" (S. L. Brock, *Tommaso d'Aquino e lo statuto fisico dell'anima spirituale*, cit., 79).

know the particular, the intelligence knows the universal, i.e., the concept or idea that is not circumscribed to this or that individual (the essence of tree is the same for the palm trees in the garden, the plantains in the city street, and the larches on the mountain slopes).

There is, then, a passage from the sense level to the intellective level, and this passage is called *abstraction*, or apprehension of essence. The universal essence is reached by abstracting or liberating sense forms from their particularity through a more or less elaborate comparison between sense images. To this end, it is indispensable that the mind remain open to reality; reality not created but illuminated by the human intellect, which, on the one hand, actively seeks to illuminate that which is intelligible and universal in the sense images and, on the other, acts as a passive force that receives and conserves the intellectual forms that have been extracted. These intellectual forms are eminently intentional, as we explained in Chapter 6. They are not what the intellect knows — otherwise they would separate us from reality — rather, they are the means by which we know reality. In other words, intellective knowledge is not limited to the abstraction of the concept but always refers back to the concreteness and individuality of reality.[3] For example, if we had encountered the famous Italian poet Giuseppe Ungaretti, we would not have stopped at the intellective knowledge of the abstract idea of man but would have intellectively known Giuseppe Ungaretti as a human being with all his own unmistakable peculiarities.

Precisely in order to gain a better knowledge of what an individual being is, we bring our various intellectual apprehensions together into a *judgment*. In this second operation of the intellect, we affirm or deny a property of a certain subject such as when we assert, "Giuseppe Ungaretti is a person," or, "My cat is not a person." It is here that truth and error come into play, for, in formulating a judgment, we can either effectively mirror reality or make a mistake.

A simple judgment, such as those just mentioned, may be articulated in *reasoning*, an operation characteristic of human intelligence, which we exercise discursively. This means that only rarely do we apprehend reality intuitively and directly, and, most of the time, in order to reach a conclusion about something, we must bring together

---

3. As Sanguineti explains, "Concepts are intentional mediators of thought and … are immanent objects *quo* (by means of which) reality is apprehended, and not *quod* objects of thought; i.e., they are not the final goal of the objectivizing operation of understanding" (J.J. Sanguineti, *Introduzione alla gnoseologia*, cit., 85).

previously formulated judgments. This happens, for example, in syllogistic reasoning in which we reach a conclusion on the basis of a premise: "My cat is an animal, and all animals are mortal; therefore, my cat is mortal."

Two further observations on this subject must be made. We have identified three operations of the intellect (apprehension of essence, or abstraction; judgment; and reasoning, or argument). This means that our intellective knowledge is progressive but not that it is fragmented. Often, precisely in order to understand the essence of something, we must formulate judgments and follow reasoning, so there is no gap between one operation and the other.

Finally, intellective knowledge can be an end unto itself or it can be aimed at some final purpose. The first of these two possibilities is called speculative, or theoretical, knowledge (for example, that of a birdwatcher who studies the flight of the quail); the second is practical knowledge (that of the hunter who studies the flight of the quail in order to position himself best). We will return to this distinction when we speak about values in Chapter 17, in Part II of this book.

3. SELF-AWARENESS, OR SELF-KNOWLEDGE

One consequence of the immateriality of the intellect is the capacity of the cognizant being to know itself, to be aware of itself, to "return to itself." By this we do not mean the kind of reflection we could define as objective by means of which we investigate the nature of the person and of his capacity for reason. Rather, we are alluding to the subjective reflection that occurs concomitantly with the action of knowing by which we could say that intelligence is present unto itself in the sense that we perceive that we are exercising intellectual knowledge and are aware that we are actually knowing something.

Why this is a consequence of immateriality is explained by St. Thomas in the following terms: "To return to its own essence means only that a thing subsists in itself. Inasmuch as the form perfects the matter by giving it existence, it is in a certain way diffused in it, and it returns to itself inasmuch as it has existence in itself. Therefore, those cognitive faculties which are not subsisting but are the acts of organs do not know themselves, as in the case of each of the senses, whereas those cognitive faculties which are subsisting know themselves."[4] Only that which is spiritual can return to itself or reflect fully upon itself because it does not intrinsically depend upon matter, which implies limitation and uni-directionality in the sense of a rigid tendency toward a specific objective. This is why animals have only imperfect self-awareness because sense knowledge intrinsically depends on an organic base and is subject to its limitations.

4. INTELLIGENCE AND SPEECH

One of the areas in which the specific nature of intelligence is most evident is that of speech, in which the symbolic capacity of the human being is expressed. In fact, we understand and symbolically represent reality through signs of various kinds, especially phonetic and graphic signs. Thanks to speech we can communicate with our fellows and express our intentional openness to the surrounding world. From this capacity derives language in the sense of an organically structured system or assembly of signs, about which we will have something to say in Chapter 16.

In order to understand why speech is a particularity exclusive to human beings, it may help to begin with an extract from Aristotle:

> Now, that man is more of a political animal than bees or any other gregarious animals is evident. Nature, as we often say, makes nothing in vain, and man is the only animal whom she has endowed with the gift of speech. And whereas mere voice is but an indication of pleasure or pain and is therefore found in other animals (for their nature attains to the perception of pleasure and pain and the intimation of them to one another, and no further), the power of speech is intended to set forth the expedient and inexpedient and therefore likewise the just and the unjust. And it is a characteristic of man that he alone has any sense of good and evil, of just and unjust, and the like, and the association of living beings who have this sense makes a family and a state.[5]

This extract highlights a fundamental characteristic of human speech: the fact that it can refer to abstract and universal objects

---

4. Thomas Aquinas, *Summa Theologiæ*, I, q. 14, a. 2, ad 1.
5. Aristotle, *Politics*, I, 2: 1253 a 10–12. The Greek text uses the term *logos*, translated as "speech," and the term *phoné*, translated as "voice."

(the good and the bad, the just and the unjust); while animal communication always refers to concrete, tangible objects.[6]

There is, in fact, a qualitative difference between the language of man and that of animals. Various experiments conducted over a period of years on chimpanzees (which possess a sufficiently developed phonetic capacity) have shown that they are able to acquire a language of gestures and even a verbal language (in the experiment to which we are referring, just four words: papa, mama, cup, up) which, however, they use only for communicating with pragmatic intent (requesting food, attracting attention, etc.).[7] In man, on the other hand, language is not acquired by simple imitation but by virtue of his capacity to recognize patterns and relationships. A child speaks to ask questions and learn about the world, and language develops by a form of retroactive control enacted by listening to the words pronounced. A child, then, is hungry for words; it asks the names of things and continually exercises its capacities, even by itself.[8]

---

6. In a certain sense echoing Aristotle's views, Heidegger writes: "Man is said to have language by nature. It is held that man, in distinction from plant and animal, is the living being capable of speech. This statement does not mean only that, along with other faculties, man also possesses the faculty of speech. It means to say that only speech enables man to be the living being he is as man. It is as one who speaks that man is man" (M. Heidegger, *On the Way to Language* [London and New York: Harper & Row, 1971], 189). And he adds, "Man would not be man if he were not able to speak — to say 'it is' — uninterruptedly, for any reason, with reference to anything, in various forms, most of the time remaining silent. In as much as language grants this power, man's being rests upon language." Heidegger does not conceive of language only as the expressive faculty of the individual; rather, though taking this into account, his ideas reveal a vision of man whose nature is not permanent but essentially historical.

7. Cf. J.C. Eccles, *Evolution of the Brain: Creation of the Self* (London and New York: Routledge, 1989), 71–78.

8. Papousek's studies of 1985 highlighted major differences between children and young chimpanzees. While chimpanzees remain largely silent, children are constantly chattering. The sounds uttered by children left alone were systematically recorded and demonstrated that they constantly exercised their capacities, with a progressive improvement in their pronunciation of phonemes: cf. M. Papousek, H. Papousek, and M. Bornstein, "The Naturalistic Vocal Environment of Young Infants: On the Significance of Homogeneity and Variability in Parental Speech," in *Social Perception in Infants* (Norwood, NJ: Allen Publishing Corp., 1985), 269–297. This situation had already been extensively described in a number of psycholinguistic studies dating back to the beginning of the last century. A child's so-called "hunger for names" appears in the twenty-third month of life when it repeatedly names the objects it has at hand. This is not simply a mechanical and mnemonic process of learning but the beginning of a relationship with the objective world (cf. E. Cassirer, *An Essay on Man: An Introduction to a Philosophy of Human Culture* [Garden City, NY: Doubleday and Co., 1953], 170–171).

At the end of the nineteenth century, progress in the study of biology and the spread of Darwinism led some people to maintain that speech and acts of linguistic expression are dictated by certain biological needs and are used in accordance with precise biological laws. In man, the theory went, there is a direct passage from mere expression of emotion to language in the true sense, and the difference between animal and human language lies only in humans having attained a higher level of evolution.

In the first place, it must be objected that this is merely a statement that explains nothing about why such diversities should exist in the first place. Furthermore, the analysis of linguistic structure highlights a radical difference between emotive language and propositional language (i.e., the language that describes or designates objects with words articulated in a proposition and that is associated with the use of the intelligence): The interjection or exclamation typical of an emotional reaction is used precisely when we cannot or do not wish to speak. Research done in this field leads us to recognize that "there is no psychological proof that animals have ever crossed the frontier that separates emotional language from propositional language."[9]

So-called animal language, as we have explained, expresses emotional states associated with the sphere of sense experience, but it does not indicate objects or actions. Its apparent similarity to human language is purely material in character and does not exclude — rather, it accentuates — its formal and functional difference. Moreover, no historical proof exists that man, even in the lowest forms of his culture, ever used a purely emotive or gestural language.

5. THE MIND-BODY PROBLEM

Among the questions that need to be dealt with through a fruitful dialogue between the sciences and philosophy is that which today is called the *mind-body relationship.* This is certainly not a new question, as it has been the subject of reflection over many centuries, but the progress made in the neurosciences has provided an impulse for it to be formulated in a new and, in a certain sense, more precise way.

---

9. Cf. E. Cassirer, *An Essay on Man,* cit., 150; cf. also *ibid,* 48.

Sometimes, but more rarely, it is described as the "mind-brain relationship," but this definition is inadequate (whatever the proposed
solution) because it induces us to think that there is an exclusive
relationship between the cerebral structures and a person's rationality, when in fact intellective capacity interacts with the entire body,
with sense experience, and with the emotions. This fact marks a radical difference between artificial intelligence and human intelligence
because the latter is never just the mere execution of operations
comparable to those of a computer. As we have said, the human
being exercises his cognitive faculty in association with the senses
and with his affective, or emotional, states as well as interacting with
the surrounding environment.

The problem could be reduced to its essential aspects by asking the
question: What is meant by the term "mind"? If by this word we
mean only a particular physical state deriving from certain neuronal processes, we inevitably fall into *materialism* or *physicalism*, to
which is associated the theory known as *eliminativism*.[10] If, on the
other hand, by the word "mind" we mean something that cannot be
reduced to matter, then various solutions open up that can be linked
to the more general problem (mentioned in Chapters 3 and 4) of
the relationship between mind and body. One of these solutions is
that of *dualism*, which distinguishes the spiritual from the physical,
but we then find ourselves with the difficulty of keeping these two
aspects together. It has been sought to solve this difficulty through
interactionism (still in a dualistic perspective), an idea supported,
for example, by J. C. Eccles who sought to explain the interaction
between body and mind on the basis of his neurological studies.
But the path of dualism is always, so to say, a path on the defen-
sive in the sense that it must seek laboriously to resolve the questions raised by personal experience itself and by the progress of the
human sciences.

There is no space here to outline all the viewpoints in the current
debate on this subject, in which there are also intermediate posi-

---

10. This theory holds that, in order to resolve the mind-body problem, it is necessary
    to "eliminate" the prescientific concepts of common sense that philosophy
    has used up to now. Only in this way will it be possible to arrive at a scientific
    form of psycho-neurophysiology: cf. S. Nannini, "*Mente e corpo nel dibattito
    contemporaneo,*" in *L'anima,* cit., 36–37. Another theory often associated with the
    materialist approach is that of functionalism.

tions with respect to the two mentioned above.[11] One of these, for example, is that of J. Searle, who has the merit of distancing himself from materialism in the strict sense and from a reductionist view of the human mind, although he does remain within the sphere of biological naturalism in his explanation of mental processes and awareness.[12] In our view, in order not to fall into an inadequate conception of the human person (and so, to all intents and purposes, to deny his freedom), the solution must be sought in the area of *dual theory* which, on the basis of Aristotelian and Thomistic philosophy, considers soul and body (and, as a consequence, mind and body) as two coprincipals of the one living individual.[13] Within the framework of this fundamental approach, to which we will return in Chapter 12, it is possible to find an answer, as various authors have sought to do, to the questions raised by the modern-day cognitive sciences.[14]

SUMMARY OF CHAPTER 8

In Chapter 6 we explained how knowledge is, in general terms, the immaterial or intentional possession of a form. In sensory knowledge, this comes about at a lower level because it has an organic base and the cognitive sense form is always individual and accidental. By contrast, intellectual knowledge is a completely immanent, and *per se* immaterial, activity.

By means of the intellect, human beings are able to know and assimilate all of reality. For this reason, Aristotle affirmed that the soul "is in a certain way all existing things." The universal nature of intellective knowledge is a sign of its immateriality because, while with the sensory faculties we apprehend only the particular aspects of a given object at a particular place and time, through intellective activity we know the essence of things, in other words, what a thing is in itself,

---

11. A recent and well-documented contribution to the topic is that of J.J. Sanguineti, *Operazioni cognitive: un approccio ontologico al problema mente-cervello*, "Acta Philosophica," II / 14 (2005), 233–258; edited by the same author, see also the thematic bibliography *Filosofia della mente e scienza cognitiva*, "Acta Philosophica," II / 14 (2005), 343–348.

12. On this matter, see the following interview: J.R. Searle, "*L'irriducibilità della coscienza: Intervista a cura di E. Carli*," in *L'anima*, cit., 105–120.

13. A concise and helpful overview of the subject is to be found in L. Borghi, *L'antropología tomista e il* body-mind problem *(alla ricerca di un contributo mancante)*, "Acta Philosophica," II / 1 (1992), 279–292. See also J.J. Sanguineti, *Introduzione alla gnoseologia*, cit., 48–56.

14. Cf. G. Basti, "*Dall'informazione allo spirito: Abbozzo di una nuova antropología*," in *L'anima*, cit., 41–65.

abstracting it from individual differences and characteristics. The operations of the intellect are abstraction, judgment, and reasoning.

The immateriality of the intellect is what makes full self-awareness of human beings possible because things limited by matter cannot reflect upon themselves. Thanks to intellectual activity, human language is *per se* different from that of animals, for, while animals communicate only emotive states and sense perceptions, human beings also communicate universal and abstract concepts such as justice and injustice, good and evil, beauty and ugliness, etc. Reflection on intellectual activity has to seek to explain the mind-body relationship, which can now be better understood thanks to progress in the neurosciences. In explanations concerning this problem, it is important to avoid reductionism, i.e., reducing humans to purely material beings in whom there is no space for freedom.

CHAPTER 9

TENDENTIAL DYNAMISM
AND FREEDOM

1. TENDENCIES AND INSTINCTS

In Chapter 7 we examined the role of an internal sense (estimative power in animals and cogitative power in human beings), which perceives the suitability or harmfulness to its own self of an individual sensory reality. In this context, we explained that this internal sense is related to the instincts and, more generally, to the natural tendencies of individuals. At this point, then, we must explain more fully what is meant by tendency and instinct.

In order to understand fully the notion of *tendency*, we must refer back to what we said about the soul as being the form of the living being and, hence, the principle of the being's development and enhancement, of its movement toward its own particular end. In the light of this notion, it may be understood that in each living being there is an orientation, or tendency, toward its own perfection. Thus, for example, a plant grows turning toward the sun, or a bee heads toward the flowers from which to extract the pollen. These are inborn inclinations; in other words, they arise from the individual's own nature and impel it toward its own vital good, toward that which it needs to achieve fulfillment.[1]

While *natural tendency* toward their own fundamental vital good (survival, reproduction, growth) is specific to all living beings, in those endowed with sensitive knowledge this intrinsic, or inborn, orientation is perfected by sense experience. Thus, they have a spontaneous inclination toward the vital good as apprehended via the senses. It is this inclination, or sense tendency,[2] that in animals is

---

1. Aristotelian-Thomistic philosophy defines this inclination as *natural appetite*, from the Latin *ad-petere*, meaning "to tend to," "to turn toward."

2. In order to distinguish it from natural appetite, in Thomistic philosophy this inclination is called *appetitus elicitus*, i.e., that which is aroused, or attracted (from the Latin verb *elicere*), by the knowledge of goodness.

called *instinct.*[3] This is why in Chapter 7 we affirmed that instinct possesses an aspect of tendency and an aspect of knowledge, for, indeed, instinctive tendency is activated, or reinforced, by reality as perceived through sense experience, and, in particular, through the two internal senses of estimative power and memory. The activation of tendency involves the entire organism such as when a cheetah prepares to chase its prey or a marmot eats large amounts of food during the warm season in order to ready itself to face its winter hibernation.

Generally speaking, instinctive tendencies impel beings, on the one hand, to seek what is pleasurable and to avoid what is harmful and, on the other, to meet any obstacles on the path to achieving pleasure or fleeing danger. For this reason, it is common to make a distinction between instinctive tendencies of the desiderative type and those of the impulsive type.[4] This distinction may be understood, if we bear in mind the fact that an instinctive tendency of the impulsive type often halts one of desiderative type and, at least in the short term, acts in the opposite direction. This is the case in many animal species where the males of the herd fight with one another in order to mate with the females and certain individuals even meet their deaths for the survival of the species. In this example, the impulsive tendency has, at least at first, the advantage over the desiderative; although it could also be argued that such behavior is simply the result of one single instinctive tendency toward the good and the survival of the species.

2. THE PLASTICITY OF HUMAN TENDENCIES

The human being is also endowed with sense tendencies, but rather than calling them instincts, we prefer (or should prefer) generically to call them tendencies or, to use a term taken from psychology, *emotional impulses.* In animals, instincts have a considerable degree of rigidity because they are predetermined for a particular end, in

---

3. Therefore, unlike the term *inclination,* the term *instinct* refers to the origin of the spontaneous movement, or tendency.

4. We adopt partly the terminology used by J.A. García Cuadrado, *Antropología filosófica: Una introducción a la Filosofía del Hombre* (Pamplona: Eunsa, 2001), 66. Aristotelian-Thomistic philosophy, on the other hand, speaks, respectively, of *concupiscible appetite* and of *irascible appetite:* cf. Thomas Aquinas, *Summa Theologiæ,* I, q. 81, a. 2, c.

accordance with the modality imposed by the species.[5] Thus, an external stimulus is followed by a perception of the senses, which activates the tendency whence derives a vegetative-motor response. The stimulus-response circuit is closed and characterized by a certain degree of automatism by virtue of which, for example, it is very difficult to keep a cat in heat closed in a city apartment, or it is inevitable that with the arrival of the summer or winter, migratory birds move from one geographical region to another.

From this point of view, animal instincts are virtually infallible under normal conditions and can give rise to certain truly remarkable responses. Think, indeed, of the migration of birds over distances of thousands of kilometers or the perfect organization of an ant nest or a beehive.

There are of course certain animal species that show some degree of adaptability and a greater capacity to accumulate sensory experiences. It is thanks to this that the domestication of certain species (such as horses and dogs) is possible, by virtue of which they can, to some extent, deal with considerable changes in their circumstances. But this involves only an enrichment of the stimulus-response circuit, for it is possible to domesticate or train an animal by making use of sensory stimuli (through reward or punishment) but certainly not by using its capacity to interiorize the reasons that explain a given form of behavior.

In human beings the tendencies or impulses[6] always possess a degree of flexibility and uncertainty. We cannot speak of a closed stimulus-response circuit because there is always some personal mediation by the intelligence; acquired habits; moral values; culture; and, in the final analysis, freedom, something we will talk about shortly. From the point of view of the external observer, this may appear as a shortcoming in human beings with respect to animals, which do not need such a long gestation period nor such pro-

---

5. On this subject see A. Malo, *Antropologia dell'affettività* (Rome: Armando, 1999), Chapter 4.

6. Psychology undertakes a very detailed analysis of human inclinations. Lersch, for example, identified an *impulse to live* (of which the impulse to act and the inclination to pleasure are part), *inclinations associated with one's own individuality* (which include egoism, the inclination to respect, and the will for power), and *transitive inclinations* (among them the impulse to produce, interest, and normative and social inclinations): cf. P. Lersch, *Der Aufbau des Charakters* (Leipzig: J.A. Barth, 1938), Chapter 4 of the general section. We will discuss normative and social inclinations in Chapter 15 where, however, we will call them *socializing inclinations*.

longed dependency on parental care. As we indicated in Chapter 4, A. Gehlen developed this idea by talking of the "incompleteness" of man with respect to the animals. But this apparent incompleteness in human beings enables the instinctive tendencies to remain open to a diversity of responses. Thus we speak of a *plasticity* of the tendencies in the sense that their activation can be modeled with a view to a certain response. We use the term plasticity in order to indicate that this capacity to orient or model the tendencies is not absolute (such as in the case of an artist, whose work necessarily depends on the characteristics of the marble or wood he uses) but must take human nature into account. For example, I can orient my tendency to nutrition by adopting a vegetarian diet, by not eating meat on Fridays during Lent for religious reasons, or by following a low-calorie diet in order to lose weight, but in any case I do have to eat.

What is the root of this plasticity? As we have just indicated, in the human being the response to the tendencies is not fixed or rigidly determined because he is endowed not only with sensitive knowledge but also with intellectual knowledge through which he knows the universal aspects of reality and, hence, understands what is good over and above the particular contingent aspects of the things he perceives. It is to goodness understood in this way that human beings orient themselves with their will, and it is about this particular tendency that we must now speak.

3. THE WILL, OR SPIRITUAL-TYPE OF TENDENCY

The fact that man has tendencies other than those of the aforementioned instinctive type can, first and foremost, be deduced from our everyday experience of conflict between what we desire with the senses and what we want rationally. For example, we feel impelled to stay in bed and sleep, but we want to get up and go to work; we long to satisfy our appetite, but we want to wait for a friend so as to have lunch together. This happens because the person not only perceives reality with the senses in its accidental and individual sensory aspects but also knows it intellectually, comprehending that which is good or true in itself as Aristotle says in the passage we quoted in the preceding chapter.

Thus, just as sensitive knowledge leads to a sense tendency that we have defined as instinctive, so intellectual knowledge leads to a tendency that we could define as being of an intellectual or spiritual type. This is the will. In general terms, then, the will is the spiritual tendency toward goodness as apprehended intellectually and, therefore, toward goodness considered in itself and not in its contingent or accidental aspects. In the two simple examples we used above, the will reveals itself to be independent from the specific good as perceived through the senses (tiredness, sating hunger) because it is oriented toward a more universal, nonmaterial good (accomplishing a duty, the faithfulness of friendship).

As such, the will is also a "natural tendency," in the sense that by nature each man has the capacity to orient himself knowingly toward perceived goodness or toward his own specific ends. Of himself, each human being wants those ends that are intrinsic to his humanity such as knowing the truth, being happy, and living, and he wants them absolutely and will not be fully satisfied with contingent results. But achieving those ends requires an evaluation of the means to be used and, hence, a choice between one path or another. Everyone wants to attain happiness and a "successful life," but some aim at it by studying philosophy and others by studying medicine. Thus, though the individual cannot but want his own fundamental good, it is up to him to desire this or that means to achieve it.[7]

4. The Voluntariness of Actions and Freedom

From a certain viewpoint, it could be affirmed that in human beings the will is the final mover of their actions. For even if it is the intellect that knows the good toward which we tend, it is the will that orients all the faculties of an individual toward goodness and can even condition the intellect. But here, too, we must be careful not to introduce a split into the unity of the person. Neither the will nor the intellect acts separately (there is no such thing as pure will or pure reason); rather, there is a reciprocal causality between the two,

---

7. The explanation given by St. Thomas concerning the relationship between intellect and will, with reference to the ultimate man's ultimate end and the means to achieve it, is still of fundamental importance: cf. Thomas Aquinas, *Quæstiones Disputatæ de Malo*, q. 6.

and both are rooted in the integrity of the individual man with his
sensibility and emotionality.[8]

This explanation is important in order to understand what we mean
when we talk about *voluntary actions*. They are actions that arise
from a principle intrinsic to the person who acts in the awareness of
the aim toward which he tends. We say they arise from an intrinsic
principle in order to distinguish them from actions that someone
might undertake under constraint (for example, under threat or in
a state of hypnosis). Voluntariness also requires an intentional, or
aware, orientation toward an end, so we can say that a voluntary
action is an action undertaken consciously.[9]

Leaving to ethics the task of studying voluntary action in more
detail,[10] from what has just been said, we can deduce that if I myself
am the principle of my own actions, then I am free. To have *freedom*
means to be masters of ourselves and our actions. This does not happen in animals, whose behavior is determined by the instincts of the
species, but it does happen in human beings who consciously orient
themselves toward their particular ends, and this is not contradicted
by the fact that human beings also have a specific nature whence
derive specific tendencies. What counts is the fact that the human
being acts from himself and for himself, voluntarily choosing the
way in which to orient himself toward an end and in the awareness
of the end toward which he inclines. It is precisely this awareness
that enables him to choose, and thus we say that reason is the root
of freedom not in order to promote rationalism (i.e., the supremacy
of the sphere of reason to the exclusion of others) but to underline
the fact that, if he did not know the end or the good in itself, man
would not be able consciously to orient himself toward it. This is

8. From an existential standpoint, the individual is always beyond that initial
   moment in which the intelligence has "constitutive" priority over the will. We can
   reconstruct this moment from a theoretical standpoint, but it has already passed
   and what we have to deal with is always a human reality in which the spiritual
   potencies are implicated together. Thus it is impossible to identify a phase that is
   purely intellective or purely volitive.

9. The conscious action, as mentioned in the text, is different from an action of which
   we are conscious. I may be conscious or aware of the digestive processes that
   take place after lunch, but they are not conscious actions in the aforementioned
   sense. Hence we distinguish between *human actions* (conscious actions in the
   above sense) and *actions of man* (those that are beyond my direct control such as
   digestion, growth, aging, and the involuntary emergence of a memory). The actions
   of man, then, are what happen in my mental-physical organism.

10. Cf. A. Rodríguez Luño, *Etica* (Florence: Le Monnier, 1992), Chapter 5;
    M. Rhonheimer, *La prospettiva della morale: Fondamenti dell'ética filosófica* (Rome:
    Armando, 2006), Chapter 2.

why classical philosophy explains that freedom, or free will, is "the faculty of will and reason" and that those actions that come from a "deliberate will"[11] (i.e., illuminated by a judgment) are free.

5. DETERMINISTIC CONCEPTS

We will give fuller consideration to freedom in Chapter 14, adopting an existential standpoint. What concerns us now is to make it clear that the subject of freedom raises a lot of queries and is undoubtedly one of the themes that has most impassioned philosophers. Some of the difficulties concern the relationships among men and of man with himself: How is it possible to be free from one's passions or with respect to society at large? Other questions concern the person's place in history: Is the individual a protagonist or a mere instrument in the progression of historical events? In order to solve these problems, deterministic solutions have often been formulated, i.e., solutions that effectively deny the existence of freedom in man. Let us briefly consider some of these positions.[12]

5.1. The Determinism of Certain Scientific Theories

As a general scientific theory, determinism was strongly propounded in the nineteenth century by P.-S. Laplace (1749–1827), according to whom it was possible to reduce astronomy to mechanics and deduce the movement of the heavenly bodies, forecasting their future and reconstructing their past. Clearly, such a theory leaves little space for the free action of man. However, universal determinism is not an observable fact or a natural law, nor is it a postulate required by science. It is, rather, a philosophical doctrine because it generalizes certain items of data and makes them absolute to the point of creating a theory that exceeds the ambit of science. Moreover, with the abandonment of universal mechanicism, developments in physics and astronomy now tend to recognize the uncertainty present in the universe.

---

11. Thomas Aquinas, *Summa Theologiæ*, I-II, q. 1, a. 1. In order to underline the difference between the free behavior of human beings and the behavior of animals, St. Thomas, with effective use of Latin and referring to St. John Damascene, explains that, while living beings endowed with intelligence "act," those endowed only with sense knowledge "are acted upon" ("*non enim agunt, sed magis aguntur*"): cf. *ibid*, I-II, q. 6, arg. 2.

12. Though very brief and with some minor ambiguities, an overview of this topic is to be found in R. Vernaux, *Psicología: Filosofía dell'uomo* (Brescia: Paideia, 1966), 189–198.

On the basis of progress made in the medical sciences, especially neurology, some people have come to consider all human actions as the result of chemical reactions and combinations or as manifestations of organic states. If this were true, then freedom would be merely apparent. Yet, however much these factors may affect the exercise of freedom, they are only the organic conditions for free action and not the seat or source of freedom, which is not measurable clinically if not in its effects. Moreover, although certain illnesses affect the exercise of freedom and in certain subjective states (such as sleep) freedom is not used, this does not mean it has been suppressed or disappeared.[13]

It must not be forgotten that human beings are not necessarily dependent upon their bodily conditions and can, for example, change their lifestyle, their source of nourishment, and so on. Indeed, one of the more evident signs of man's emergence over matter and over animals is his tendency to find alternatives, to identify and resolve problems, and to make use of empirical data in order to achieve original and creative results. In the face of difficulties and needs, animals react instinctively and fairly predictably, while human beings think up solutions or discover new opportunities, which they are capable of conserving, passing on, and augmenting. In this way, as Leonardo Polo observes,[14] man is an open system; in other words, he is a structured entity that can be reorganized and perfected. He is not in a state of homeostatic stability but of dynamic equilibrium.[15]

In order to underline the fact that there is no deterministic rigidity even at the neurological level, we can point out that certain areas of the brain show a considerable capacity to substitute others in cases of damage, and that cerebral development itself is not completely predictable in its outcomes, not even genetically (despite

---

13. Cf. J. Cervós-Navarro, "*Libertà umana e neurofisiologia,*" in *Le dimensioni della libertà nel dibattito scientifico e filosófico* (Rome: Armando, 1995), 25–34. For references to other theories arising from neurophysiology that have serious implications for human freedom, see L. E. Echarte, *Limiti e classificazione del nuovo campo della Neuroetica: Identità, responsabilità, informazione e manipolazione del cervello, "Medic — Metodologia didattica e innovazione clinica: Nuova Serie,"* 2/12 (2004), 19–20.

14. Cf. L. Polo, *Quién es el hombre: Un espíritu en el tiempo* (Madrid: Rialp, 1998), 116–117.

15. The principle of homeostasis, which has applications in physics and biology, indicates the state of equilibrium established between an external stimulus and an interior response. In opposition to Freud, Viktor Frankl highlights how this principle is reductive toward man because it overlooks his teleology (cf. V. E. Frankl, *Man's Search for Meaning* [Boston: Beacon Press, 2006], 110).

certain superficially flaunted supposed discoveries). Concerning the uniqueness of the human being, Eccles spoke in terms of an "infinitely improbable genetic lottery."[16] In order to demonstrate the relationship between freedom and the material conditions it has to deal with, Popper cited two interesting examples: firstly, that of Beethoven, who composed his great symphonies overcoming the objective limitations arising from his progressive deafness. Indeed (and this is the second example), man with his freedom faces the circumstances of his life like a mountaineer, who may choose to climb the Himalayas or the Andes but in reaching the peak is inevitably held back and limited by his own physical capacities and by the route he has chosen.[17]

Two famous cases in the history of science, much studied in the late nineteenth and early twentieth centuries, are those of Helen Keller and Laura Bridgman. Both were deaf and blind (Keller became so soon after birth) and managed to learn the use of words thanks to the help of their teachers. Their lives show that the human relationship with the world (i.e., the development of culture and the attainment of universal concepts through intelligence) involves overcoming the simple association between sensory stimulus and individual response.[18]

To explain what we have just said, we can use the now classic distinction between "freedom from" (which is never absolute in man because he is constrained and limited) and "freedom to" (which means adopting a certain stance, orienting oneself toward an end); the former is negative, the latter positive.

5.2. Sociologism and Psychologism

A deterministic-type solution can also be applied to the problems that emerge in the life of man and society. Although we will consider this subject in Chapter 15, let us now make it clear that if excessive importance is attributed to the pressures and structures of society, we reach the *de facto* conclusion that human conduct is infallibly predictable on the basis of social-cultural statistics and influences, and this once again would be to deny the existence of freedom. This

---

16. J.C. Eccles, *Evolution of the Brain: Creation of the Self*, cit., 248.

17. Cf. K.R. Popper, *The Open Universe: An Argument for Indeterminism* (London: Hutchinson, 1982), 128.

18. Cf. E. Cassirer, *An Essay on Man: An Introduction to a Philosophy of Human Culture* (Garden City, NY: Doubleday and Co., 1953), 52–56.

does not mean, on the other hand, that we must ignore the influence of society, environment, or education, but we do have to recognize that the real lives of individual human beings negate theories of this kind. Statistics, for example, refer only to the exterior results of actions (actions matured internally and freely by each individual); they register merely the sum total of the results of individual decisions.

Certain psychological theories also sometimes go so far as to subordinate individual behavior to unconscious impulses,[19] and according to some observers the characterial elements of the personality follow well-defined laws. Yet we must ask ourselves whether characterial habits and tendencies are not themselves freely acquired, at least in part. Moreover, all the information that can be gathered about an individual man does not enable us to go beyond mere probability in predicting his conduct. As Frankl observes, any apparently obvious and unreflective action represents the final link in a long chain of decisions, of which the first was probably conscious.[20]

In other cases attempts are made, often from the viewpoint of social psychology, to establish a necessary and deterministic link between individual social factors that exist in infancy and certain situations or forms of conduct that arise in adolescence or in adult life. Undoubtedly, it is possible to establish such connections *a posteriori*, but these factors do not *a priori* negate the individual's "freedom to," although they do constitute limits on his "freedom from." Hence, the historical background to a situation of deviancy (family problems, inadequate education, tension, or traumas) must of itself be considered as an "indicator of nonspecific risk": "This means that these prior conditions, though identifiable in many cases of deviancy, remain open to other quite different and nondeviant outcomes."[21]

---

19. In Freudian psychology, for example, although neither the freedom of the individual nor the moral imperative is denied in principle, a theory is created that excludes effectively the central role of freedom of action: cf. A. Lambertino, *"Aspetti della teoría freudiana dell'uomo,"* in *Immagini dell'uomo: Percorsi antropologici nella filosofia moderna* (Rome: Armando, 1997), 63–76.

20. Cf. V. E. Frankl, *Homo patiens* (Brezzo di Bedero: Salcom, 1979), 99.

21. G. De Leo, *"Vuoto esistenziale e devianza minorile: Elementi per una lettura psico-sociologica,"* in *Giovani, vuoto esistenziale e ricerca di senso: La sfida della logoterapia,* (Rome: Las, 1998), 30.

SUMMARY OF CHAPTER 9

Every living being has tendencies, that is, natural or inborn tendencies toward its own enhancement and development; they are natural tendencies in the sense that they are inherent to the nature of the being (be it plant, animal, or human). The natural tendencies of living beings possessing sensory awareness are called instincts, and instincts can be either desiderative (searching for pleasure) or impulsive (such as reactions to something harmful). In human beings the natural sense tendencies are generally called emotional impulses because, thanks to the mediation of the intellect, they show a notable degree of plasticity.

The will is an intellectual or spiritual tendency. It is thanks to the will that human beings can orient themselves not only toward a specific and contingent good perceived through the senses but also toward goodness or truth in themselves. The will enables the individual to act freely and voluntarily, i.e., to undertake actions with the awareness of seeking a certain goal. Thus, we say that to be free means to be the source, principle, and master of one's own actions. In the history of philosophy there have been certain views that effectively deny the freedom of the person; such views are called "deterministic" because they maintain that human action is entirely "determined" by society, by physiological and neurological structures, or by the unconscious.

CHAPTER 10

AFFECTIVE DYNAMISM

1. PHILOSOPHICAL REFLECTIONS ON AFFECTIVITY

When we speak of "affectivity," or the emotions, the first impression we may have is that of dealing with a dimension that is of great relevance for human beings but that, at the same time, is difficult to define with precision. It is no exaggeration to say that, among the many recently published studies on this subject, there is an almost unanimous consensus in recognizing its importance but, at the same time, considerable disagreement on the basic approach to take. It may be believed that affectivity has only become an object of study in recent times and that the thinkers of antiquity and the Middle Ages ignored it almost completely. Yet such a view would be incorrect.

The Greek philosophers (mainly Aristotle and Plato but also the Stoics, Epicureans, and Neo-Platonists) discussed the affections. St. Augustine also gave considerable attention to the subject as did St. Thomas Aquinas in the Middle Ages. It is true that, in some cases, these authors adopted a prevalently ethical rather than anthropological perspective, but it is also true that any ethical study presupposes anthropological foundations as we explained in Chapter 1, and thus, also in these works, is it possible to find important reflections on the subject of affectivity.

2. TERMINOLOGICAL CLARIFICATION

Before giving a brief presentation of the main aspects of human affectivity, it is important to make a number of observations concerning terminology. We often speak indistinctly of "feelings," "emotions," "passions," and "affections." These expressions and others like them are not synonyms, but neither are they complete antonyms: Their meanings have something in common, but they imply different nuances. To define these nuances exactly is very difficult because the use of the terms changes depending on the school of thought and the author. Consequently, we will limit ourselves to offering the minimal clarifications necessary in order to follow the explanations given in this chapter.[1]

As may easily be deduced, each of the above expressions refers to affectivity but from a different standpoint. In fact, we tend to speak of "feeling" to refer to a mental phenomenon that is stable and regular, while we invoke "emotion" to indicate a complex state in an individual that involves profound mental and physiological changes. The term "passion" is usually adopted to denote passivity at the level of the senses toward a stimulus of great intensity, while the word "affection" indicates an analogous phenomenon but at the spiritual level. Today, this entire sphere is often alluded to indistinctly with the term *heart*. In any case, generally speaking we can say that what modern psychology calls "emotions" or "affections" corresponds in its essentials to what classical philosophy called *passiones* (passions) — from the Latin verb *pati*, to suffer — underlining how the individual suffers or undergoes a specific reaction. In this chapter, we will speak of feelings and affections, using the two terms as synonymous.

This initial clarification enables us to infer three basic characteristics of affectivity: Affective dynamism is part of the sphere of the tendencies as the principles of action, it implies a certain passivity in the subject, and it manifests itself differently at the level of the senses and at that of the spirit.[2]

3. TENDENCIES AND AFFECTIONS

"To experience a feeling" is something that can happen in different ways, but it always involves the attraction of a subject toward an object: "I like to travel," "I'm afraid of flying," "I'm happy that you're with me," "I like someone," etc. As far as affections are concerned, the individual, rather than "doing" something, "feels moved" toward something. This does not mean that affection is merely passive but that its activity fundamentally consists in "reacting" in the face of something that arouses attraction or repulsion.

---

1. A useful summary is to be found in J. Vicente Arregui and J. Choza, *Filosofía del hombre: Una antropología de la intimidad* (Madrid: Rialp, 1991), 223 ff.

2. On the subject matter of this chapter, much benefit may be gained from reading A. Malo, *Antropologia dell'affettività* (Rome: Armando, 1999); for a clear and concise explanation, see also F. Rodríguez Quiroga, *La dimensión afectiva de la vida* (Pamplona: Cuadernos de Anuario Filosófico, 2001).

Attraction and repulsion are the ways in which the tendencies relate to their object (i.e., a good to be obtained or an evil to be avoided), while passivity is the fundamental characteristic of the organic faculties. Hence, the *affections* or feelings could be defined as the operations specific to the sensory tendencies,[3] in other words, the activation of those tendencies. For example, the fact that man tends toward woman, and vice versa, is something naturally present in all individuals, but it is toward a specific person that we experience attraction as a consequence of the activation of the tendency.

Affectivity, then, is not to be considered as secondary to knowledge or to the tendencies but as the exercise of the tendential faculties.[4] And so the sensory tendencies, about which we spoke in the preceding chapter, are called simply "tendencies," while "affections" is the generic name for their acts. They are, then, not separate faculties, but operative potencies or their own operations.

4. SENSATIONS, FEELINGS, AND MOODS

We have established, then, that affections, or feelings, are the acts or operations of the sensory tendencies. Hence, affectivity will interact, on the one hand, with knowledge and, on the other, with the body.

In fact, as we explained earlier, tendency always follows knowledge, in keeping with the classic theory that "no one tends toward something that is not already known to him."[5] Hence our sensory tendencies make us tend toward things we know, and the way these tendencies are activated is precisely through the affections, or feelings. Thus, for example, I may know a chocolate cake by looking at it or tasting it; I may then feel attracted by it, and this attraction expresses itself as a feeling of desire, or pleasure: "I'd love to eat a slice!" or, "This cake is delicious!" Feelings of desire or of plea-

---

3. As St. Thomas observes, we can also speak of affections to refer to the operations of the spiritual faculty of the will, but in the spiritual field affections are more "active" and less "passive" because they do not have an organic base: cf. Thomas Aquinas, *Summa Theologiæ*, I-II, q. 22, a. 3, c. It must be borne in mind that, what we are here calling affections, in Thomistic anthropology are referred to as "*passions*" precisely to underline how the individual becomes aware of these reactions as if "suffering" them (from the Latin verb *pati*) or undergoing their influence: cf. M. Rhonheimer, *The Perspective of Morality: Philosophical Foundations of Thomistic Virtue Ethics* (Washington, D.C.: The Catholic University of America Press, 2011), 168–175.

4. Some philosophers (such as I. Kant in *The Critique of Judgment*) have assigned to affectivity or sentiment the role of "third faculty" alongside the intellect and the will. But from the standpoint of classical anthropology, the affections are acts and not operative potencies.

5. Cf. Thomas Aquinas, *Summa Contra Gentiles*, I, 5, n. 2.

sure — like other feelings — are, then, the "realization" of the tendencies, i.e., their activation.

Consequently, it is important not to confuse *feeling* with *sensation*. They are both forms of sense activity, but the former is tendential, while the latter is merely cognitive. I could, at least in theory, know something without experiencing any feeling toward it. Becoming aware of the qualities or values of a reality is not the same as feeling inclined toward it. As a tendential activity, affection, or feeling, has its origin in knowledge, but it is not reducible to knowledge.

Although feelings draw their origins from knowledge, not all forms of knowledge can stimulate the tendencies but only those that give rise to an evaluation and that are, hence, predisposed for action. For example, if I am full I will examine the window of a cake shop with a certain lack of interest, but if I am hungry I will examine it to see which cake attracts me most. As we know, this kind of knowledge is supplied by the intentional internal senses — cogitative power and memory — which are capable of apprehending the sensory values of suitability and conserving them. Only in the measure to which I know something as good for me at the present moment can it arouse my tendencies, and it is from their activation that feelings derive.

The sensory tendencies are organic faculties, and this means that their use is associated with the disposition of the body. We have all experienced how a single phenomenon can provoke different affective reactions in different people, or in the same person at different moments depending on his physical state. If I am ill, I will probably not experience any feeling when faced with something I like. This state of affairs is indicated by a commonly used word: mood, which describes a physiological-affective condition that is influenced not only by specific spiritual dispositions but also by certain physical conditions such as tiredness, atmospheric pressure, and hormonal imbalance.

Thus, it becomes clear that the feelings have a dual role. On the one hand, they refer to objective sensory values; in other words, they register the suitability or harmfulness, the difficulty or ease, of individual sense realities. Fear, for example, is a response to a real situation of danger, and joy is the reaction to a real situation of harmony. Individual sense realities, then, are apprehended in their relationship with our own nature, and, although our affective reactions are not always proportional to the external stimulus, nonetheless our evaluation does not refer only to our subjective interior state but to the relationship that is established between ourselves and reality.[6] On the other hand, however, the feelings are also the expression of subjective physiological and psychological dispositions in that they manifest the state of the body and the mind, conditions that may be transitory or permanent. An affective response of one kind or another highlights, to a greater or lesser degree, the character of an individual, his mood, and even his state of health.

5. THE DYNAMISM OF THE FEELINGS

How, then, does a feeling arise? As we have seen, it depends fundamentally on sensory knowledge of sense values as apprehended by the cogitative power and conserved in the memory. This knowledge arouses the tendency, attracting it toward the acquisition or rejection of a certain reality, and it is precisely this kind of reactive movement that is called feeling. Subsequently, tendency, through the activation of the affections, acts on other faculties, provoking an impulse to act either to attain or to avoid the reality known. Thus, a circuit is established among knowledge, affectivity, and action.

In the case of human sensory affectivity, the feelings are normally insufficient for action because there are other demands, greater than those of sense experience, that intervene in our behavior. In fact, human activity derives from a deliberated will that is not necessarily regulated to follow the impulses of sense experience; i.e., a feeling of dislike does not *per se* lead to aggressive behavior toward another. Nonetheless, the affections have an important role in activity because they reinforce the influence of the tendencies on the other faculties. For example, the desire to be with the person he loves may lead a man to undertake a journey in order to see her, to work longer hours in order to buy her a present, etc. We can, then, speak of feelings as reinforcing the tendencies. Being the act of tendential potencies, feelings favor the passage from tendency to activity, from a simple "tendency" to an "action."

6. This means that the feelings can never be exclusively subjective or arbitrary. As Lewis observes, the judgment, "I like," cannot be reduced to the judgment, "I have pleasing feelings"; rather, it implies an objective reference to reality: cf. C.S. Lewis, *The Abolition of Man* (London: Fount, 1999), 1–16.

5.1. The Affections as Immanent Sensory Actions

Considered as the consequence of tendential activities, the affections are immanent operations that cannot merely be equated with physical events or vegetative functions. Sadness at the death of a friend is not reducible to the secretion of tears or the activation of certain neurotransmitters. The immanent nature of the feelings or affections implies intentionality, which means that they have a content, that they refer to something;[7] i.e., feelings are always "feelings for" or "feelings with respect to" the thing that arouses them, as we have already explained. Even if we wished to maintain that an affective condition could exist with respect to nothing,[8] that nothing itself would be considered — by being processed in the intellect — as a certain object or content of the affection.

At the same time, the sensory nature of affectivity implies the involvement of the organism and, hence, a certain degree of transitive activity. Thus, when we are emotional we also undergo somatic phenomena of various kinds such as increased heart rate, agitation, sweating, shivering, or tears. The polarity between these two aspects, the immanent and the transitive, corresponds to the traditional distinction between the "formal" and "material" components of the feelings.[9] The former is their specific and particular dimension, which consists in a tendency of cognitive origin and, hence, in an immanent activity. The latter refers to their substratum and, so to speak, to their means of transmission, i.e., physiological changes.

The feelings, in fact, being sensory actions, necessarily involve somatic changes. As we have seen, each sense faculty constitutes a single unit with its organ just as form unites to matter. Hence, we affirmed that the organic reactions associated with affectivity are notably influenced by prior somatic conditions. For example, we do not have the same emotional reactions when we are tired as when we are rested, when the weather is cold or hot, when the sun is shining or when it is raining, or in spring or in winter. In other words, the dispositions of the body condition the activity of the tendential faculties, as happens with other organic potencies. This

7. Remember what we explained in Chapter 5.
8. This, for example, is one of the connotations with which Heidegger describes the feeling of anxiety, although his analysis concerns a level very different from that of the anthropology of affectivity: cf. M. Heidegger, "What Is Metaphysics?" in Basic Writings (San Francisco: Harper One, 1993), 100–106.
9. Cf. Thomas Aquinas, Summa Theologiæ, I-II, q. 37, a. 4, c; ibid, q. 44, a. 1, c.

particular bond between the affections and physical condition leads to difficulties not only in conceptualizing the affections but also in dominating them. Feelings are never fully transparent or completely under our control.

It must also be borne in mind that the organs are the material substratum of the faculties and that the faculties can only act through the organs. This means that the bodily reactions associated with the feelings are always proportional to affective activity itself and cannot be understood separate from it. In other words, even if such reactions are influenced by the external physical environment (temperature, air pressure, climate, and so on) or by subjective physiological conditions (for example, state of health), they nonetheless occur in correspondence with the tendential movements, which are immanent actions.[10]

By virtue of this dependency, the body and the organic movements are an expression—we might call them the "language"—of affectivity. If the affections were a mere organic response to the influence of external reality on the body, in keeping with the stimulus-response model,[11] or if they were simple expressions of the subject's internal processes, independent of his knowledge of reality,[12] then they would be an incomprehensible language. The fact is, though, that, despite our difficulty in understanding feelings, we are accustomed to interpreting them. Tears, sobbing, and the contraction of the face, for example, represent the somatic aspect of what we call "crying," and even at the cinema or theatre we know that these gestures correspond to a particular psychological state and express certain feelings. What emerges, then, is a correlation among known reality, feelings, and somatic reaction.

5.2. The Cognitive Value of Feelings

Tendential acts, which include the affections, possess a particular form of intentionality with respect to cognitive acts. They refer not only to an object but also to the measure with which that object concerns the individual (they identify the object as suitable or harmful, as difficult or easy). For example, the desire to drink may direct

---

10. Cf. Thomas Aquinas, *Summa Theologiæ*, I-II, q. 37, a. 4, c.

11. This is the thesis behind certain behaviorist and functionalist theories, such as those of the psychologists W. James and F.A. Lange. A critical appraisal of behaviorist theory is to be found in A. Malo, *Antropología dell'affettività*, cit., 39–65.

12. Kant's anthropological thesis could be held to reflect this view.

itself toward a glass of water, but it considers it as something that can satisfy the thirst experienced by the individual. This is why the feelings, as we have already suggested, refer not only to real sense values but also to subjective sensory dispositions. In a certain sense, we could say that they are the "thermometer" of those dispositions. Hence, we can speak of an "indirect" cognitive role of the affections, a role that refers both to the reality and to the subject. They express reality through the subject's evaluation thereof, or the subject's disposition toward that reality.[13]

In the final analysis, the affections, and the somatic reactions associated with them, depend upon apprehended values, which are what motivates them. Generally speaking, "motivation," or "motive," is used to describe the formal and final causes of a movement (in this case, emotional reaction) but not the efficient cause (i.e., the cause that provokes the movement in real and practical terms).[14] To be "motivated" means to be attracted, not to be pushed, and it is in this way that the sense values move the tendency, and the tendency generates feeling. Affectivity's dependence on knowledge makes it possible to orient the emotions and to have some control over them. The fact that this dependence is formal and final but not efficient means that it is not possible to exercise a rigid control over affectivity but rather to guide it. In other words, we cannot perfectly regulate the emergence, intensity, and duration of feelings, but we can, so to speak, steer them.

We have spoken about the motivation and the orientation of feelings. This raises two very important questions that concern affectivity: the education of the feelings and their role in ethics. But before going into this matter, it may be useful to introduce a number of further clarifications regarding the nature of feelings.

6. TYPOLOGY OF THE AFFECTIONS

Many classifications for the feelings have been suggested based on different criteria. These criteria may be condensed into two fundamental categories: the relationship of the tendencies to their specific object and the reactions provoked in the subject by their activity. The

---

13. Cf. J.A. García Cuadrado, *Antropología filosófica: Una introducción a la Filosofía del Hombre* (Pamplona: Eunsa, 2001), 102–103.

14. As we will see, this coherence with the causal relationship established between knowledge and tendency is in the realization of acts: the influence of knowledge is formal and final, whereas that of tendency is efficient.

first of these can be considered as essential because it concerns the acts of the faculties themselves, acts which are specifically distinguished on the basis of their objects. Indeed, in order to understand the nature of a faculty, it is necessary to identify the object of its operations. However, the second of these criteria (i.e., the subjective reactions) must be considered as accidental because it concerns the consequences of tendential activities in the subject and not the activity in itself. This criterion may be subdivided depending on whether consideration is given to mental reactions,[15] somatic or physiological reactions,[16] or to other aspects such as intensity and duration.[17] Finally, there may also be mixed classifications that take both the object of the tendencies and the subjective reactions into account.[18]

Thus, from the point of view of their essence, the affections are categorized on the basis of their object. This is the criterion we will follow since it concerns the very nature of the feelings.[19] On this basis it is possible to categorize feelings into three levels: generically, on the basis of the diversity of the tendential faculties; specifically, on the basis of the relationship of each tendency with its own object; and accidentally, on the basis of the intensity of the influence of the object or on the basis of its specific content.[20]

A first distinction between the affections derives from the diversity of the sense tendential faculties. As we have explained, a tendency of the desiderative type makes the subject tend toward the possession of what is suitable and the rejection of what is harmful, whereas a tendency of the impulsive type moves the subject to overcome the obstacles that separate himself from what is pleasurable or appe-

---

15. This is the approach characteristic of the phenomenology of Max Scheler.

16. This is the prevalent perspective of experimental psychology.

17. These points of view may be applied both to mental and somatic reactions, whence derives, for example, the distinction between simple feelings and moods; cf. P. Lersch, *Der Aufbau des Charakters* (Leipzig: J.A. Barth, 1938), 126–133.

18. One example of such classification is to be found in the first part of the book by P. Lersch, *Der Aufbau des Charakters*, cit.

19. This is the criterion followed by Thomas Aquinas. Nonetheless it must be remembered that, although St. Thomas's works contain various more or less detailed classifications, he does not seek to give an exhaustive presentation of the contents of the affections. A detailed description of these contents is, rather, the task of a phenomenological analysis, which, we think, is fully compatible with his point of view. His classification may, of course, seem to be of little descriptive use precisely because he is not seeking to offer a description, yet we feel that the flexibility of his approach may prove useful as a foundation from which to develop a phenomenological analysis.

20. Cf. Thomas Aquinas, *Quæstio Disputata De Veritate*, q. 26 a. 4 c.

tizing, and to stand firm against what is harmful.[21] The movements of desiderative tendency refer, then, directly to the sensory object, while those of impulsive tendency refer more directly to the means that concern the object. In the case of the former feelings, the possession of the object is perceived as something immediate; in the case of the latter, the possession of the object is mediated by facing certain difficulties. The impulsive tendency presupposes, or follows, the desiderative tendency.

Secondly, the distinction between the affections is determined by the relationship of the tendencies with their object. This relationship depends on two aspects: the contrariety of the object with respect to the tendency and its degree of proximity thereto. Indeed, the sensory tendencies can have a positive or negative relationship with their object: The desiderative tendency apprehends the object's suitability or harmfulness, while the impulsive tendency apprehends the congruousness, or lack of congruousness, of the means to attain the object. Thus, the impulsive tendency relates to its object, considering it, if something good, as achievable or unachievable and, if evil, as avoidable or unavoidable.

Moreover, a tendency can orient itself toward its object in varying degrees. In the case of desiderative tendency, the first degree is that in which it is attracted by what is good or repulsed by what is bad (love / hatred); the second, that in which it is moved effectively to possess what is good or effectively to reject what is bad (desire / rejection); the third, that in which it enjoys what is good or suffers the effects of what is bad (pleasure / pain). In the case of impulsive tendency, the first degree is taken as given, as we have said, while the second degree consists in the movement toward what is good but not yet possessed, being achievable or unachievable (hope / desperation), or toward what is bad but not yet suffered, being avoidable or unavoidable (daring / fear). In the third degree, the impulsive tendency concerns evil as avoidable (anger), but has no movement with respect to an evil present but unavoidable nor with respect to the good already possessed since in both these cases there are no longer means to be employed or obstacles to be overcome.[22]

---

21. Remember that desiderative and impulsive tendencies are called, in Aristotelian-Thomistic philosophy, *concupiscible appetite* and *irascible appetite*.
22. Cf. Thomas Aquinas, *Summa Theologiæ*, I-II, q. 23, a. 4; *Quæstio Disputata De Veritate*, q. 26, a. 4.

Finally, the third distinction between the affections is the accidental distinction, which depends upon the intensity of the affective
movement or upon its object. For example, love may be more or
less enflamed, hope more or less confident, and joy more or less
euphoric. Moreover, we may be sad with regard to the evil suffered
by others (compassion) or to the good enjoyed by others (envy).
Nonetheless, this is of secondary importance in defining the various
kinds of affections since it concerns their nature only accidentally.[23]

Taking the object of the tendencies as his foundation, Thomas
Aquinas offers the following classification of the affections:[24]

In tendencies of desiderative type:
    1. With respect to good in general: *love*
    2. With respect to evil in general: *hatred*
    3. With respect to future good: *desire*
    4. With respect to future evil: *flight*
    5. With respect to present good: *joy*
    6. With respect to present evil: *sadness*

In tendencies of impulsive type:
    7. With respect to achievable future good: *hope*
    8. With respect to unachievable future good: *desperation*
    9. With respect to avoidable future evil: *daring*
    10. With respect to unavoidable future evil: *fear*
    11. With respect to avoidable present evil: *anger*

In this list, certain points arouse particular interest. Certain aspects
of activity, which we are used to considering as acts of the will (love
and hatred) or as ethical virtues (joy, hope, and daring), are listed as
feelings. Why? In order to understand this, it must be remembered
that the affections are, properly speaking, acts of the sensory tendencies. However, human sense experience does not exist separate
from rationality but in continuity with it. From this fact derive two
important consequences: On the one hand, such continuity makes it
possible for the affections to exist at a higher level (i.e., in the will);
on the other, it means the affections are the matter, or content, of
certain ethical virtues.[25] Therefore, we feel it may be helpful to give

---

23. A systematic, though not exhaustive, explanation of the various accidental
    classifications is given by St. Thomas in his *Scriptum Super Libros Sententiarum,*
    lib. 3, d. 26, q. 1, a. 3, c.

24. Cf. Thomas Aquinas, *Summa Theologiæ,* I-II, q. 23, a. 4.

25. It is the role of virtue to guide a human act so that it may be accomplished in the
    best way. If we bear in mind the distinction we made in a footnote of the preceding

some consideration to the education of feelings and their role in moral life.[26]

7. Affectivity and Freedom

We have said repeatedly that feelings are sense activities and, hence, distinct from spiritual, tendential activity that depends upon the intellect and the will.[27] However, it would be wrong to believe that the affections have to be "overcome" by voluntary acts. Human beings cannot dispense with their feelings just as intellectual activity cannot dispense with the senses, which would be to suppose that an individual can manage without his body.[28] Human nature "essentially" includes the spiritual and corporeal dimensions.

Thus, on the one hand, we must remember that the feelings are different from the acts of the will. We become aware of this when we freely take a reluctant decision, i.e., one that contrasts with the emotional reaction of the moment. But, on the other hand, we must never forget that the feelings always accompany voluntary acts, sometimes reinforcing them.[29] It is this relationship that induces us to reflect upon the morality of the affections.

7.1. The Feelings and Moral Responsibility

Moral evaluation is a practical judgment that holds an action to be good or bad in the degree to which it is recognized as being directed

---

chapter between "human actions" and the "actions of man," we must conclude that, of themselves, the feelings fall into the latter category. It follows that certain virtues guide human actions while others integrate the actions of man in the sphere of his freedom.

26. On this subject, see, among others: M. Rhonheimer, *The Perspective of Morality*, cit., 168–182; A. Rodríguez Luño, *Ética* (Florence: Le Monnier, 1992), 144–148, 260–262; E. Colom and A. Rodríguez Luño, *Scelti in Cristo per essere santi: Elementi di Teologia morale fondamentale* (Rome: Edizioni Università della Santa Croce, 2003), 141–171, 217–218.

27. But, as St. Augustine and St. Thomas explain, it is not incorrect to speak of spiritual feelings, or feelings of the will, because of a certain similarity with the effects of the sense tendencies: cf. St. Augustine, *De Civitate Dei*, IX, 5; Thomas Aquinas, *Summa Theologiæ*, q. 22, a. 3, ad 3. It must be borne in mind that, while sense tendency is attracted by the object and its activity denotes passivity, spiritual tendency actively moves toward the object.

28. St. Thomas makes the following important observation: "The good operation of man is with *passion*, even as it is produced with the body's help" (*Summa Theologiæ*, I-II, q. 59, a. 5, ad 3).

29. Obviously, at least in theory, there may be extraordinary circumstances in which affective movements are reduced to a minimum as the consequence of some psychological condition or as the result of excessively rigorist behavior. But a background "affective tonality" is inseparable from human life.

(or not directed) at the good of the person. In order for an action to be directed to a certain end, the agent must be its cause in the proper sense and not merely a passive subject of its effects. This is not fully the case for the affections, which, as we have said, are *per se* something that happens to me, not something I do, although, of course, this does not mean complete passivity to certain stimuli. However, it is the actions freely undertaken in the light of reason that are, in the full sense, caused by the person. Hence, only voluntary acts are, properly speaking, moral and may be evaluated as being good or bad in the radical sense (on the basis of their relationship with the final and total end of the person).

Thus, feelings are not subject to direct moral evaluation (i.e., considered isolated and in themselves), but this does not mean that they are ethically irrelevant. What it does mean is that their moral value depends upon how they share in the activity of the higher faculties, i.e., the intellect and the will.[30] For example, to experience a feeling of annoyance during a long and boring talk may be a natural reaction, especially if we are tired, but, if we willfully brood on our emotional reaction and use it as a reason to offend the speaker or criticize him behind his back, then, at that point, freedom and, hence, moral responsibility come into play. As may be seen, then, it is not the feeling in itself that is morally good or bad but the voluntary act that derives from it. In fact, the will cannot remain indifferent toward affectivity for the simple reason that it is not indifferent to the values that the feelings — consequences of cognitive sensory activity — present to it.

It follows from this that the relationship between the affections and reality is, in some way, the prerequisite of free action in both a positive and a negative sense. The feelings are the psychological condition for free (and, hence, morally responsible) action. For example, a person who reacted incoherently toward the values of reality would be unable to make completely voluntary decisions. To remain indifferent while suffering physical harm, to feel fear in the absence of danger, or to find pleasure in cruelty are states we may consider as pathological and that limit freedom of action.[31] And if such incoherence were the fruit of a freely chosen attitude, it would

---

30. Cf. Thomas Aquinas, *Summa Theologiæ*, I-II, q. 24 a. 1 c. On the relationship among reason, will, and affectivity, with reference to Aristotelian-Thomistic anthropology, see: A. Malo, *Antropología dell'affettività*, cit., 213–258.

31. Cf. Thomas Aquinas, *Quæstiones Disputatæ de Malo*, q. 3, a. 9 c.

be evaluated as morally negative conduct. On the other hand, when affective reactions are balanced and coherent with real values, it is possible to make a free and mature decision.

We cannot continue here to dwell on the moral relationship between affective reactions and voluntary acts: That task falls to ethics and moral theology on the basis of adequate psychological data. We will limit ourselves to underlining one important question that has just emerged, i.e., the relationship between feelings and the values of reality. This relationship is partly natural and spontaneous and partly falls into the sphere of the free self-realization of the individual. In fact, a person can educate his affectivity through his habits, and it is to this we will now turn to conclude this chapter.

7.2. The Education of Affectivity

Although there is a natural connection between the affections and the sense values of reality, the individual can modify this connection nonetheless, at least to some extent, by educating or perverting his feelings. For example, it is natural to feel compassion toward the suffering of others, but I could train myself to suffocate my compassion and assume an attitude of impassibility, at least as much as possible.

This can come about for at least two reasons. The first is the circuit connecting knowledge, tendency, and action, which is specific to cognizant beings. In fact, as we will see, the actions reinforce, through the habits, knowledge and tendency. Actions of the same kind make a certain evaluation and a certain tendential movement more natural. The second reason is specific to man: Human knowledge and sensory tendencies are open to the reason and to the will in the sense that the latter two can orient the former two. This reason, which we also mentioned earlier, is of considerable importance, and we will try to explain it more fully.

As we have seen, each tendential act depends, in the final analysis, on a cognitive act in such a way that the tendencies can be regulated on the basis of knowledge. Knowledge exercises a formal and final influence because its role consists in presenting the forms and the values that attract the tendencies. But since the sensory tendencies are organic faculties, it is not possible to exercise complete control over them, only to guide them. This is why Aristotle observed that we can have political but not despotic rule over our tendencies.[32] Despotic rule is that exercised by a master over a servant who cannot oppose his control or act autonomously. The relationship between soul and body could be compared to such rule because the body without its vital principle would no longer be a living body and could do nothing. Political rule, on the other hand, is that exercised by free agents who have the capacity to act for themselves and to oppose the control of the master. The relationship of the intellect and the will with the feelings is analogous to this form of rule. This is so not because the tendencies and the affections associated with them can act with complete independence but because their movements also depend on the imagination and on the external senses. For example, I may know it is beneficial to take a medicine, and I may want to take it, but I perceive it as foul tasting and, therefore, feel repulsion toward it. Or I know that overeating is harmful to the health, and I would like to avoid certain foods; nonetheless, those foods still appear to me as pleasurable and attract me strongly. In both these cases the affective reaction cannot be completely modified, and free action has to take account of this.

It is a common experience to feel as if our emotions escape our control, but we also know that it is possible to be aware of them and guide them. We cannot repress or suffocate them (because our rule over them is not despotic), but we can, aware of their reactivity, orient them toward the attainment of a certain objective. It follows that certain attitudes are wrong: hedonism in the general sense, according to which the good of the individual consists in sensory pleasure and any kind of pain is a radical evil, and rigorism, which holds that any kind of pleasure implicates an evil. Both these attitudes presuppose a vision that runs counter to the unity of the human person, who can achieve his perfection only through all his dimensions: the sensory, the affective, and the rational.

In order to understand how the *political rule* of the affections is possible, we must remember that the operative potencies of the intellect and the will are capable of enhancing themselves in the exercise of their acts. Such enhancement, stably maintained, is called *habit*. From an anthropological-moral point of view, *the habits* are

---

32. Cf. Aristotle, *Politics*, I 2, 1254 b 2. We must, of course, recognize that the expression "rule," which arises on a number of occasions in this section, has negative connotations, and only with great reserve would it be accepted by modern philosophy. Using a concept to which we will refer in Chapter 11, we could, rather, speak of the "integration" of affectivity into the totality of the person.

stably acquired perfections of the operative potencies through which the influence of the rational sphere is exercised on the sensory and affective sphere. To say that they are stably acquired perfections does not mean that they are irremovable because the dynamism of the person requires continuous enhancement and, if the habits were not improved, they would tend to disappear.

Therefore, the education of affectivity essentially consists in the acquisition, conservation, and strengthening of the habits. However, the habits cannot be educated in a morally neutral way, i.e., ignoring their reference to good or evil. Being the result of free action, they will always be either good or bad: in the case of the former, they will be virtues; of the latter, vices. The growth of a virtue implies the diminution of its opposing vice and, vice versa, the diminution of virtue implies the increase of vice.[33]

We can, then, say that the man of virtue is master of his own acts and is capable of guiding his own feelings. However, the man of vice does not dominate his feelings; rather, he is himself dominated by the sense objects that present themselves to him and trigger an emotional reaction. In the presence of a positive aspect of reality, for example, the man of virtue is capable of controlling his reactions and enjoying that good in conformity with his own good. The man of vice, on the other hand, is not capable of controlling his reactions but remains dependent upon the reality that attracts him even if it involves something bad for him. In the final analysis, educating the affections means augmenting freedom and moulding the virtues; affective education is an important part of moral education. For example, it is not enough to want what is good; rather, we must know how to achieve it with courage and strength — moral qualities that include the feelings of hope and daring (to refer to the list we gave earlier).

Before concluding this chapter, we must observe that the affections have the merit of being a particularly appropriate expression of the substantial unity of body and soul, of spirituality and sensibility. Nonetheless, they are not the root of the enhancement of the person. The individual cannot act without the feelings, but he cannot achieve his own enhancement without ordering his affections

---

33. Vice, then, is not only the lack of virtue but also the real and effective presence of a habit that disposes us to evil and truly hinders the achievement of good.

through his freedom. Affectivity is guided by the intellect and the will through the virtues.[34]

SUMMARY OF CHAPTER 10

In the preceding chapter we explained what a tendency is and what kinds of tendency are to be found in human beings. The affections, or feelings, may be defined as the operations of the tendencies: when a known object activates one of the individual's natural tendencies, then an emotion arises in him in response to that stimulus. Thus, the affections are always associated with sense knowledge (the object may be present or merely remembered or imagined). On the one hand, the emotional reactions of the individual refer to the sensory aspects of reality, but, on the other, they also depend on the individual's subjective sensory dispositions (physiological and psychological).

There is a close relationship among knowledge, affectivity, and action: The feelings can reinforce or hinder the decision to undertake a certain free action, but they can also lead to an impulsive and not entirely voluntary action. Therefore, it is important to educate affectivity and to learn to know our emotional reactions so as to regulate our feelings with a view to our own moral enhancement.

---

34. On the subject matter of this section, see A. Rodríguez Luño, *La scelta ética: Il rapporto fra libertà e virtù* (Milan: Ares, 1988); M. Rhonheimer, *The Perspective of Morality: Philosophical Foundations of Thomistic Virtue Ethics*, cit., 167–223.

CHAPTER 11

SEXUALITY

1. CORPOREITY AND SEXUALITY

In Chapter 4 we considered the subject of corporeity and explained how each human being experiences himself as a corporeal-spiritual individual. The manner in which I exist in the world and establish relations with others is characterized by my corporeity with its spatiality (my lineaments, my figure, and so on), temporality (including my age and state of development), and sexuality (femininity or masculinity). Corporeity concerns the whole person in the sense that our mind and our spiritual activities also depend upon our bodies. It follows that sexual identity is not just an anatomical configuration but marks the entire existence of the male individual and the female individual. For this reason, we often distinguish between *sex* and *sexuality*. The former is a mere biological physiological fact; the latter is the configuration of the entire person in accordance with a male or female identity.[1]

Understood in this way, sexuality is yet another expression of the unity of the entire human person, in whom body, mind, and spirit cannot be separated comprehensibly. A body, sexually identified but considered as pure matter, risks being reduced to an object for experimentation or exploitation; a mind not correlated to the body and to spiritual tensions could be reduced to a heterogeneous assemblage of impulses; spirituality not referred to body and mind may appear as an ideal and unattainable state. At the same time, the fact that sexuality affects the entire person means that the individual also has a very specific duty: that of integrating his or her masculinity or femininity into the overall framework of his or her life as we will explain below. To describe this as a duty means that it is not something automatic or taken for granted; i.e., sexual tendency — like the other sensory tendencies but perhaps more strongly — can be a source of disintegration and conflict.

---

1. This distinction is clearly explained by, among others, S. Palumbieri, *L'uomo, questo paradosso: Antropologia filosofica II: Trattato sulla con-centrazione e condizione antropologica* (Rome: Urbaniana University Press, 2000), 198–199.

The unitary vision of the person enables us not to fall prey to another form of reductionism, which could be defined as the "reductionism of culture" or the "reductionism of freedom," which in the final analysis is a product of individualism.[2] It is true that human beings are not compelled necessarily to follow their natural tendencies, including sexual tendencies, but this does not mean that no account must be taken of their physical constitution and that it can be transformed according to subjective taste.

If arbitrary and subjective preferences prevailed, we would be reducing corporeity (understood as one dimension of the totality of the person) to a body to be manipulated and exploited, and this would have a disintegrating effect on individual life. In fact, the complementarity of man-woman and the openness of sexual union to procreation are not forms of "biological conditioning" to be overcome but data inscribed from the beginning into the very anthropological structure of individuals and, consequently, of society. Moreover, the position we have described as the "reductionism of culture" would involve a dualistic vision of the person because it would mean presenting the body as a prison, or an enemy, to the "I" that seeks to affirm itself.

2. RELATIONS BETWEEN MAN AND WOMAN

There should be no need to underline the fact that the difference between man and woman is, from the anthropological point of view, a primary datum. However obvious it may be, let us reiterate that things did not begin with sexually indistinct individuals who, over the course of the centuries and through cultural transformations, became sexuality differentiated. Moreover, it is evident that the difference between the sexes is part of the general context of reproduction in living beings, even allowing for all the peculiarities and complexities of the animal and plant worlds. Yet we must

---

2. Examples of the "reductionism of culture" include certain extreme positions in recent discussions on the question of *gender* that minimize the role of bodily difference and overestimate that of subjective culture. When in this text we speak of "sexual inclination," we are not referring to what today is called "sexual orientation," i.e., an inclination of a sexual nature that is exclusively subjective and circumstantial. Of itself, "sexual orientation" is not a criterion upon which to base a claim for rights because the expression can be used to refer to any impulse to which we may be prey. Thus, for example, a phrase of the kind "we must not allow discrimination on the basis of sexual orientation" is too ambiguous to be admitted; after all, pedophilia is also a "sexual orientation," but it would not be discriminatory not to employ a pedophile as a primary school teacher.

ask ourselves whether it can be said that the significance of sexual difference in human beings begins and ends with its reproductive goals, i.e., whether it can only be understood from a biological-physiological point of view. And once again we must respond that this point of view alone does not do justice to the particularity of the human individual.

Human beings are structured with very precise identities (an onto-logically founded identity as we will see in Chapter 13), part of which is sexual difference, i.e., femininity and masculinity. When we said the difference between man and woman is a primary datum, what we meant was this: that not only at the origin of each human being, in the course of history, lies a union between a woman and a man but also that the human person fulfills and understands him- or herself thanks to the reciprocity between man and woman, the reciprocity between the male person and the female person. This self-understanding and self-fulfillment involves all the dimensions of the individual: that of the body (with the development, discovery, and knowledge of sexualized corporeity), that of the mind (with its various stages of maturation), and that of the spirit (with its incessant enhancement).

Because the duality of the sexes is a primary datum, woman and man enjoy equal dignity as persons, although history has frequently witnessed the subordination of the former to the latter. This is an evident sign of disorder, of the conflictive roots in relations between individuals,[3] something upon which we cannot dwell here but that has provoked a counter-movement by feminist groups over recent decades. Such achievements as obtaining equality of rights must be considered as a conquest, but an antagonism has at times been created that seems to blur the difference between the sexes and, as a consequence, the specificity of the roles of man and woman in society and the family.

The goal that women should seek clearly cannot be that of identi-fying themselves completely with men (or vice versa). If they took men as their model of reference, they would lose sight of their own identity. Thus, it must not be forgotten that the duality of the sexes implies a specificity, a particularity in the male person and the

---

3. Christian Revelation goes to the root of this conflict with the narrative of Original Sin in the Book of Genesis. One commentary of fundamental importance for biblical anthropology is that of St. John Paul II, *Man and Woman He Created Them: A Theology of the Body* (Boston, MA: Pauline Books and Media, MA, 2006).

female person that cannot be reduced to mere biological aspects but that also involves a duty of the entire person toward others and toward society. The tendency to level out differences, which is manifested in so many ways in modern culture, could lead to an irreparable impoverishment of the family, of the social community, and of individuals. Suffice to remember the undeniable fact that the married couple and the family are founded on sexual difference and on the fecundity of the union between the sexes.

3. Integrating the Sexual Impulse into the Idea of Love as a Gift

As we explained in Chapter 9, the sensory inclinations that are called instincts in animals should be called emotional impulses in human beings because the way they are translated into action is not rigidly determined by the species but characterized by a certain plasticity. To speak of plasticity is to refer to the freedom with which the individual orients himself toward his own particular end, i.e., self-determination and self-realization. Therefore, human beings do not have a merely animal sexuality, one forced to follow mechanisms that are uncontrolled and independent from the voluntary or rational sphere. The sexual tendency that each individual has by nature must be progressively humanized. In other words, it must be integrated into that which is specifically human, i.e., the sphere of freedom and of love as a gift. To put it another way,

> When we speak of the sexual urge in man, we have in mind not an interior source of specific actions somehow "imposed in advance" but a certain orientation, a certain direction in man's life implicit in his very nature. The sexual urge in this conception is *a natural drive born in all human beings, a vector of aspiration* along which their whole existence develops and perfects itself from within....
>
> Man is not responsible for what *happens* to him in the sphere of sex since he is obviously not himself the cause of it, but he is entirely responsible for what he *does* in this sphere. The fact that the sexual urge is the source of what happens in a man, of the various events which occur in his sensual and emotional life independently of his will, shows that this urge is a property of the whole of human existence and not just of one of its spheres, or functions. This property permeating the *whole* existence of man is a force that manifests itself not only in what "happens" involuntarily in the

human body, the senses and the emotions, but also in that which takes shape with the aid of the will.[4]

This passage highlights the difference, which we noted earlier, between the human dynamics that are not directly controlled by the individual and the free actions. Applied to sexuality, this difference shows that certain emotional and physiological reactions can be activated spontaneously, but it is up to each one of us to orient our sexual inclination to the enhancement of the entire person, as must also be the case for the other sensory inclinations.

We will dwell at some length on the free enhancement of the person in Chapter 14. For now, we can say that the human individual achieves appropriate self-fulfillment when he guides all his own structures and dynamics toward his own good. It is in this way that he manifests his capacity for self-possession, which is an indispensable precondition for freedom because, if I were not master of my own self, I would not be free. It follows that the fullest expression of freedom is the giving of self to others either through marriage or to God: Possessing all of myself (my aspirations, my tendencies, my past, and my future), I give myself because I can only give that which is mine. A gift, then, is always a gratuitous gesture born of love and not of calculation. When we give, we do so forever (not with the intention of taking back what we gave) and exclusively (not bartering our gift).

If we understand the relationship between love and giving in this way, then the integration of the sexual impulse means giving that impulse a sense of totality because, by virtue of its intensity, it is an inclination capable of involving the bodily and mental energies of the individual. As Karol Wojtyła explains, "The Latin word 'integer' means 'whole'—so that 'integration' means 'making whole,' the endeavor to achieve wholeness and completeness. *The process of integrating love relies on the primary elements of the human spirit — freedom and truth.*"[5] It is free will and an inner orientation toward truth, which does not depend upon ourselves, that constitute the essence of love and the motor of the process by which the sexual impulse is integrated.

---

4. K. Wojtyła, *Love and Responsibility* (San Francisco: Ignatius Press, 1993), 46–47; emphasis in original.

5. *Ibid*, 116; emphasis in original.

4. Sexuality and the Maturation of the Person

It must not be forgotten that the integration to which we referred above is a process in the sense that it follows a gradual development and is not a definitively acquired state. This is evident if we think of the growth of human beings from a physical and mental point of view through their various stages of childhood, adolescence, and old age. In each of these "phases" of life, the sexual impulse is manifested in very specific ways, and, therefore, the task of integrating it will take place differently each time: from gaining an awareness of one's own sexual identity, to understanding the peculiarities of the other sex, to accepting the "language of the body."[6]

In the course of this personal maturation, the individual develops his capacity for self-possession, which also means discovering and safeguarding his own intimacy—not only physical intimacy but also spiritual intimacy. In this sense, *modesty* is not shame or demureness but the awareness of a treasure that is freely communicated only to those held to be worthy of trust and affection. Part of this treasure is one's own sexualized body and sentiments, which, if exposed to the world, become trivial, a mere commodity to be bartered away.

As we have said, it is self-possession that makes love and giving possible. From this we may deduce that the essence of the reciprocal exchange of gifts between woman and man, upon which the family is based, is constituted by the inner freedom of the individual who recognizes the truth of the other. Sexual union between man and woman is the full bodily expression of such freedom, and for this reason it has meaning only in the context of total giving that is specific to marriage. Outside the context of a reciprocal, total, and exclusive gift (i.e., without limit of time or circumstance), sexual union between man and woman is a falsification.

---

6. In the integration of sexuality, as in all formative processes that involve the person, there is an interaction among various factors: physiological aspects, character, family, society, culture, and so on. Consequently, results are not achieved automatically, and imbalances or deficiencies may arise. Despite all attempts to demonstrate its genetic roots, homosexuality is to be attributed to a psychological disturbance of an affective-educational nature. On this subject, it is possible to consult studies by G. van den Aardweg and by husband and wife J. and L.A. Nicolosi, including: G.J.M. van den Aardweg, *Homosexuality and Hope: A Psychologist Talks About Treatment and Change* (Ann Arbor, MI: Servant Books, 1985); G.J.M. van den Aardweg, *The Battle for Normality: A Guide for (Self-) Therapy for Homosexuality* (San Francisco: Ignatius Press, 1997); J. Nicolosi and L.A. Nicolosi, *A Parent's Guide to Preventing Homosexuality* (Downers Grove, IL: InterVarsity Press, IL, 2002).

Love between husband and wife in marriage is not the only way to experience the self-giving that involves a person's entire existence. The capacity to give oneself may be oriented transcendently toward an ideal or toward God, renouncing sexual activity. This does not mean that sexuality is inhibited but that it is integrated at a more exalted level.[7] The fact that all human beings have in themselves a male or female sexual identity indicates that each person is called to live life oblatively, i.e., called to express the idea of love as gift. This is, in fact, the most radical vocation of the human being—that each person exists thanks to love, and he or she lives to love and to be loved.

Before concluding this chapter we must make it clear that we have reflected on the subject of sexuality from an anthropological and not from a moral point of view. In other words, our aim was that of outlining, within the limits we assigned ourselves for each chapter, the anthropological elements that may be useful in understanding the role of sexuality in the life of the person. It is these anthropological elements, among others, that serve as the foundation for the moral reflections that are the focus of study in ethics and moral theology, which draw more directly from Christian Revelation.

SUMMARY OF CHAPTER 11

Sexuality is not just an anatomical configuration (male or female) but characterizes a human being's entire existence. In this sense, it expresses the unity of the human person, made up of body, mind, and spirit. The complementarity of man and woman and the openness of their sexual union to procreation are inscribed into the very origins of the anthropological structure of individuals and, as a consequence, of human society.

Therefore, there is no purely animal sexuality in human beings; the sexual inclination that each individual has by nature must always be humanized in the sense that it must be integrated into that which is specifically human, i.e., into the sphere of freedom and the idea of love as a gift. This integration of sexuality into the totality of

---

7. As Dr. Wanda Poltawska observes: "From the point of view of the physiology of the human body, renouncing sexual activity does not represent the mortification of a specific requirement because the body does not possess mechanisms that force it to such activity" (W. Poltawska, "Il celibato sacerdotale alla luce della medicina e della psicología," in Solo per amore: Riflessioni sul celibato sacerdotale [Cinisello Balsamo: Paoline, 1993], 90).

existence is a process of gradual development and not a definitively acquired state.

CHAPTER 12

SPIRITUALITY, DEATH, AND IMMORTALITY

1. MONISM, DUALISM, AND DUALITY

In Chapters 3 and 4 we turned our attention, respectively, to the soul and the living body. We also constantly reiterated the fact that they are coprinciples, i.e., two principles that operate together in the constitution of the human individual. Alone, neither the body nor the soul constitutes a human being. We likewise observed that it is not easy to exemplify the unitary reality we perceive in ourselves and in our fellow creatures because our imagination always tends to present two "things," one alongside the other or, at most, mixed together. This difficulty is reflected in the various ways in which, over the history of philosophy, attempts have been made to explain in conceptual terms the coexistence of human beings in their corporeity and their spirituality.

One frequently used approach is that of *monism*, which reduces human reality to a single dimension, be it material or spiritual. *Materialism* holds that we can only know that which is corporeal and, therefore, effectively denies that human beings can possess any real principle of a spiritual nature, i.e., one that cannot be reduced to calculable, measurable, or testable dimensions. There may exist, though it is much less frequent, a contrasting form of monism: either spiritualistic or idealistic, which, though unable to deny the evidence of corporeity, bases its understanding of man only on his spiritual or rational life, sometimes denying a real distinction between material events and mental events.[1] However, this latter position inevitably ends up in dualism, as we will now explain.

Dualism, in fact, recognizes that human existence is characterized by the presence of spiritual reality and material reality but does not want or is unable to present them in their unity. In this view, matter and spirit are two distinct, often contrasting, elements, which, despite their heterogeneity, exist contemporaneously in the individ-

---

1. Cf. J.J. Sanguineti, *Introduzione alla gnoseologia* (Florence: Le Monnier, 2003), 49.

ual. It is clear, then, that while monism (at least apparently) defends the unity of the individual, dualism introduces a fracture that is difficult to mend.

Dual theory, on the other hand, draws on the ideas of Aristotle and Thomas Aquinas to present the human being as a bidimensional whole, that is, as a being characterized by the cooperation of spirit and body. Such cooperation has emerged in many of the arguments thus far presented such as when we spoke of the necessary relationship between rational activity and sensory activity or of the link between the dynamism of the senses and that of the spirit. This cooperation expresses the duality of the human being, which implies that the spiritual principle cannot be understood without reference to the body, which is thereby permeated, and that the body cannot be understood without reference to the spirit, which is therein incarnated. As we saw, especially in Chapter 3, in order to understand the unity of the person we must adopt a perspective that extends to the ultimate principles of reality, i.e., the metaphysical perspective that enables us to understand the substantial unity between soul and body. The radical principle of the person, the perfection that makes all his perfections possible, is the act of being communicated by the soul to the body.[2]

We will return to this topic in the next chapter. Now, however, we must consider a question that tests the validity of the theories about the unity of the person, that is, the problem of death.

2. THE EXISTENTIAL, OR PHILOSOPHICAL, PROBLEM OF DEATH

It is not easy to perceive the problem of death when we view it detachedly or from a distance. On the other hand, we do perceive it as a problem when it touches us personally either because we feel its approach in ourselves or we see it touch someone near to us. It is in situations such as these that we acquire a complete awareness of our mortal state and anxiously question ourselves about the meaning of life, the value of our actions, the transitory nature of things, and the persistence of the self beyond earthly existence. One particularly problematic aspect is the contrast between the ineluctability of

---

2. A brief presentation of dual theory, which also responds to some of the most recent objections, is to be found in G. Basti, "*Dall'informazione allo spirito: Abbozzo di una nuova antropologia,*" in *L'anima* (Milan: Mondadori, 2004), 41–65. Cf. also J.J. Sanguineti, *Introduzione alla gnoseologia,* cit., 54–56.

dying and the desire of the individual to persist into the future and uninterruptedly to prolong his love for others.

As long as death remains just one subject among many others, a subject to be studied detachedly, we do not feel directly involved. Referring to the philosophy of Kierkegaard, Pareyson with his characteristic tone explains that "if it is only a question of defining death, then it is soon done, and even a youth can manage it without too much experience. But if it is a question of saying what is the value of death as orientation for life, what is the concrete meaning of death for a real specific individual, then it is necessary to have carried the idea of death inside oneself for a long time, to have deposited it in the conscience as a living seed of interior reflections and exterior actions."[3]

Sometimes it is literature, rather than philosophy, that best demonstrates how the approach of death in man, or near him, can effect profound changes. One masterly example of this is in a novella by Tolstoy in which the protagonist is overwhelmed by the inexorable advance of his disease:

> The example of the syllogism he had learnt from Kieseveter's logic: "Caius is a man, men are mortal, therefore Caius is mortal," had seemed to him all his life correct only as regards Caius, but not at all as regards himself.... "Caius really was mortal, and it was right for him to die; but for me, little Vanya, Ivan Ilych, with all my feelings and ideas, for me it's a different matter. It cannot be that I ought to die. That would be too awful." Such was his feeling.[4]

Such existential doubts lead to other queries that call into question the philosophical conception of the human person. Is everything in the individual, then, material and therefore corruptible? How can we explain the persistence of "something" of the individual after death? In order to find an adequate response, we must return to the elements of the dual theory of the person and arrive at its metaphysical nucleus.

3. MORE ON THE SOUL-BODY RELATIONSHIP

The human person is a whole whose existence is made possible by two coprinciples: the soul and the body. We explained this, first

---

3. L. Pareyson, *Kierkegaard e Pascal* (Milan: Mursia, 1998), 156.
4. L. Tolstoy, *The Death of Ivan Ilych and Other Stories* (New York: Barnes & Noble, 2004), 121–122.

by defining the soul as the "form of the body" in accordance with Aristotle, and then by specifying that the soul is the "substantial form of the body." In other words, the soul is the radical principle of the living being in the sense that it does not merely confer certain secondary properties but "conforms" matter, making it a living body (in the case of man, a human body), an organism capable of undertaking certain vital operations. Therefore, it is the union of soul and body that causes the individual to exist as a complete substance.

But we must underline the fact that, for human beings, the adjective "substantial" united to the noun "form" takes on a particular significance because, in this case, it means that the human soul is the form of the body and that, at the same time, it is subsistent. To affirm that the human soul is subsistent means that it possesses being and communicates it to the body. We reach this conclusion on the basis of the observation that there are immaterial operations in man, i.e., actions whose accomplishment depends on the senses only extrinsically (as regards the object apprehended by the senses) but not intrinsically. This relative independence from matter leads to the assertion that the human soul acts of itself, in the sense that it is the principle of its own actions. Now, since each being acts in the degree to which it is "in act," it follows that the intellective soul (that is, the form of the body) possesses being of itself.[5] It communicates being to the body, and it is by virtue of this one act of being that the human person subsists.

4. IMMATERIALITY AND IMMORTALITY

From what we have just said and on the basis of the explanations provided in Chapter 8, we must conclude that the human soul is an immaterial, or spiritual, principle. Plato reached this same conclusion with great clarity and precision.[6] Hence, notwithstanding the various forms of materialism, this is a truth that is part of the perennial heritage of the history of philosophy.

The immateriality of the human soul implies its incorruptibility, and this can be demonstrated in various ways. Firstly, the soul is *simple* in the sense that it is not composed of form and matter. From a metaphysical point of view, corruption means precisely the separation

---

5. Cf. Thomas Aquinas, *Quæstio Disputata De Anima*, a. 1, c; *Summa Theologiæ*, I, q. 76, a. 1.

6. Especially in his dialogue *Phaedo*.

of these two principles, as happens when substantial changes take place in a subject that loses its substantial form, for example, wood that becomes ashes or a flower that rots. But the human soul is a subsistent form, and its subsistence is not annulled by the corruption of the body because the body receives its being from the form. Moreover, it may be considered that, while the body is subject to the action of other agents, the spirit is not "corroded" by external agents of material kind. Through intelligence, we can know all of reality, but this does not erode the spirit in itself; on the contrary, the more we progress in knowledge, the more acute our intellect becomes.

In support of the idea of the subsistence of the soul as coprinciple of the human individual, other (epistemological) arguments could be used, as we outlined in Chapters 4 and 8. The intellect is capable of receiving all sense forms, while the body is always determined by matter. The intellect knows universal and abstract forms, or concepts (justice, evil, good, beauty, hatred, generosity, and so on), which transcend the material conditions of the objects perceived. The intellect is capable of complete self-reflection.

Nonetheless, in order to understand the spirituality of human beings (precisely by virtue of their spiritual principle), anthropological arguments are also very effective. Thomas Aquinas, for example, highlights how each individual wishes to exist in a way specific to himself and how, since what is specific to humans is to live according to reason, the human being desires always to exist because, through reason, his knowledge of reality can overcome the limits of time and space, i.e., contingent circumstances. This *desire for perpetuity* does not derive from material factors but from the spiritual nature of the human soul.[7] For his part, St. Augustine places the emphasis on the *desire for happiness* that is inherent in each human person, a desire that surpasses all limited and temporary forms of satisfaction because it longs for endless and imperturbable happiness.[8]

In the same context, we can reflect upon the capacity for *self-transcendence* by human beings, who constantly tend to surpass themselves in their self-realization, to project themselves beyond time (with hopes and plans for the future), and to turn toward God over and above worldly uncertainties. As we will see more fully in Chap-

---

7. Cf. Thomas Aquinas, *Summa Theologiæ*, I, q. 75, a. 6.

8. On this subject, see Agostino, *La speranza* (Rome: Città Nuova, 2002).

ter 14, self-transcendence implies the emergence of the spirit over materiality.

It should, then, be evident that to speak of the immateriality and incorruptibility of the human soul means to support the idea of its immortality. But here an apparent problem that arose earlier emerges once again: Is it the soul that is immortal or is the person immortal? The problem is only apparent and can be resolved by recalling what we said about intellectual knowledge. The one who knows the truth or extracts a universal concept is the person, but it is not wrong to affirm that "the intelligence knows" because such a phrase highlights the role of the immediate principle of the action, i.e., the rational soul. In the same way, the root of immortality in the person lies in his substantial form. And so, in maintaining that the human soul is immortal it is implicit that the person is immortal by virtue of his spiritual principle.

The person survives death—the corruption of the body—with his individual characteristics, with his "I." But the condition of the "soul separated from the body" is unnatural because each soul is made to exist with its body. And hence we may see, in the light of reason, the feasibility of the resurrection of the flesh as laid down by Christian Revelation.

Thus, also as concerns immortality, it is as well not to overlook the existential perspective, which invites us not to reduce the subject to some irrelevant erudite discussion because it is in fact a decisive question. Kierkegaard observes that

> raising the problem of *one's own immortality* is, at the same time, for the living subject who raises the problem, an *action*, and certainly not one for the distracted who every now and again ask themselves if they are immortal in an entirely general way.... He asks how he must behave in his life in order to express his immortality, and whether he effectively expresses it or not; and until receiving new orders he contents himself with this task which, given that it will embrace all eternity, can certainly embrace an entire life.[9]

5. At the Origin of the Person

Having said what we have said, a spontaneous question arises concerning the origin of the person with his two constituent principles

9. S. Kierkegaard, *Postilla conclusiva non scientifica alle "Briciole di filosofia"* (Bologna: Zanichelli, 1962), Vol. I, 370; emphasis in original.

of soul and body. Although we will return in part to this subject in the following chapter, some explanations can be given here.

The question concerning the origin of the person would be easy to answer if we wished to maintain a materialistic viewpoint. If human beings were mere matter, then the study of genetics and embryology would suffice to understand where they come from. But we have thus far sought to show that one of the constituent principles of man is not material, and thus scientific research manages to explain how the human organism is formed and develops but not where its spiritual principle comes from. This principle, precisely because it is spiritual, cannot come from the reproductive process in the sense that it is not transmitted by the parents, who do, however, transmit an individual's genetic heritage.[10] If this were not true, i.e., if we were circumscribed to a material process, we would not have a principle intrinsically independent of matter.

To seek to understand where the human soul comes from, how it "arises" to conform the person, we must also refer to the distinction between the human soul and that of irrational beings.[11] In the case of plants and animals, the form, or soul, is conveyed in the reproductive process through the potency of an appropriate biological material. The soul of irrational beings does not have existence of itself, but thanks to it an individual comes into being. As we have said, its function is limited to conforming the body and enabling it to undertake the bodily actions specific to the species. The human soul, on the other hand, possesses a perfection that surpasses the properties of matter, so its origin cannot be explained only on the basis of material elements. This perfection is shown in the accomplishment of such actions as free will and intelligence, which are not *per se* corporeal even though they make use of an organic base.

In the light of Christian Revelation, we reach the conclusion, glimpses of which were already evident in Greek philosophy, that the human spirit derives from a Principle that is itself spiritual, that is, from God. Therefore, at the origin of the human soul, which communicates its being to a body specific to itself, is a creative act of God. In speaking of the human soul as substantial form, we made

---

10. The view that holds that the soul is transmitted by reproduction is called *traducianism*; one of its supporters was Tertullian, but the theory was propounded again in the nineteenth century.

11. On this subject, see the concise explanation in Thomas Aquinas, *Quæstio Disputata de Spiritualibus Creaturis*, q. 1, a. 2, ad 8.

it clear that, by using this concept, we do not wish to establish a temporal priority of the soul over the body (i.e., the soul does not preexist somewhere to be then "infused" into an unformed body) but to indicate an ontological preeminence, i.e., the fact that it is the soul that transmits the being possessed by the body.

From the point of view of theology and philosophy, the above conclusion requires further clarifications, which, however, we cannot go into here. We will limit ourselves to saying that this conclusion presupposes the simultaneous intervention (in some sense, a kind of cooperation) between the parents and God with his creative action. The parents prepare the matter to receive the form, which is directly created by God.

SUMMARY OF CHAPTER 12

In philosophical reflection upon the human person, it is important to avoid materialist monism, which concentrates only on the person's bodily dimension, but it is equally important to avoid dualism, which considers the person as an amalgam of two different substances (body and spirit), accidentally united to one another. By contrast, emphasis must be given to the duality of human beings, recognizing that they possess two coprinciples (corporeity and the spiritual soul) united to form a single substance. The spiritual principle cannot be understood without reference to the body of which it is the form, and the body cannot be understood without reference to the spirit, which is therein incarnated.

Precisely because of the human being's unity, death emerges as a problem not just from an existential but also from a philosophical point of view. Death poses forcefully the question of who the human being is and whether the individual survives the destruction of his body. The human soul is *per se* incorruptible because it is the principle of immaterial activities that do not intrinsically depend upon the body (free actions and intellectual knowledge). Proving the immateriality and incorruptibility of the human soul leads to sustaining the survival of the self after death. This thesis can also be upheld by reflecting on the desire for perpetuity and for complete happiness, which is inherent in each individual.

Since the human soul is spiritual, it cannot derive from matter. Rather, being a spiritual principle, it derives from a spiritual Principle, i.e., from God.

CHAPTER 13

WHO IS THE PERSON?

1. THE CENTRALITY OF THE PERSON

Underlying the debates on the most important ethical questions (from respect for human life to defense of the environment) lies a very precise conception of who the person is, even if this is not specifically recognized. To admit, for example, that it is lawful to reproduce and select the human individual in a laboratory does not only mean to decide on the use of a particular form of technology but also to maintain that man may be manipulated in the same way as a computer or a doll. This also holds true for other fundamental problems facing culture, society, and politics.

Therefore, it is understandable that particular attention should be paid to the human person today even if we often speak on the subject without clarifying exactly what we mean, that is, without making it clear from a conceptual standpoint why and how the human person is different from other living beings. And yet it is necessary to arrive at a notion of the human person that can act as a foundation, a clear point of reference, when facing the problems discussed in the fields of philosophy and law, psychology, education, and sociology. Indeed, it may be said that in any science involving man it is necessary to proceed on the basis of an appropriate conception of the human person as we highlighted in Chapter 1.

2. PHENOMENOLOGICAL PERSPECTIVE AND METAPHYSICAL PERSPECTIVE

We have just said that transformations in modern culture must encourage us to ask ourselves about the roots of the dignity of the person in order to answer the question: Who is man?[1] We can

---

1. Posed in this way, the question expresses the correct attitude toward man because it immediately highlights his peculiarity. It would be reductive to ask ourselves "what" man is because such a formulation would risk reducing the human being to one more thing among many others. Classical philosophers (for example, Richard of Saint Victor and Alexander of Hales, both from the twelfth century) underlined the fact that the philosophical notion of person answers the problem of *quis est* ("who is") the individual man.

attempt to respond to this query by following two philosophical itineraries, which, as we will see, are not mutually exclusive.

In the first place, it is possible to show specific characteristics that make the human being entirely original and unmistakable in the world in which he lives and, therefore, deserving of an esteem that cannot be shown to other living beings, which are nonetheless worthy of respect.

We could define this approach as a phenomenological-existential process because it is based on the observation of typically human phenomena[2] and on reflection about the distinct features of human existence. It focuses on observable facts in order to examine and throw light on the ways in which man manifests and fulfills himself. In this way, various characteristics emerge that enable us to give a number of definitions of man on the basis of his capacities. Most of these definitions are not entirely comprehensive but include one or more of the fundamental aspects of the human person. Among them is the old formulation that defines man as *animal rationale* (rational animal), i.e., the animal capable of knowing reality and extracting universal concepts therefrom.[3] In the same way, it could be said that man is the only being who knows how to laugh,[4] showing his capacity for detachment from himself and from the events in which he is involved. Or again, he is the only mortal being[5] on the basis of the assumption that the event of death (not reduced to its biological aspects) does not truly concern other animals. Or that he "knows

---

2. From the Greek *phainómenon*, "that which appears." Here we use the expression "phenomenological" in a generic and not a technical sense, i.e., not limited to a particular philosophical school of thought.

3. Though more or less accurate (because man is scientifically classified as part of the animal kingdom), this definition is inadequate because the meaning of *animalitas* in man is different *per se* to that in animals (cf. E. Coreth, *Antropología filosófica* [Brescia: Morcelliana, 1991], 67). With such a definition, in fact, we run the risk of attributing to the common notion of animal the extrinsic gift of rationality (cf. H. Arendt, *The Human Condition* [Chicago: The University of Chicago Press, 1958], 284) as if to say that just as the chameleon is the animal capable of changing color, so man is the animal capable of reasoning. But to proceed in this way would mean to lose sight of who man is because it would mean putting him at the same level as other animals and so denying his particularity.

4. Cf. H. Bergson, *Il riso: Saggio sul significato del comico* (Rome and Bari: Laterza, 1994), 4.

5. Cf. H. Arendt, *The Human Condition*, cit., 18–19. This affirmation is also to be found in other philosophers, among them Heidegger, who notes that death in man is an existential phenomenon that cannot be reduced to the physical-biological datum of the cessation of vital activities: cf. M. Heidegger, *Being and Time* (New York: Harper & Row, 1962), Division two, Chapter 1 §§ 49–53. Elsewhere he says: "To die means to be capable of death as death. Only man dies. The animal perishes": *id.*, "The Thing," in *Poetry, Language, Thought*, 176 (New York: HarperCollins, 2001).

how to say no" and, therefore, does not depend unequivocally and absolutely on the reality before him.[6] Or that he is "the being who acts"[7] in the sense that he assumes positions and also has the capacity of deciding for himself.

Each of these affirmations highlights a fundamental trait of the human person, but it is clear that, in following this first itinerary, we are using a method that is prevalently descriptive or comparative, one that supplies significant information because it presupposes, more or less consciously, an underlying notion of the human person. What is needed, then, is a second itinerary that starts from the human person's constitutive foundation in which the potentials that man manifests in his life are already contained *in nuce*: This perspective is specific to metaphysics, which concerns itself with the ultimate principles of reality. We could say that, in the above affirmations ("man is a mortal being," "man is the being who knows how to say no," and so on), the phenomenological-existential analysis concentrates on the predicate of the proposition, while metaphysical analysis focuses on the verb "is," on personal existence.

Clearly, the metaphysical perspective alone is not enough to understand all the richness of human existence because, as we will see in coming chapters, the person would not be comprehensible without considering the way in which he relates to others, exercises his freedom, gives of himself, lives in time and history, achieves self-fulfillment, and transforms the surrounding world. Nonetheless, these personal dimensions necessarily imply an ontological identity from which they stem. Put another way, the ontological dignity of the human person, his personal existence, does not depend on a specific capacity or characteristic; the fundamental rights of the person (the right to life or to religious freedom, for example) do not derive from an individual's specific gifts or moral rectitude but from his very existence, from which all the other perfections derive. In other words, the human individual is worthy of respect not because he is capable of laughter or because he is mortal (to refer to two characteristics mentioned above) but because he is a person.

From what we have said, however, it is evident that the metaphysical and phenomenological-existential perspectives are not mutually

6. Cf. M. Scheler, *"Die Stellung des Menschen in Kosmos,"* in *Gesammelte Werke,* 44, (Bern: A. Francke, 1976).

7. Cf. A. Gehlen, *Man: His Nature and Place in the World* (New York: Columbia University Press, 1988), 24, 48.

exclusive; rather, they complement one another. A kind of circularity must be established between them that they may reciprocally clarify each other. To this end we will now seek to penetrate to the original nucleus of personal existence and then, in coming chapters, turn back to consider the various levels of existence. To do this we must use some apparently difficult concepts, but the effort required to understand them will not be in vain.

3. Metaphysical Analysis of the Notion of Person

We will leave until the end of this chapter certain historical explanations as to how the metaphysical notion of person developed. For now, in order to reach the abovementioned ontological nucleus, we can start with Thomas Aquinas's affirmation: "'Person' signifies what is most perfect in all nature: that is, a subsistent individual of a rational nature."[8] This is a metaphysical assertion because the dignity of the person is not based directly upon how he acts but on what he is as such (we will explain this more fully later) independently of whether all his potentials are expressed or not. From this affirmation it follows that the value of human life, or of the human person, is incommensurable. Its intrinsic value does not depend on and is not increased by other qualities, nor is it comparable with them. What each individual is worth as a man does not admit comparison with a specific technical ability or physical performance.

Alongside this statement of Thomas Aquinas, we can place the classic definition of Boethius, according to which the person is "an individual substance of a rational nature."[9] Both affirmations contain three important metaphysical notions: individual, nature, and substance. In order to understand the person from a metaphysical point of view, it is not enough to affirm that he is something individual because individuality also belongs to accidental properties,

---

8. "*Persona significat id quod est perfectissimum in tota natura, scilicet subsistens in rationali natura*" (Thomas Aquinas, *Summa Theologiæ*, I, q. 29, a. 3). St. Thomas condenses the notion of person into the expression *subsistens rationale*; i.e., subsistent rational being: cf. A. Milano, "*La Trinità dei teologi e dei filosofi: L'intelligenza della persona in Dio*," in *Persona e personalismi* (Naples: Dehoniane, 1987), 56–61. On the conception of the human person in St. Thomas, see J.A. Lombo, *La persona humana en Tomás de Aquino: Un estudio histórico y sistemático* (Rome: Apollinare Studi, 2001).

9. "*Naturæ rationalis individua substantia*": S. Boethius, *Liber de persona et duabus naturis contra Eutychen et Nestorium, ad Joannem Diaconum Ecclesiæ Romanæ*, Chapter III, PL 64, 1343.

i.e., to what exists as a perfection or characteristic of a subject. For example, weight or color, which do not subsist in and of themselves but inhere in something else (white and yellow do not exist in general but as a white page or a yellow flower).

Likewise, it is not enough to say that the person is a substance, i.e., something that subsists in itself and not in something else, nor that he is a "a nature" because this is a generic and abstract concept. Nature indicates something common to all individuals and, hence, belongs to a species, whereas, in reality, "a nature" always subsists in individualized form, i.e., with characteristics that make it a specific individual of its species and which are not *per se* part of the definition of a specific nature (in other words, not "horseness" or "dogness" but this horse or that dog exist in extramental reality).

Thus, uniting the three notions (individual, substance, and nature) with the term person, we are referring to an individualized substance of a rational nature. As regards human nature, the person is singular, unique, and unrepeatable. The ultimate foundation of this uniqueness and unrepeatability is the possession of a specific act of being (*actus essendi*), which confers actuality to the substance and to its determinations. Everything the person knows, everything he wants, and everything he does stems from the act by virtue of which he is. Although this subject can be interpreted in various ways, let us seek to draw some basic outlines.

What do we mean by the expression "act of being"? We mean the metaphysical principle by which something really *is* — not existence *as man*, *as cat*, or *as rock*, which derives from its nature, or essence — but *being*, simply and radically. In truth, of course, being belongs to all individual subsistent substances, but of these the person shows a higher level of subsistence because he acts "*propter se*," as the principle of his own actions. With respect to other subsistent individuals, his act of being is possessed more "specifically."

The irreducible dignity of the human person lies not so much in abstract reason (as could seem at first glance in Boethius's definition) but in the rationality or spirituality possessed by a concrete individual who subsists by virtue of an act of being. It is evident that the individual human goes through various stages of development, but there is a continuity in his existence. Either he is a human being or he will never become one however many perfections may be externally attributed to him and however many the external circumstances in which he may find himself. It is not phenomenological-existential properties that determine personal existence but the other way round: From personal existence arise the specific characteristics of the human person that can be studied from a phenomenological-existential perspective.

The human person possesses the act of being in himself and for himself but not from himself; that is, he does not, from an ontological viewpoint, create himself. His existence is granted by the Subsistent Being, in other words, God. Drawing from Christian Revelation and in accordance with what we explained in Chapter 12, we can say that at the origin of each human person is a free creative act of God, who institutes that person as a "novelty in existence," in his image and likeness. The dignity of the person derives, then, from his origin and from his actual being.

Let us see now the main metaphysical properties that follow from such a conception of the human person. These properties, which were already implicit in our earlier analysis,[10] are highlighted by many personalist and existentialist philosophers, and here, too, we will pass frequently from one level of analysis to the other. This is further proof that, in order to understand these properties correctly, they must be examined in a metaphysical perspective. We will have to return to some of these characteristics in later chapters.

3.1. Inalienability

To begin, let us examine the two characteristics that derive from the first fundamental aspect of the human person, i.e., from his subsistence.

Firstly, the *inalienability* of the human person derives from the fact that he does not inhere in something else but subsists in himself and for himself:[11] My being a person is inalienable in the sense that it cannot be taken away from me. One person cannot be assumed by another because each person possesses his own ontological identity,

---

10. For a clear and more detailed explanation of what we have said, with precise reference to the works of St. Thomas Aquinas, see C. Cardona, *Metafisica del bene e del male* (Milan: Ares, 1991), especially Chapter 3, "*L'atto personale di essere*," 62–93.

11. In classical terminology, this quality was identified with the name of "incommunicability." This term, however, can give rise to misunderstandings because it may be forgotten that it refers to the metaphysical level and not to the existential level of relations between people.

an identity that enables him to assume a role or a task.[12] From this attribute derives the classical definition according to which the person is *sui iuris et alteri incommunicabilis*[13] (which we could translate as "the person belongs to himself and is inalienable").

That which makes an individual being *this particular thing* is not transferable or communicable to others, and this is especially true of the person, who enjoys an entirely unique form of individuality.[14] Indeed, what makes Socrates a man (i.e., his nature, or essence) can be communicated to many others, but what makes him *this* man can be communicated only to one person, to himself.[15] The species propagates itself, not the person. For the same reason, as we have said, my "being a person" cannot be taken from me even though I can lose a particular role or certain physical characteristics.

This concept, upon which Christian philosophy lays much emphasis, represents a fundamental difference with respect to pantheistic or mystical philosophies, which conjecture the annulment of the person in the whole, in nature, or in the divinity. The individual remains himself before God.[16] In the light of Christian Revelation it is easier to understand that the creature is wanted, guided, and protected *"propter se"*[17] ("for himself").

3.1.1. Unrepeatability

One feature of the inalienability of the human person is his *unrepeatability* because the individual person is not merely a single instance of a universal norm like one square among the infinity of geometrical figures having four sides of equal length set at right angles. He is not like one of the innumerable reproductions of Donatello's David

---

12. Cf. Thomas Aquinas, *Commentum in Librum III Sententiarum*, d. 5, q. 2, aa. 1 e 2.

13. As K. Wojtyła has observed, implicit in this phrase are the self-possession (*sui juris*) and self-control (*alteri incommunicabilis*) characteristic of the person who, consequently, decides about himself using his own will (cf. *The Acting Person* [Dordecht: D. Reidel Publishing Company, 1979], 106–107).

14. Cf. Thomas Aquinas, *Summa Theologiæ*, I, q. 29, a. 1.

15. Cf. *ibid*, q. 11, a. 3.

16. It is in this sense that we can understand Augustine's words: "When I come to be united to thee with all my being… my life shall be a real life, being wholly filled by thee" (*"Cum inhæsero tibi ex omni me… viva erit vita mea tota plena te,"* [Augustine, *Confessions*, 10, 28, 39]); my being is not taken away from me by the definitive union with God.

17. Thomas Aquinas, *Summa Contra Gentiles*, III, 112. Just how much an adequate understanding of the human person is linked to the relationship with God is concisely explained in R. Guardini, *"Conosce l'uomo chi ha conoscenza di Dio,"* in *Accettare se stessi*, 35–72 (Brescia: Morcelliana, 1992).

or Michelangelo's Moses. Rather, we could say that he is an original, imitable but not in himself repeatable. For even if we could precisely reproduce the bodily characteristics of a person, we would not have the same person because he is an individual who exists in his own original and unrepeatable singularity.[18]

In philosophical terms this may be more clearly understood if we consider that, while the concept of nature embraces only the essential elements of a thing and is a part with respect to the whole of the individual creature, the concept of person means something else, something that exists and includes everything there is in the human being with the individual characteristics that distinguish him from others. Peter is not a person because he is *a man*, he is a person because he is *this man*. Nor is it correct to say that "man is a person"; rather, we must affirm that "this man is a person";[19] in the same way "the human person" does not exist; rather, "this, or that, human person" exists. Hence, as we have explained, personal dignity does not derive from humanity or rationality considered in abstract terms but from concrete, real, and individual existence that derives from a specific act of being.

3.1.2. The Consequences of Inalienability

In emphasizing the inalienability and the unrepeatability of the person, we are affirming the primacy of individuality. Humanity, Society, Absolute Spirit, Nation, and Cosmos (or, to use more everyday terms, public opinion, the masses, the group, and so on) are categories that cannot be considered as independent from or in opposition to the value of the individual man.[20] In these totalitarian concepts (i.e., concepts that stress the whole or the entirety), the individual would, to use a fitting expression of Sciacca, be nothing

---

18. According to Crosby, the unrepeatability characteristic of the human person may be considered as a consequence or expression of his spirituality, in other words, of the fact that the person cannot be completely reduced to the spatial or material dimension, and that in him the whole is superior to the individual elements, which of themselves may appear negligible (cf. J.F. Crosby, *The Selfhood of the Human Person* [Washington, D.C.: The Catholic University of America Press, 1996], 43–44, 52–53).

19. Cf. Thomas Aquinas, *Commentum in Librum III Sententiarum*, d. 10, q. 1, a. 2.

20. Cf. C. Fabro, *Riflessioni sulla libertà* (Segni: Edivi, 2004), 200. This aspect is effectively explained by E. Mounier, who uses the term "vocation" to describe it: "The significance of each person is such that he cannot be replaced in the place he occupies in the universe of persons" (*Il personalismo* [Rome: A.V.E., 1974], 73).

more than a "a scrap of cloth" distinguished only by its dimensions with respect to the whole.[21]

The primacy of individuality can also be diminished by rigid and materialistic evolutionary theory, according to which the individual human being is subordinated as a mere means or instrument to the progress of the species. At the same time, however, the individual must not be closed in on himself and made an absolute. The human being's unrepeatability and dignity reveal themselves precisely in his inherent relationality with transcendence in the fact that he has a personal relationship with the world, with others, and with God. As we will soon see, unrepeatability and relationality can be fully understood only by comparison with others. Only by considering myself and others in our respective unrepeatable individuality (i.e., not as mass-produced and infinitely multipliable individuals) is it possible to recognize the dignity of each man and to treat him as an individual, unique in himself.

Guardini adds certain other existential characteristics possessed by individuals on the basis of their metaphysical inalienability: They are self-belonging, irreplaceable, and self-guaranteeing. This he explains as follows:

> "Person" means that I, in my being, definitively cannot be possessed by any other entity but belong to myself.... Person means that I cannot be inhabited by any other, but that, in relation to myself, I am alone with myself; I cannot be represented by any other but am my own guarantor; I cannot be replaced by anyone else but am unique.[22]

From an anthropological and phenomenological point of view, the inalienability and ontological inviolability of the person are reflected in the phenomenon of modesty.[23] Indeed, inalienability suggests a profound and inviolable intimacy that the person tends to protect. Moreover, this metaphysical property of human beings shows itself to be very important in the study of freedom, for, in fact, the self-

---

21. M. F. Sciacca, *Morte e immortalità* (Palermo: L'Epos, 1990), 39; Sciacca is here referring to the philosophy of Spinoza, but he uses the same image in his *L'uomo questo "squilibrato"* (Palermo: L'Epos, 2000), 109.

22. R. Guardini, *Persona e libertà: Saggi di fondazione della teoría pedagogica* (Brescia: La Scuola, 1987), 181–182. See also how these ideas are presented in B. Mondin, *L'uomo: chi è: Elementi di antropología filosófica* (Milan: Massimo, 1989), 374–375.

23. Cf. K. Wojtyła, *Love and Responsibility* (San Francisco: Ignatius Press, 1993), 190–191. Though, in a strictly metaphysical context, Mounier also emphasizes the bond between a person's self-possession and the feeling of modesty: cf. E. Mounier, *Personalism*, cit., 66–67.

determination and self-control that distinguish free acts are rooted in the self-possession that derives from inalienability: The action arises from the being that possesses itself (in keeping with the classic principle *operari sequitur esse*, which means: "action arises, or derives, from being"). Hence, moral acts, in other words, the actions deriving from the exercise of freedom, can be defined as a free affirmation of our being.[24]

3.2. Completeness

A second characteristic to derive from the subsistence of the human person is *completeness*. This should not be understood in material-quantitative or logical terms but in the sense that, by virtue of the richness of his act of being, the person is a complete reality; i.e., he is not simply a part with respect to a whole but a whole in himself. Although from birth to adulthood he will go through various stages of development, from an ontological point of view he never lacks anything to be a person. Therefore, to avoid misunderstandings, it would perhaps be better to speak of *fullness*, or *integrality*.

It would be reductive to say, for example, that the person is only a part of the universe or that he has no other task than that of being a part of society. The person is not just an individual at the service of the species;[25] he is not destined simply to be "like others." To use Kierkegaard's paradoxical expression: A thousand men are less than one man.[26] In other words, individuals are not simply elements, which, added together, constitute humankind, nor is it the final sum that establishes the value of the individuals. This fact is denied — in theory and, sooner or later, in practice — by all totalitarian ideologies, according to which the individual is only relevant in order to

---

24. Cf. A. Millán-Puelles, *La libre afirmación de nuestro ser: Una fundamentación de la ética realista* (Madrid: Rialp, 1994).

25. This also means that the person cannot be understood only in terms of quantitative relationships with his fellow men. This is an aspect of which St. Thomas seems already to have been aware when he wrote, *"ratio partis contrariatur rationi personæ"* ("the concept of 'part' is opposed to that of 'person'"), *Commentum in Librum III Sententiarum*, d. 5, q. 3, a. 2; cf. J.F. Crosby, *The Selfhood of the Human Person*, cit., 50. Shortly afterwards, he wrote: *"Ad rationem personæ exigitur quod sit totum et completum"* ("in the concept of person it is implicit that 'person' means an integral and complete reality"), *Commentum in Librum III Sententiarum*, d. 5, q. 3, a. 2, ad 3.

26. Cf. S. Kierkegaard, *Diario (1847–1848)* (Brescia: Morcelliana, 1980), Vol. 4, IX A 91, n. 1791.

accomplish social progress, the march of history, the realization of some political or demographic project, and so on.[27]

To say that the person is a whole in himself does not mean to recognize some supposed ontological self-sufficiency in him. That is, it does not mean thinking that the individual is the author and principle of his own being. Rather, it indicates, as Kant observes,[28] that the person is an end unto himself and never simply a means; he is an end that exists *per se* and cannot be used as a mere instrument subordinated to other ends.

The importance of considering the person with respect to his inherent value, as a totality, becomes evident if, for example, we consider two events in man's life such as death and birth.

In an idealistic perspective, or in the Marxist version of the Hegelian dialectic, the value of the individual is effectively denied. It comes as no surprise, then, that Marx should write of death in these terms:

> Man's individual and species-life are not *different* however much — and this is inevitable — the mode of existence of the individual is a more *particular* or more *general* mode of the life of the species or the life of the species is a more *particular* or more *general* individual life.... Death seems to be a harsh victory of the species over the *particular* individual and to contradict their unity. But the particular individual is only a *particular species-being* and as such mortal.[29]

From a materialistic viewpoint such as that of Marx, the individual is effectively subordinated to the progress of the species because nothing in him escapes the determinism of the laws of nature. However, it is precisely when faced with death that the human being experiences his own totality. As we suggested at the beginning of the chapter, death is not just a biological fact but an event in which I find myself alone with my whole self, quite independent from the

---

27. It is as well to underline the paradoxical nature of Kierkegaard's aforementioned expression, which, if detached from the other fundamental characteristics of the human person, could lead to the danger of passing from a metaphysical level to the ambit of vitality, individual gifts, originality, beauty, and exalted cultural values. This would open the way to individualism, which, in fact, does lurk in certain existentialist positions (cf. R. Guardini, *Das Ende der Neuzeit: Ein Versuch zur Orientierung* [Basel: Hess, 1950], 76–77).

28. Cf. I. Kant, *Fondazione della metafisica dei costumi* (Milan: Rusconi, 1994), section II, 141–145.

29. K. Marx, *Economic and Philosophic Manuscripts of 1844* (Moscow: Progress Publishers, 1959); emphasis in original.

events of the species or of humanity. It is with this sense of uniqueness that relatives and friends perceive the death of a loved one.[30]

A similar argument could be made concerning the birth of the person. The value of the individual coming into the world is not limited to the process of propagating the species. The baby establishes a unique relationship with its father and mother, and the parents are not indifferent as to whether one or other of their children should survive.

Progress in genetics makes it ever more urgent and important to understand the incomparable value, with respect to the species, of the individual human being who comes into the world. Technology such as artificial fertilization and cloning (applied to man) may lead us to consider the human being not for his nontransferable, personal identity but for his biological qualities, which can be arbitrarily manipulated, programmed, and selected. In the case of artificial fertilization, the "human product" would seem to be worth more in terms of what it represents to the people who commissioned it than in terms of *what* it is. This significantly increases the danger that a birth be used as a means to placate one's own feelings, to satisfy the desire to have a child, or to fill a sense of emptiness.

Let us, nonetheless, reiterate the fact that the metaphysical characteristic of a person's completeness has to be seen in association with his constituent relationality. The human person is a whole who must fulfill and possess himself in relation with others.

3.3. Intentionality and Relationality

Apart from subsistence, the metaphysical analysis also throws light on another fundamental aspect of the human person, that is, rationality, understood as the capacity to assimilate cognitively everything that exists and apprehend the intelligibility, beauty, and goodness of existence.[31] Associated with rationality are, first and foremost, *intentionality* and *relationality*, in other words, openness to reality and to others.

It is a fact that human beings are relational, their first relationship being with God and their parents. But relationality also means

---

30. Cf. J. Gevaert, *Il problema dell'uomo: Introduzione all'antropología filosófica* (Torino and Leumann: Elle Di Ci, 1989), 255–256; J.F. Crosby, *The Selfhood of the Human Person*, cit., 51–52.

31. Cf. A. Campodonico, *Ética della ragione: La filosofía dell'uomo tra nichilismo e confronto interculturale* (Milan: Jaca Book, 2000), 29–31, 216–218.

a capacity to establish relationships, to orient oneself toward the world and toward others, to give of oneself. This capacity can be directly associated with rationality but must also be seen in terms of metaphysical inalienability and of the fundamental self-belonging mentioned above. If this latter quality were lacking, only exterior relationships would be established, not personal relationships (that is, between a "me" and a "you"). On the basis of his profound intimacy and self-possession, man is not just one among many but establishes relationships that are unique and specific to himself. He is not isolated and closed: The concept of person implies both the relationship with self, or self-belonging, and the relationship with that which transcends the self (other people or God).[32]

At first sight this property, which is as essential as others, would seem to be somewhat disregarded in the metaphysical analysis of the person. It is, however, given considerable emphasis by many modern philosophers who study the person. We will not dwell on the subject any longer here but return to it from a different point of view in Chapter 15.

3.4. Autonomy

Rationality in human beings is also associated with their autonomy. Returning to what we outlined above we could say that in the person, in a certain way, nature is at the service of the individual or, better still, of the singular, as Kierkegaard says.[33] It is not natural instincts that decide each man's destiny but the individual who uses his natural instincts, knowing their purpose, to direct the course of his life.[34] As we have said, rational individuals show a particular form of singularity because they have control over their own actions; they do not act like others but act *per se* ("essentially"),[35] thus demonstrating their own inalienability.

---

32. This aspect is highlighted in Pareyson's notion of the confluence of self-relation and hetero-relation in the person: cf. L. Pareyson, *Esistenza e persona* (Genoa: Il Melangolo, 1985), 229–230. For a philosophical-theological study of relationality, also with reference to what is known as "dialogical or relational philosophy," see M. Serretti, *Natura della comunione: Saggio sulla relazione* (Soveria Mannelli: Rubbettino, 1999).

33. Cf. S. Kierkegaard, *Diario (1850)* (Brescia: Morcelliana, 1981), Vol. 7, X2 A 426.

34. See also how a very similar observation appears in Thomas Aquinas, *Summa Contra Gentiles*, III, 113.

35. Cf. *id, Summa Theologiæ*, I, q. 29, a. 1. In this sense it could be said that while rational individuals act (*agunt*), nonrational individuals are directed or moved (*aguntur*): cf. *ibid.*

This property recalls the classical principle whereby actions, in the final analysis, belong or are to be attributed to living individuals. Thus, just as we said that Peter is a person in the degree to which he is *this man*, so we must say that he is this person who can act and does act, carrying out personal actions: It is the same unique subsistent subject who is, feels, wants, and knows.[36] We experience this truth subjectively in the exercise of our freedom when we feel, so to speak, alone with ourselves in making certain choices or performing certain actions, something we will consider in the next chapter.

4. HISTORICAL EXPLANATION OF HOW THE METAPHYSICAL NOTION OF PERSON DEVELOPED

4.1. The Greek and Latin Notion of Person Before Christianity

The history of the notion of person, in its semantic and conceptual aspects, is an intricate and complex affair; here we can give only a brief glimpse that may nonetheless be helpful in tracing a basic outline of the subject.[37]

Person in Greek was at first πρόσωπον, which, from meaning theatrical mask (literally "that which is before the eyes"), came to designate the theater actor himself, the one who wore the mask. Originally this word did not designate man at all—either in a general sense or, even less so, in an ethical-spiritual sense—but the "character," the part played by the actor who used the mask to present himself with a face different from his own.

This meaning is also present in the Latin word. The mask made it possible to communicate with the public (thus, *personare*, according to some scholars, comes from *sonus*, an allusion to the amplification of the voice, whence derives the verb "to personify") and denoted the role of the actor in the action taking place on the stage. This accommodated certain fixed roles in Latin comedies, for example, since women were not permitted to act in the theater, the mask enabled men to personify women.

36. St. Thomas says as much with the simple phrase "*hic homo intelligit*" ("this man knows intellectually"), *Summa Theologiæ*, I, q. 76, a. 1, with which he confuted the existence of a universal intellect for all men. The phrase highlights the fact that, despite the existence of various faculties in the soul, in actions it is the entire person that intervenes, i.e., there is unity in human activity.

37. For more detailed explanations, see the essay by J.A. Lombo, *La persona humana en Tomás de Aquino: Un estudio histórico y sistemático*, cit., 31–165.

In Roman law, the term "person" was used to designate someone who, by virtue of a name, was recognizable and could play a role in society. But that role, and the dignity of being a citizen, was subordinated to certain external conditions, such as birth, wealth, and lineage. A man without a name, who did not belong to a known lineage and without a voice, i.e., without the right to vote, was a *caput*; that is, an anonymous individual.[38]

In very general terms, we can say that in Greek culture, too, the individual's value was secondary or subordinate with respect to the universal, to the cycle of history, to the city-state, to the patriarchal family, to destiny, or to the will of the gods.[39]

Plato (427–347 BC), in fact, held that only Man, and not this man, is truly real and knowable. It is the idea of man that is eternal, unchangeable, and necessary, while individuals are temporary and accidental. Ideas relegate the animate, living individual that contemplates them to a secondary level. One example of this is to be found in the following extract: "You, little man, are one of those who ceaselessly look to the whole and tend toward it. . . . You fail to understand how each act of generation comes about that the essence of happiness may be present in the life of the whole. Thus, it is not for you that it exists; rather, it is you who exist for the life of the whole."[40] It is no surprise, then, that in the fifth book of his *Republic*, Plato theorizes that wives and children should be held in common, arguing that procreation is exclusively a function for the good of the State.[41]

In a similar way, Plotinus (AD 205–270) also seems to subordinate human freedom to Providence which, in the name of overall harmony, designates some men as good and others as bad.[42]

Our purpose here is not to devalue more than seven centuries of philosophy, only to highlight briefly that, in the light of Revelation, earlier philosophical conceptions were no longer enough to provide an adequate foundation for the notion of person. Nonetheless, the

---

38. Cf. B. Albanese,"*Persona (storia)*"in *Enciclopedia del Diritto* (Milan: Giuffrè, 1983), Vol. XXXIII, 169–181.

39. Cf. É. Gilson, *The Spirit of Mediæval Philosophy* (New York: Charles Scribner's Sons, 1940), Chapter X, 189–208.

40. Plato, *Laws*, X 903 C. St. Thomas points out that for Plato only the "separate" man is the true man; man as he exists in matter is man only by participation: cf. Thomas Aquinas, *Summa Theologiæ*, I q. 18, a. 4, ad 3.

41. Cf. Plato, *Republic*, V 459 A– 462 C.

42. Cf. Plotinus, "On Providence" I, in *Enneads*, III, 2, 10–11.

philosophy of Socrates with its call to interior life and to "know thyself"; that of Plato with its recognition of the primacy of Good; that of Aristotle with its masterly study of ethics; and, in the Latin world, the stoicism of Seneca with its focus on the virtues of the wise provided the necessary foundations for speculation to continue.[43] In this context, it is significant that St. Clement of Alexandria (150–215) should have considered Greek philosophy as a second revelation, though incomplete, or as a river flowing into the New Testament. It should not, in fact, be forgotten that ancient philosophy had its own anthropology and its own ethics. To cite another example of the value of the thinkers of antiquity, in the stoic-cynic philosopher Epictetus (50–138), the term πρόσωπον, even in its definition as theatrical mask, takes on clear ethical-anthropological connotations: Man is an actor who did not choose his role but must play it well. A similar idea is also to be found in Seneca.

Here we have made brief mention of Greek and Latin philosophy; limiting ourselves, that is, to Western thought. It remains to be asked whether and how Eastern thought contains an adequate notion of the person. But to do so it would be necessary to embark on a historical-critical study in order to identify what philosophical notion of person existed before Christ, and whether the spread of Christianity subsequently influenced certain aspects of "Eastern philosophy." This, however, is something we cannot do here.

4.2. The Contribution of Christianity

With Christianity the individual emerges in all his value, as the recipient of the Revelation, object of love, and adoptive child of God. Man is rational and free precisely because he is created in the image of God. He is autonomous by virtue of the creative act which, making him a participant in an infinitely wise and free power, creates each individual and endows him with the light of knowledge, the initiatives of will, and the capacity to love.[44] The contents of Revelation — and especially the truths of filiation and divine providence — help us see the meaning of person with fresh clarity. Thus,

---

43. Even Gilson, whom we mentioned earlier, highlights the "effective contribution" made by Greek and Latin philosophy in this field: cf. É. Gilson, op. cit., 243.

44. On this subject, see G. Reale and D. Antiseri, *Il pensiero occidentale dalle origini ad oggi* (Brescia: La Scuola, 1985), Vol. I, Part 8. "*La rivoluzione spirituale del messaggio biblico.*" Mounier's explanation about the cultural novelty of Christianity as it regards the concept of person is also useful: cf. E. Mounier, *Personalism*, cit., 14–18.

as Guardini observes, if our relationship with the living and personal God of Christianity fails, it is still

> certainly possible to recognize a gifted, cultured, and efficient individual but not the authentic person that is an absolute designation of each man over and above his psychological or cultural qualities. Thus, knowledge of the person is linked to Christian faith. Recognition and respect may last a little after faith is lost, but then they are gradually lost.[45]

The change introduced by Christianity made itself felt not only at the level of philosophical speculation but first and foremost in society and culture.

According to some scholars, the influence of Christianity is evident in Roman law in various fields of legislation but particularly as concerns the rights of the person. This is most noteworthy, as is only to be expected, in the period between Constantine and Justinian, during which the influence of Christian ethics came to be added to the earlier influence of stoicism. Examples of the influence of Christianity include the spread of the practice of manumitting slaves (*favor libertatis*); the ban on owners alienating a slave by separating him from spouse and children, and recognition for the families of slaves. In the same way, property rights and the right to legitimate defense came to be moderated by respect for others.[46]

4.2.1. The Philosophy of the Fathers up to St. Augustine

The lack of adequate conceptual categories in the philosophy of the time tasked the reasoning of the Fathers of the Church, who drew from the Greek and Latin philosophical heritage to define the notion of person. The occasion arose, above all, with the theological disputes on the Trinity and the Incarnation. The history of this speculative development is long and complex, and we will give only a brief outline.

It is important to bear in mind the fact that what Christian thinkers sought to do was answer the theoretical questions that emerged from their reflections upon Revelation. Going beyond the ideal of the virtuous man as understood by the Greeks and Latins, it became necessary to attempt to translate into philosophical terms the truths

---

45. R. Guardini, *La fine dell'epoca moderna: Il potere* (Brescia: Morcelliana, 1984), 99.

46. Cf. S. Riccobono, *Lineamenti della storia delle fonti e del diritto romano* (Milan: Giuffrè, 1949), 178–190; M. Talamanca, *Lineamenti di storia del diritto romano* (Milan: Giuffrè, 1989), 556, 575.

of man's status as creature, his divine filiation, and the Incarnation in the Second Person of the Trinity. How can we explain in conceptual terms that God truly became man? How can we define the singularity and individuality of the human person? In what does his being in the image and likeness of God consist? What is his dignity and upon what does it rest? Can we speak of "person" in God and in man?

Sts. Gregory of Nazianzus (329/330–390) and Gregory of Nyssa (335–395) detached the notion of person from that of "mask" and were among the first to use the term πρόσωπον (which had given rise to misunderstandings and heresies that saw in the Persons of the Trinity only "modes" of God) as equivalent to υποστασις.

An important contribution to systematizing the question was made by St. Augustine (354–430) in his studies on the distinction and unity of the divine Persons. But in his day there was no terminological consensus on the use of the term "substance" as a synonym of "person." Despite this, he reveals a considerable grasp of the notion when he writes: "Person does not signify species but something singular and individual,"[47] and: "Each individual man ... is one person."[48] We must not, however, seek in his works a full and complete definition of person nor a specific study of its analogical use, to be able to apply the concept of person to God and to man.[49]

4.2.2. Boethius's Definition

The most famous expression to indicate the metaphysical notion of person was that coined by Severinus Boethius (480–526), who held important positions in the court of Theodoric and translated and commented on works by Plato and Aristotle. It would certainly be inappropriate to consider his as a true and complete definition in the modern or scientific meaning of the word. It is, rather, an expression that systemizes the use of certain terms and presupposes an entire concept of the world and of man. He arrived at it in the context of certain theological disputes against the Nestorians (who held that there are two natures and two Persons in Christ, united by a purely moral bond) and the Monophysites (who, inspired by Eutyches, held that Christ had only one, divine, nature). As we indicated above,

---

47. *"Personæ nomine non speciem significari, sed aliquid singulare atque individuum"*: Augustine, *De Trinitate*, VII, 6, 11.

48. *"Singulus quisque homo... una persona"*: ibid, XV, 7, 11.

49. Cf. A. Trapè, *"Introduzione: Teologia,"* in Augustine, *La Trinità*, Vol. IV. (Rome: Città Nuova, 1987), XXXVI–XXXVII, LXII–LXIII.

Boethius "defined" the person as "an individual substance of a rational nature."[50]

We examined the meaning of the individual terms earlier in this text, but will briefly mention them again though without entering into the various interpretations the definition has been given. "Substance" indicates that which exists in itself, as opposed to "accidents" (weight, color, size), which are the inherent characteristics of a subsistent subject. This substance is "individual," i.e., it exists with characteristics that distinguish it from other individuals of the same species. The term "nature" means the essence (that by which a thing is what it is), being the principle of operations. On this nature depends "rationality," in other words, the capacity to know the surrounding world and to extract universal concepts therefrom.

Boethius's definition arranges and systemizes the Greek and Latin concepts as in a mosaic. It specifies the totality of the subsistent subject, in other words, his species and the accidents that inhere thereto.[51] To reach this point he first had to clarify—and it is here above all that his merit lies—the distinction between the two terms "nature" and "person," which at the time were being used incorrectly and confusedly.

This definition makes no claim to illuminate the entire truth about man. It should be understood only as a theoretical peak in a broader vision of the person and the world that is not limited to a single formula. Subsequently, its implicit limits would be highlighted, among them the difficulty of applying such a notion of person, at one and the same time, to God, to the angels, and to man or a certain ambiguity in the term *substantia*.[52]

4.2.3. St. John Damascene and St. Bonaventure

St. John Damascene (ca. 675–749), almost like a forerunner of existentialism, wrote that "the person is he who, expressing himself

---

50. "*Naturæ rationalis individua substantia*": S. Boethius, *Liber de persona et duabus naturis contra Eutychen et Nestorium, ad Joannem Diaconum Ecclesiæ Romanæ*, Chapter III, PL 64, 1343.

51. Spaemann gives a very good explanation of the ontological import of Boethius's definition: "An individual existing in this way cannot be displayed in full by any possible description. No description can replace naming. A person is *someone*, not *something*, not a mere instance of a kind of being that is indifferent to it" (R. Spaemann, *Persons: The Difference Between "Someone" and "Something"* [Oxford: Oxford University Press, 2006], 29).

52. This question is examined in J.A. Lombo, *La persona humana en Tomás de Aquino: Un estudio histórico y sistemático*, cit., 69–114.

through his own operations and properties, presents a manifestation of himself that distinguishes him from others of the same nature as him."[53] His is an interesting definition because it shows, among other possible examples, that the personalist and existentialist dimensions were by no means absent in classical thought on the human individual. Mention must also be made of Richard of Saint Victor (d. 1173), who defined the human person as "individual or incommunicable existence of a rational nature"[54] and the divine Person as "incommunicable existence of divine nature."[55]

St. Bonaventure (1217–1274) may be considered one of the finest interpreters of what is known as Christian personalism. In his view, the idea of person implies the idea of individual and that of a certain dignity due to his specific form. He acutely perceived the profound root of the person: "This is the distinction of the person in the third chapter of Exodus: I am who I am."[56] Personalism, then, is founded on the "metaphysics of Exodus." Here, the revelation throws a shaft of light on divine being: Personality is the sign of existence in its highest degree of perfection. We are persons because we are the work of a Person. We share in the divine personality, just as we share in his perfection and his providence, just as we share in his being.

4.2.4. The Philosophy of St. Thomas Aquinas

We have made repeated reference to the philosophy of St. Thomas Aquinas (1224/5–1274). He returned to Boethius's definition, but we have seen how he also defined the person as a *subsistens rationale*, or as that "which subsists in an intellectual or a rational nature,"[57] because such a notion can also be attributed to God. The term "subsistent" encapsulates the three elements: individual, nature, and substance.

His comments on Boethius's definition throw light on its profound implications as concerns, for example, individuality and subsistence. In underlining the dignity of the human person in his concrete indi-

53. *Dialectica*, c. 43, PG 94, 613.
54. "*Rationalis naturæ individua [vel incommunicabilis] existential*": *De Trinitate*, lib. IV, cap. 23, PL 196, 946. The author uses the term "*existentia*" with a very precise meaning to indicate originality and substantiality.
55. "*Divinæ naturæ incommunicabilis existential*": *ibid*, cap. 22, PL 196, 945.
56. "*Ecce, personalis distinctio; Exodi tertio: Ego sum, qui sum*": *Commentarius in Evangelium S. Joannis*, VIII, 38.
57. "*Omne subsistens in natura rationali vel intellectuali*": Thomas Aquinas, *Summa Contra Gentiles*, IV, c. 35; cf. *Summa Theologiæ*, III, q. 2, a. 2.

vidual state, St. Thomas recalls how actions always belong to the singular subsistent individual (the *suppositum*), never to nature, and that the *suppositum* is the whole which possesses the specific nature as its formal or perfective part.[58] With a vision that runs counter to any form of Platonism, he affirms that the existence of a man is truer in his own nature than in the divine mind because the fact of existing in the material state is part of the truth of man, and this is not the case for the divine mind.[59]

4.3. The Role of Personalism

This brief overview will suffice. It is not, of course, a complete history of how the metaphysical notion of person developed but does show some of the phases of the process whereby it was affirmed and defined. We have focused above all on certain philosophical stages of the metaphysical perspective; in coming chapters we will examine other important aspects of the conception of the human person, aspects which emerge more fully in the perspective we have defined as phenomenological-existential.

To conclude this brief inquiry, we must make some reference to the fact that in the twentieth century, under the influence of specific historical circumstances, the attention of many thinkers came to be focused on the person. Indeed, the tragedy of the two world wars, especially the second, showed what extremes of contempt for man can be reached in the name of an ideology. And the same can be said about historical examples of exploitation and abuse of individuals in the name of capitalism, communism, or nationalism. Faced with such events, it is natural that one should ask: How is it possible to go so far as to lose sight of the value of the individual human being? What concept of the human person can be used as a foundation and not a provisional foundation for his dignity?

These questions, arising from the lessons of history, together with other philosophical and cultural factors, gave rise to a number of schools of philosophy collectively known as "personalism," which developed especially during the first half of the twentieth century.[60] Thinkers of sometimes very different tendencies came to be part of the movement (including, to mention just two, Emmanuel Mounier

---

58. Cf. *id*, *Summa Theologiæ*, III, q. 2, a. 2.

59. Cf. *ibid*, I, q. 18, a. 4, ad 3.

60. The first to use this expression was Charles Renouvier (1818–1903), who in 1903 wrote a work entitled *Le Personnalisme*.

and Paul-Louis Landsberg). They sought to place the value of individual existence at the center of their reflections and gave a positive impulse to debate on this question among the intellectuals of their day. That impulse, at least in its unitary sense, has now perhaps lost a lot of its energy, but the importance of studying the human person can never diminish and fortunately, in fact, it is still with us today.[61]

SUMMARY OF CHAPTER 13

The two fundamental questions raised in this chapter are, "Who is the human person?" and, "What notion of the human person can serve as an adequate foundation for his dignity?" We can give a phenomenological-existential response based on those characteristics of human life that distinguish it from the lives of other living beings, or we can give a metaphysical response that seeks to reach the ultimate foundation of personal ontological identity. These two approaches are not mutually exclusive, but the metaphysical perspective is the one that offers a definitive answer to the two fundamental questions mentioned above. Metaphysical reflection leads us to consider the person as an individual being of a rational nature, and analysis of this notion shows that the human being is inalienable, unrepeatable, complete in himself, intentional, and relational, autonomous in his actions. Development of the metaphysical notion of the person has been a long, historical process in which Christianity has played a decisive role. The historical events of the twentieth century have led many thinkers to examine the centrality of the human person.

---

61. In 1983, Ricoeur wrote a brief article with a deliberately provocative title, "*Meurt le personnalisme, revient la personne…*," in which he affirmed that the idea of person is still the most relevant terrain in which to consider the juridical, political, economic, and social problems of today while it would be ineffective to appeal to the ideas of "conscience," "subject," or "self" (the article was republished in P. Ricoeur, *Lectures 2: La contrée des philosophes* [Paris: Seuil, 1992], 195–202).

CHAPTER 14

FREEDOM AND SELF-FULFILLMENT

1. THE TASK OF SELF-FULFILLMENT

In the preceding chapter we sought to understand the metaphysical nucleus of the notion of human person, at the same time highlighting the importance of not stopping at that result but, on the foundation thereof, also examining man in his existential dimensions, in other words, in his dynamism.[1]

To introduce our subject, we may begin with a very effective passage from St. Gregory of Nyssa:

> All beings that are subject to the passage of time never remain identical to themselves but pass continually from one state to another in a process of change that is always at work, for good or for bad.... Now, to be subject to change is to be reborn continually.... But, in this case, birth does not come about by external intervention, as is the case in corporeal beings.... It is the result of a free choice, and thus we are, in a certain way, our own parents, creating ourselves as we wish and through our choices giving ourselves the form we wish.[2]

This passage refers not only to the fact that human existence goes through various phases of physical-biological development (infancy, childhood, and so on) but also alludes to the entire physiognomy of the person — spiritual and corporeal — which is called to self-fulfillment. Thus, we say that man is *causa sui*, cause of himself, not in an ontological sense because the finite individual cannot create himself from nothing but in the dynamic-existential sense, i.e., in

---

1. We will dwell on this question at some length because our explanations will serve as a reference for a number of future chapters, especially as regards culture and cultural values.

2. Gregory of Nyssa, *De Vita Moysis*, II, 2–3: PG 44, 327–328. The same expression, also referring to freedom, is to be found in *Homilia* 6: PG 44, 702–703: "We are in a certain sense our own parents." For his part, St. Augustine contrasts spiritual birth and growth with physical birth and growth: "Age or stature of the body is not at one's own will. A man does not grow in respect of the flesh when he will any more than he is born when he will, but where the being born rests with the will, the growth also rests with the will" (Augustine, *In Epistolam Ioannis ad Parthos*, III, 1).

operational terms. Each free action configures me in a particular way, positively or negatively, forming my personality. The same idea can be expressed thus: Each person is a task unto himself; we are necessarily free, and, therefore, whether we like it or not, the fulfillment of our lives depends upon us.

Obviously, this does not mean that we are the cause of ourselves in an absolute sense, i.e., with no reference to the individual (bio-psychological) and historical-sociological factors that distinguish us, but our free self-fulfillment does interact with those factors.

In order to understand this better, it may be helpful to delve briefly into neurology, limiting ourselves to seeking an intuitive comprehension of what we affirmed above. The development of the personality (that is, of the dynamic-existential aspect of the person) is linked, on the one hand, to the growth processes of nerve tissues and, on the other, to cerebral plasticity. The former are responsible for the specialization of areas of the brain, especially the linguistic areas; the latter, which is not limited to one period of life, lies at the basis of all processes of learning and adaptation. Mozart is considered to be an excellent example of such plasticity, i.e., of the capacity to model and orient the development of specific areas of one's own brain. From the earliest years of his life, he revealed an extreme aptitude (determined onto-genetically) for music. His father understood this immediately, and, thanks to a constant musical education, before Mozart reached puberty, his neurones (the area of the brain known as the neo-cortex) underwent a reorganization that made him one of the greatest musicians of all time.[3]

This example shows that, in achieving self-fulfillment, man must take account of the dispositions of his own body, which, thanks to his freedom and creativity, he can use to reach the goals he has set for himself. It also shows that self-fulfillment does not concern only the strictly spiritual aspect of man but also involves his body. Indeed, it could be no other way given the corporeal-spiritual unity of the human person.

It is important that our reflections on the free self-fulfillment of an individual life take place *after* having undertaken a metaphysical

---

3. Cf. J.C. Eccles, *Evolution of the Brain: Creation of the Self*, cit., 225. For a brief explanation of the concept of cerebral plasticity from a neuro-psychiatric viewpoint, see C.L. Cazzullo, "*La libertà nell'interpretazione della struttura e della dinamica della personalità*" in F. Russo and J. Villanueva (eds.), *Le dimensioni della libertà nel dibattito scientifico e filosofico*, 44–45 (Rome: Armando, 1995).

analysis of the human person, in order not to lose sight of his onto-logical nucleus. Otherwise, we may come to think that everything in the individual is variable and relative, that changes and choices influence each of us to such an extent as to prevent us knowing what the person, as such, is. From a metaphysical perspective, however, it is easy to understand that each individual has a permanent onto-logical identity, which is the foundation that makes him recogniz-able as a person, although the characterizations that he periodically assumes in his life may change.[4]

In this context we speak of a "personalistic foundation of freedom" in order to underline the fact that freedom can be fully understood and justified only on the basis of an adequate understanding of the human person, and, just as progress has been made in efforts to understand the essential nucleus of the notion of person, so there has been a parallel progress in reflections upon freedom.

Setting aside the conclusions he reached, Hegel recognized that the influence of Christianity, with its speculative efforts to formulate an adequate conception of the human person on the basis of Revela-tion, was decisive to the understanding of freedom:[5]

> Whole continents... have never had this idea.... The Greeks and Romans, Plato and Aristotle, even the Stoics did not have it. On the contrary, they saw that it is only by birth (as, for example, an Athenian or Spartan citizen) or by strength of character, educa-tion or philosophy (the sage is free even as a slave and in chains)

---

4. Many existentialists and some personalists highlight that one is a person and one autonomously manifests oneself as such when one exercises one's own freedom. But a positive conception of freedom has to be founded on a metaphysical notion of the person; otherwise, our position becomes a mere description, or parenthesis, which then turns out to be an insufficient basis for ethics. As we have said, from an ontological point of view, either one is a person or one will never become one. It is true that freedom is exercised in time and goes through various stages of maturation, but there is no ontological leap in the existence of the individual human being. It is evident that many authors wish to avoid the danger of what is called "substantialism," but the term substance, as used in classical philosophy, should not be understood as an immobile substratum of a static individual but as a source of autonomy and inviolability that belongs to the act of being. An interesting analysis of the relationship amogn person, freedom, and nature with reference to certain positions of modern philosophy is to be found in P. Sabuy Sabangu, *La question du dualisme anthropologique: Une analyse d'après Robert Spaemann, "Acta Philosophica,"* II/9 (2000), 241–265; *Persona, natura e ragione: Robert Spaemann e la dialettica del naturalismo e dello spiritualismo* (Rome: Armando, 2005).

5. See the comments of the following authors on the radical change in the conception of freedom between Greek and Christian culture: G. Reale, "*Libertà,*" in *Storia della filosofia antica,* Vol. V, 152–155 (Milan: Vita e Pensiero, 1980); M. Pohlenz, *Freedom in Greek Life and Thought: The History of an Ideal* (Dordrecht: Kluwer Academic Publishers, 1966), 161 ff.

that the human being is actually free. It was through Christianity that this idea came into the world. According to Christianity, the individual *as such* has an *infinite* value as the object and aim of divine love, destined as mind to live in absolute relationship with God himself, and have God's mind dwelling in him, i.e., man is *implicitly* destined to supreme freedom.[6]

2. AUTHENTIC EXISTENCE

Having established our premise for examining man's self-fulfillment, we must now add a number of clarifications in order to understand, first of all, what direction free self-fulfillment must take.

To understand this, we must first recognize that the following interpretation of freedom is very widespread: Someone is free if he is able to choose anything, without being subject to any criteria of evaluation or to the judgment of others. Individual choice is above criticism because individuals are free to fulfill themselves as they wish, however they like, and no rules or models can be imposed upon them. From this viewpoint, the self-fulfillment we mentioned above is understood as a capacity to adopt any kind of lifestyle without having to justify oneself to any higher authority, to nothing and to no one.

Without going into the historical-philosophical roots of this approach,[7] it is clear that this is an infantile notion of freedom, as if being free meant neglecting one's own power of judgment, making capricious and whimsical decisions, and being incapable of taking any responsibility in our dealings with others. Clearly such behavior denotes not only immaturity but also the triumph of selfishness, of an individualism impenetrable to any kind of discussion, the overriding power of the "self" superficially expressed in such phrases as, "I do just as I please," and other similar claims.

---

6. G.W.F. Hegel, *Encyclopedia of the Philosophical Sciences* § 482. See also observations on this subject by C. Fabro, *Riflessioni sulla libertà* (Segni: Edivi, 2004), 16. Gadamer also says that, in the world of classical Greece, freedom was "the freedom of action and choice of one who was his own master, unlike the slave who followed not his own will but the whims of his master. Freedom in this sense was a characteristic of political 'status': the condition of being a free man" (H. G. Gadamer, "*Kausalität in der Geschichte?*" in *Gesammelte Werke*, Vol. IV, 113 [Tübingen: J.C.B. Mohr, 1987–1995]). From this viewpoint, then, there is a limitation to the sphere of freedom.

7. Yepes, whose reflections on this subject are very clear, refers to J.S. Mill's theories on freedom: cf. R.Yepes, *Fundamentos de antropología: Un ideal de la excelencia humana* (Pamplona: Eunsa, 1996), 165–166.

To confute such a position it should be enough to observe that absolute freedom understood in such terms is unrealistic because it overlooks the fact that all our choices are made in the presence of precise conditions and circumstances and effected under the burden of our past and our aspirations for the future in such a way that any supposed spontaneity is merely apparent. Moreover, our own personal experience belies this thesis for, if we were truly capable of making any choice with complete indifference, our lives and those of others would not be seen as problematic or as dramatic as they sometimes are. The truth is that, at least in some circumstances, we are aware that it is not easy to make a decision: We ask ourselves what would be the best thing to do and, in turn, judge the decisions of others, recognizing them as worthy of praise or blame. In brief, we come to realize that free self-fulfillment cannot mean indifferentism or emotivism.

Indifferentism and emotivism would arise if, for example, we set ourselves to try any experience, the more the better, under the misapprehension that one is as good as another. To do so would be to fall into superficiality and dispersion, experiencing inner emptiness and an inevitable sensation of tedium and meaninglessness because it would mean losing sight of why we act and the values toward which we are directed. The truth is that it is not having experiences that counts but the way in which we undertake them and their content. Thus, we can say that, in order to live an authentic life, we need "to know how to manage the yeses and noes,"[8] i.e., to give an adequate response, either positive or negative, to the alternatives that present themselves in our lives. We need to recognize that our individual choices, inasmuch as they are ours and free, can be right or wrong. Seen in this way, authentic action contrasts with artificial action, with the unreflective adaptation to dominant norms, with, in a word, conformism.[9]

As Spaemann observes, in order to consider oneself authentic it is not enough to say, "I do as I please," or, "I do however I like." These are obvious and meaningless remarks both because one who acts according to conscience does, in the final analysis, act just as he likes and because they contain the implicit risk of acting under the effect

---

8. Cf. *ibid*, 169.
9. On this subject, consult R. Yepes, *La persona come fuente de autenticidad, "Acta Philosophica,"* I/6 (1997), 83–100; C. Taylor, *The Ethics of Authenticity* (Cambridge, MA: Harvard University Press, 1992).

of a momentary impulse.[10] The specifically human attitude is to ask *why* I want something, for it is, in fact, specific to man's dignity to act according to reason.[11] This does not, however, mean that only reason is human; rather, reason must be the principle coordinator of a conduct oriented toward happiness.[12]

It is for this reason that it is possible to evaluate whether a form of conduct is authentic or not, that is, whether the individual is fulfilling himself in a singular and nontransferable way, orienting himself toward the end specific to him. In fact, as we will see in Chapter 18, people act in accordance with a kind of table of values, which each person can structure in a different way and that constitutes the objective guide for his own life project. Hence, it is with reference to these rationally knowable values that the authenticity of individual conduct can be judged.

These observations on authenticity can be associated with one of the metaphysical properties of the person about which we spoke in the last chapter, that is, the unrepeatability of the individual. This unrepeatability is made manifest not only in eating, growing, experiencing pleasure, sleeping, etc., but above all in those choices that are a conscious expression of our autonomy, which involve the entire person in a serious and intense commitment (loving someone, giving of oneself, deciding one's own future, taking on a role or a task). These are important actions in the sense that they are important to me, and their intensity derives more from the fullness of meaning with which they are accompanied than with the physical effort they involve.[13] If, in the final analyses, these traits are to be found in all free actions, it is nonetheless true that there are some actions in

10. Cf. R. Spaemann, *Basic Moral Concepts* (London and New York: Routledge, 1989), 22–23, 34–35, 60. Recall also Max Scheler's observation, quoted in Chapter 13, to the effect that man is the one who knows how to say no; in other words, he knows how to orient his actions over and above the stimulus-response model.

11. Cf. Aristotle, *Nicomachean Ethics*, I, 7, 1098 a 1–3; *ibid*, X, 7, 1177 b 27–38.

12. Cf. M. Rhonheimer, *The Perspective of Morality* (Washington, D.C.: The Catholic University of America Press, 2011), 91–92. Sciacca explains: "Man's humanity is greater than, but not without, his rationality" (M.F. Sciacca, *L'uomo questo "squilibrato"* [Palermo: L'Epos, 2000], 24).

13. Cf. R. Yepes, *La persona come fuente de autenticidad*, cit., 89, 93. For this reason, St. Thomas Aquinas observes that truly human actions are those for which the individual is freely and consciously responsible: cf. *Summa Theologiæ*, I-II, q. 1, a. 1. An important theoretical contribution to the subject of authenticity has been made by A. Rigobello, *L'estraneità interiore* (Rome: Studium, 2001).

which they are more evident because they are without indifference and emotivism.

3. COHERENCE AND FAITHFULNESS

The danger of conformism, to which we have referred, reminds us that man's growth, his accomplishment of the task of self-fulfillment as a person, automatically takes place in truth and toward truth, toward the good as wished and chosen in the light of truth. Hence, truth must be known profoundly.[14] A form of behavior cannot be authentic if it runs counter to the good of man or it could be so only subjectively, which would, however, highlight the incoherence among what man is, what he holds himself to be, and what he expresses of himself.

The authentic self-fulfillment we are talking about here is not the same thing as the mere accomplishment of a free act; rather, it depends upon the moral value of that act. Man authentically fulfills himself not by the simple fact of carrying out a free action or choice but because he makes himself good (or, put another way, truly and authentically man) when the action is morally good. Here, self-transcendence comes into play, i.e., the growth or surmounting of the self toward truth and goodness.[15] If I did not orient myself toward goodness and truth — which do not depend upon me but are located at a higher level — I would not achieve transcendence. In surmounting the self, an increase in freedom also takes place because there is a greater capacity for self-determination.

Alongside this need for intimate coherence, we must remember that the exercise of freedom, which lies at the foundation of the authentic behavior we have been talking about, must always come about dialogically (that is, in dealings with others); otherwise, it is easy to slip from the idea of authenticity into subjectivism and individualism.[16] It is precisely in opening up to others and in recognizing our fellow man that we are able to comprehend and affirm our own selves more fully. Authenticity is strengthened and guaranteed by

---

14. Cf. K. Wojtyła, *Perché l'uomo: Scritti inediti di antropologia e filosofia* (Milan: Mondadori, 1995), 80.

15. Cf. K. Wojtyła, *The Acting Person* (Dordrecht: D. Reidel Publishing Company, 1979), 155–156, 179–180. We will speak more fully about self-transcendence in section 8 of this chapter.

16. Cf. C. Taylor, *The Ethics of Authenticity*, cit., 55–69. We will consider this aspect in greater depth in Chapter 15.

the development of the interpersonal dimension, of relationality, which, as we saw in the last chapter, is an essential characteristic of man.

Harmony among a person's interior world, his conduct, and the truth (or goodness) of man makes it possible to persevere in the commitment to completing a freely assumed task, one that involves the entire individual. Behavior is, then, authentic when it reflects this coherence and gives proof of faithfulness. A person behaves faithfully when, in the light of truth, he remains oriented toward the future realization of his own life project, freely enacted in the present in continuity (which may be continuance or rectification) with what has been done in the past.[17]

4. PERSONS AND INDIVIDUALS

Precisely in order to underline man's duty to fulfill himself in a manner that accords with his dignity, many philosophers, especially of the existential school, make a distinction between the concept of person and that of individual. We mention this because it is a widespread approach not ineffective in underlining our responsibility of authentic self-fulfillment, though it does, as we will see, have certain potential limits[18] if its context is not made amply clear. We will refer to just two authors, but it may be observed that, in a trait shared by the various definitions, the term person is used above all as an ethical category, indicating the adequate degree of human fulfillment man must reach if he does not wish to remain at the level of mere individuality, which is an ethically insufficient or not ethically definable condition.

For N. Berdyaev (1874–1948), "Personality is not a biological or a psychological category but an ethical and spiritual."[19]

> The individual is a category of naturalism, biology, and sociology.... Man certainly is an individual, but he is not only an indi-

---

17. With much greater incisiveness, St. Josemaría Escrivá writes: "A husband, a soldier, an administrator who faithfully fulfils at each moment, in each new circumstance of his life, the duties of love and justice which he once took on will always be just that much better a husband, soldier, or administrator. It is difficult to keep this keen sense of loyalty constantly active... but it is the best defence against ageing of the spirit, hardening of the heart, and stiffening of the mind" (J. Escrivá, *Conversations with Monsignor Escrivá de Balaguer* [Sydney: Little Hills & Scepter, 1993], 1).

18. Cf. S. Cotta, *"Persona (filosofia del diritto)"* in *Enciclopedia del diritto,* Vol. XXXIII, 162–167 (Milan: Giuffrè, 1983).

19. N. Berdyaev, *Slavery and Freedom* (London: G. Bles, 1943), 25.

vidual.... There are not two separate men, but one and the same man is both an individual and a personality. That is not two different beings but two kinds of qualitativeness, two different forces in man.... Man, as an individual, endures the experience of isolation, egocentrically engulfed in himself.... Man as a person, the same man, gains the mastery of the egocentric self-confinement [and] discloses a universe in himself.[20]

"Personality is not in any case a ready made datum, it is the posing of a question, it is the ideal of a man";[21] it is "my whole thinking, my whole willing, my whole feeling, my whole creative activity."[22]

E. Mounier also uses this distinction. Although he maintains that the two concepts cannot be clearly contrasted or separated, he observes that the individual is dominated by dispersion and by covetousness; the individual is the person reduced to his purely material aspects, a subject without interior life, a being without generosity who seeks only to seize everything for himself. He lives a life of superficiality and selfishness. The person, on the other hand, incarnates generosity and interior life; he gives and gives of himself, his prospects are open.[23]

More or less similar arguments are to be found in L. Lavelle, G. Marcel, M. Blondel, M. F. Sciacca,[24] as well as in J. Maritain. It is an approach, which, if seen in the context of the aforementioned remarks on the task of self-fulfillment in accordance with an authentically human existence, has a certain validity. But it is evident that man cannot be neatly divided into levels by making observations, which, when all is said and done, remain external and arbitrary. Are there, then, individuals who will never become persons? Does the dignity of the person depend only upon his actions? Are there fields in which it is enough to behave as mere individuals? Precisely in order to avoid these uncertainties, it is important not to lose sight of the metaphysical perspective we mentioned earlier.

---

20. *Ibid*, 35–36.

21. *Ibid*, 23.

22. *Ibid*, 25.

23. Cf. E. Mounier, *Personalism*, cit., 46–53, 64.

24. For the latter, see particularly M.F. Sciacca, *L'uomo questo "squilibrato,"* cit., 42–45, 52–72.

5. The Experience of Freedom

What we have said about the self-realization of the person implies that everyone experiences himself as being free, responsible for the choices he makes. This responsibility, especially at certain moments of life, makes its weight felt. As Lévinas writes:

> To be Me / Ego thenceforth signifies being unable to escape from responsibility as if the whole edifice of creation stood on my shoulders. But the responsibility that empties the Ego of its imperialism and egoism — be it ego of salvation — does not transform it into a moment of the universal order; rather, it confirms the uniqueness of the Self. The uniqueness of the Ego is the fact that no one can answer in my stead.[25]

Responsibility is always an appeal to freedom, and it is to this fundamental dimension of the human person that we must now turn our attention. Freedom can be given a philosophical foundation on the basis of the dynamism inherent to human nature, but it is also possible to reach the same conclusion, in keeping with what we have said up to now, by what may be defined as the experiential way to freedom.

This approach is to be found in various authors, including, to mention two examples chronologically distant from one another, R. Descartes and H. Bergson. For Descartes we know nothing with more certainty than we know freedom,[26] and, according to Bergson, freedom is among the things we know most clearly.[27] Although the underlying argument he uses is completely different, Kant also reaches a similar conclusion: The autonomy of the will is clearly evident in the face of moral law. Man intuits his moral duty and the possibility of transgressing it, and thus he gains awareness of being free.[28]

It can, then, be asserted that the interior experience we have of our free will in our free acts is directly apparent and represents the *fondamentum inconcussum* (the solid foundation) for the affirmation

25. E. Lévinas, *Humanism of the Other* (Chicago: University of Illinois Press, 2003), 33.
26. Cf. R. Descartes, *I principi della filosofía*, Pars Prima, XLI (Torino: Bollati Boringhieri, 1992), 92.
27. "Freedom is, then, a fact and, among the facts we are able to observe, none is clearer": H. Bergson, *Essai sur les données immediates de la conscience* (Paris: PUF, 1970), 145.
28. Cf. I. Kant, *Critique of Practical Reason* (Mineola, NY: Dover Publications, 2004), 2.

that freedom is effectively present in those acts.[29] Indeed, each of us is individually aware of the lability of the will when we experience the condition commonly described as "being spoiled for choice," when we are faced with alternatives that do not offer decisive motivations. In order to overcome the indecision, self-determination of the will is necessary, which may be considered as the "motor" of the self-fulfillment we are discussing.

Many existentialist authors tackle this subject with great energy, including Guardini, whose views on the matter are very significant. He, too, holds that awareness of being free is a direct result of experience: In freedom, we experience that which is invariable, irrevocable. Being free presents itself to me as a fact, and I have interior experience of this not if I consider the question abstractly but if I reflect in concrete terms on my own actions, in which case I recognize they belong to me (this is the essence of freedom) in the sense that action arises in me and from me.[30] I experience myself as the living starting point of actions, the source of causal links, in keeping with two modalities that find expression in the phrases, "I am my own master," and, "I am myself." The freedom-affirming value contained in these two affirmations (or in others like them) remains evident even if they are expressed in the negative ("In those circumstances I wasn't my own master," "I'm not myself any more").[31]

---

29. Cf. A. Millán-Puelles, *La libre afirmación de nuestro ser: Una fundamentación de la ética realista* (Madrid: Rialp, 1994), 207. Explaining that, precisely because of its obviousness, freedom is not susceptible of proof and requires none, the author explains how a similar conclusion is to be found not only in Descartes and Kant (though with certain caveats) but also in Aristotle, St. Thomas, and Jaspers (cf. *ibid*, 208–217).

30. Cf. R. Guardini, *Persona e libertà: Saggi di fondazione della teoría pedagogica* (Brescia: La Scuola, 1990), 58–99. "Freedom is self-belonging. I know I am free when I realize that I belong to myself; when I realize that in acting I depend upon myself, that the action does not transit through me and therefore belongs to another entity but arises in me, and therefore it is mine in that specific sense; and in it I am my own" (*ibid*, 101).

31. Cf. *ibid*, 99–102. St. Thomas also mentions the self-belonging conferred by freedom: "*Homo liber dicitur esse sui ipsius. Et hoc est quod Augustinus dicit,*" *Super Ioan.* (Tract. XXIX, super VII 16 [PL 35, 1629]): "*Quid tam tuum est quam tu?*" ("A free man belongs to himself. And as Augustine says, 'What is more yours than yourself?'"), *Summa Theologiæ,* I, q. 38, a. 1, ad 1; St. Thomas makes these remarks in the interesting context of his explanation as to why the Holy Spirit can be called "Gift."

6. The Experience of Evil

Reflections upon our experience of freedom, on the way in which each man perceives himself as being free, cannot be separated from reflections on the experience of evil. Evil cannot be set aside by devising a falsely optimistic anthropology and giving the impression that personal self-fulfillment follows a path of continuous ascent without setbacks or failures.

The tragedy of the Holocaust, Bosnia, and Rwanda (to mention just some dramas of the twentieth century) must stand as warnings, fomenting a culture of memory that encourages man to transcend himself toward what is good. In the society of databases and information storage, there is a risk, as J. B. Metz and H. M. Enzensberger note, of falling into a culture of amnesia because to store really means nothing other than to forget.[32] To remember, however, does not mean to nourish a culture of resentment; rather, it means acquiring an awareness capable of opening itself to forgiveness and change.

The catastrophic consequences of evil in history must lead the individual to ask himself about the evil he faces in the context of his own life. The arguments used to support the idea of the experience of freedom can also be adopted to recall the tenacious presence of negativity, transgression, and the voluntary abandonment of goodness as it is known and presented. Perhaps it is literary figures who most effectively call our attention to this aspect of human existence. Think, for example, of the hero of Camus's novel *The Fall*, who discovers evil not only in his surroundings but also within himself, or of the psychological insight of Dostoevsky, who "places man's life in the context of the struggle between good and evil."[33]

> Against the facile, idealistic, and positivist optimism of the nineteenth century, according to which evil is nothing more than a dialectic element destined to be overcome or a transitory episode in the triumphal march of humankind, he recalls that the reality of evil and pain, of sin and suffering, of guilt and retribution, of crime and punishment is, unfortunately, a real and inescapable fact.[34]

---

32. Cf. J. B. Metz, "*Tra la memoria e l'oblio: La Shoah nell'epoca dell'amnesia culturale*," in E. Baccarini and L. Thorson (eds.), *Il bene e il male dopo Auschwitz: Implicazioni etico-teologiche per l'oggi* (Milan: Paoline, 1998), 53–55.

33. L. Pareyson, *Dostoevskij: Filosofia, romanzo ed esperienza religiosa* (Torino: Einaudi, 1993), 60.

34. *Ibid*, 27.

In the history of philosophy, there has been no lack of attempts to project man's interior conflict onto the external world. The clearest example of this is the Manichæan theory; St. Augustine, in his combat against it, maintained that the conflict between good and evil is not due to the existence of two impersonal opposing principles but is interior to the will like a radical sickness of the spirit that is marked by Original Sin and in need of an extraordinary intervention of grace. His writings reveal a kind of duality of the will: "Whence is this monstrous thing? And why is it? The mind commands the body, and it obeys immediately; the mind commands itself, and is resisted."[35] And a little later, he adds: "I, when I was deliberating upon serving the Lord my God now, as I had long purposed, I it was who willed, I who was unwilling. It was I, even I myself."[36] Elsewhere he makes it clear that evil is not something into which one falls but the very act of falling itself.[37] There is, in short, no created reality that is evil in itself.

In the passages we have quoted, the Bishop of Hippo is describing what, with great anthropological acumen, St. Paul had already written:

> For I know that nothing good dwells within me, that is, in my flesh. I can will what is right, but I cannot do it. For I do not do the good I want but the evil I do not want is what I do.... So I find it to be a law that, when I want to do what is good, evil lies close at hand.[38]

To recognize the experience of evil in these terms helps us to understand that there is no validity in the intellectualist viewpoint (only partly of Socratic-Platonic origin) that holds that perfect knowledge necessarily generates a perfect action. If this were true, it would follow that ignorance is the only cause of evil (which would thus be reduced to the status of mere error) and that all evils may be resolved through progress and science. This is falsely optimistic and takes no account of the truth about man. Hence, Karol Wojtyła,

---

35. Augustine, *Confessions*, 8, 9, 21; cf: *ibid*, 8, 5, 10. On this subject see also L. Alici, R. Piccolomini, and A. Pieretti, *Il mistero del male e la libertà possibile*, vol II: *Linee di antropologia agostiniana* (Rome: Institutum Patristicum Augustinianum, 1995); L. Alici, *L'altro nell'io: In dialogo con Agostino* (Rome: Città Nuova, 1999), 177–182.

36. Augustine, *Confessions*, 8, 10, 22. This, moreover, is also a recurrent observation in non-Christian literature; suffice it to recall Ovid's famous verses: *"Aliudque cupido, mens aliud suadet: video meliora proboque, deteriora sequor"* ("Reason pulls one way, burning lust another; she sees and knows what's good, but she does neither"), Ovid, *Metamorphoses*, lib. VII, 19–21.

37. Cf. Augustine, *De Civitate Dei*, 12, 8.

38. Rom 7:18–19, 21.

drawing on Scheler but partly criticizing his conclusions, also highlights the presence of a "drama of the will," an interior struggle in
the concrete experience of good and evil and in the experience of
moral obligation.[39]

7. THE "CHECKMATE" OF PAIN

In following the path of self-fulfillment, we inevitably have to come
face to face with pain (physical or moral, our own or that of others).
This often presents itself as an obstacle as our projects and aspirations are "checkmated" and we are obliged to reorder our lives. It
could be said that the person who suffers undergoes a change of
perspective that brings him to question his own identity, his relationship with the world, and his relations with others. These three
fundamental elements of self-fulfillment are put to the test and, in
some cases, thrown into turmoil. The image we have of ourselves
and our capacities may change; the way we look at the world and
what it offers us (and, apparently, denies us) may alter. Our relations
with others can collapse, consolidate, or grow.

Suffering can provoke a self-interrogation of such depth as to com-
pel us to call into question the very foundations of our existence.[40]
In this context, "to put to the test" also acquires the meaning of
corroborating the authenticity and genuineness of our relations and,
as a consequence, revealing, on the one hand, false securities and
inauthentic attitudes and, on the other, deep bonds and true personal qualities.

It is precisely for this reason that the ineluctable encounter with pain
also involves the nontransferable responsibility of the individual in
the face of the situations and events of his life. Seen in this light,
suffering becomes a call to surpass oneself and to maturation and
can, in unimagined ways, accelerate the complete fulfillment of self.[41]

---

39. Cf. K. Wojtyła, *Perché l'uomo: Scritti inediti di antropologia e filosofia*, cit., 161–162.
    The expression "drama of the will" here refers to the dynamism of that faculty.

40. What we have called self-interrogation is more effectively described, in
    autobiographical terms, by St. Augustine, who, sorely tried by the death of a dear
    friend, tormented himself continually in his pain: "I became a great puzzle to
    myself and asked my soul why she was so sad" ("*factus eram ipse mihi magna
    quæstio et interrogabam animam meam*" [Augustine, *Confessions*, 4, 4, 9]).

41. This does not alter the fact that pain bursts into life as a "scandal" and that,
    considered at a personal level, it always conserves a background of "mystery."
    See the essays contained in the volume R. Esclanda and F. Russo, *Homo patiens:
    prospettive sulla sofferenza umana* (Rome: Armando, 2003).

8. SELF-FULFILLMENT AND SELF-TRANSCENDENCE

The responsibility with which each person assumes his task of "becoming man" and the commitment with which he truly fulfills himself as a person are signs of his constant self-transcendence, that is, of his projection beyond the particular situation and beyond himself. This is a fundamental characteristic of the human person, one that can be expressed using Pascal's famous phrase: "Man infinitely transcends man,"[42] meaning that we discover in ourselves an "instinct" toward happiness, toward goodness, and toward truth. All of these are beyond us, though; we do not possess them absolutely, and we cannot dispose of them at our pleasure. Even having an awareness of one's own misery is a sign of greatness because it presupposes the idea of what one aspires to be; i.e., it presupposes the idea of and the desire for truth and goodness.[43]

Another author who placed self-transcendence at the center of his reflections was the psychiatrist and philosopher Viktor E. Frankl, who wrote:

> The essence of human existence lies in "self-transcendence."... And by self-transcendence I mean the fact that being man fundamentally means being oriented toward something that transcends us, toward something that is beyond and above us, something or someone, a meaning to fulfill or another human being to meet and love. Consequently, man is himself in the degree to which he surpasses and forgets himself.[44]

Thus man's existence lies in a context of self-transcendence.[45] This is observable in various fields, where we find what we might call the "symptoms" of the freedom and spirituality of the human person. Let us consider a number of examples.

---

42. B. Pascal, *Pensées* (Paris: Cerf, 1982), 371; cf. *ibid*, 369.

43. Cf. L. Pareyson, *Kierkegaard e Pascal* (Milan: Mursia, 1998), 242.

44. V. E. Frankl, *Alla ricerca di un significato nella vita* (Milan: Mursia, 1990), 72.

45. Palumbieri makes an apt distinction between "self-transcendence," which is the basic dynamic structure of human beings, and "self-transcending," which is the process that derives from that structure (cf. S. Palumbieri, *L'uomo, questo paradosso: Antropologia filosofica II: Trattato sulla con-centrazione e condizione antropologica* [Rome: Urbaniana University Press, 2000], 40. The mainstay of our entire analysis in this essay is "self-transcending").

8.1. Dynamism and Tension

By virtue of his capacity for self-transcendence, the human person is characterized by dynamism. As we have seen from the beginning of this chapter, his existential personality is an ongoing conquest that is never fully completed; it is a result achieved as he goes along but never definitive. Luigi Pareyson, in analyzing the constituent traits of the person in existentialist terms, writes that the person can be described using the conceptual binomial of totality and insufficiency, indicating the two poles of a living dialectic.[46]

This means that, at any given moment of his life, man appears as a finished whole with a well-defined validity while remaining, nonetheless, insufficient, i.e., susceptible to amendment, rectification, or enrichment. Like an artistic creation, the individual may be considered as a work (in a certain sense, a self-made work), which, however perfectible it may be, is of itself worthy of recognition.[47]

This dynamism is also evident in the fact that in man there is a constant tension to surpass himself, to go beyond and outside his own self. Sometimes this is experienced as an imbalance between what one is and what one would like to be, between the effective result of an action and its original objective. Maurice Blondel analyzes the conflict the will has to face when it feels itself to be contradicted and defeated: The person aspires fully to be what he wants but is unable to be so absolutely; he would like to be sufficient unto himself but cannot. We have to make allowance for this apparent failure of our desired action.

There is a perennial dissymmetry between the action we undertake and our will. The conceived ideal is surpassed by the real operation, but, in its turn, the reality thus obtained is surpassed by an ideal that is being recreated constantly. All this, according to Blondel, is proof of our own poverty, of the fact that the perfection and intelligence we see in ourselves are not our own: "We discover, as in an imper-

---

46. Cf. L. Pareyson, *Esistenza e persona* (Genoa: Il Melangolo, 1985), 200.

47. Cf. *ibid*, 200–201. "The person, captured in one of his instants, frozen in his incessant process of development, identified in one of his acts that capture and condense him, is the finished result of an entire process of operations: he is a finished and defined work with his individual and unmistakable character. He is not one of many (i.e., individual) but unique, nor is he part of a whole (i.e., particular) but entire" (*Id, Estetica: Teoria della formatività* [Florence: Sansoni, 1974], 184). This appears even more clearly if we reconsider what was said in Chapter 13 about the metaphysical "completeness" of the person.

fect mirror, this inaccessible perfection."[48] This conflict in activity can, then, open man to God, to transcendence. Such openness, though we may be unaware of it, distinguishes our every action and shows itself in our natural aspiration toward the best, in our perception of having a role to fulfill, in our search for the meaning of life.[49]

The individual's incessant efforts at perfection, though fundamentally interior and nonquantifiable, appear in all dimensions of the person and become evident to others in ways that are sometimes surprising, arousing admiration. Romano Guardini, an attentive observer of the dynamics of education, gives an acute description of this phenomenon:

> Here is a man with a defined and clearly penetrable disposition. The calculation of his energies seems clear and apparent. Whoever knows him knows his character and his possibilities and knows more or less what course his development will follow. This man does his job; he toils for what is right and good; he lives his human life. In his intimate self, however, lies the secret of his willingness and, through everything he consciously does and wants, a metamorphosis comes about from his inner self. There is something there that makes him increasingly open to things which before were closed to him. Beyond all calculable psychological capacities, he becomes broader, richer, more transparent and benevolent. A slow metamorphosis takes place, so silent that he himself is not aware of it and perhaps only his friend, at times almost frightened by the comparison, sees what has happened. Everything achieves a profundity, a translucency, a luminous energy. The metamorphosis even reaches the face, even the tone of voice. This is the spirit.[50]

8.2. Interiority and Exteriority

The dynamic tension of the person, an expression of his self-transcendence, is evident in the relationship between interiority and exteriority. We experience this when we are unable to give adequate expression to our feelings or when harsh words and gestures make it impossible for us to scrutinize the hearts of others. St. Augustine examines this relationship and shows how interiority exceeds and

---

48. M. Blondel, *Action (1893)* (Notre Dame, IN: University of Notre Dame Press, 2007), 320.

49. Cf. *ibid*, 326.

50. R. Guardini, *Persona e libertà: Saggi di fondazione della teoria pedagogica*, cit., 157.

surpasses exteriority.[51] The concept of interiority is not the same as that of soul; rather, it refers back to the Pauline image of the interior man who renews himself day after day, also in contrast with the decline of the exterior man.[52]

Interiority is not a static quality. It is not a state in which we come to find ourselves but a dynamic projection toward a goal. This means that the person transcends his own acts, that his interior universe cannot be completely expressed because what is spiritual cannot fully be fixed and inserted into a material sign. This is why "we can become privy to the secrets of conscience only in so far as these are disclosed to us, and so far only do we judge."[53]

Returning to the theme of the imbalance of exteriority and interiority in man, St. Augustine observes that, while God is absolute simplicity because by virtue of the fullness of his being he is what he has, in the human person's existential vicissitudes what prevails is the dimension of having, which implies changeableness and contingency.[54] Thus, he exhorts people: "Do not look for what you have but for what you are,"[55] wishing to recall that the dimension of possession belongs, of itself, to exteriority, while what counts is fulfilling that which we are called to be.

Therefore, the unifying center of human existence in the process of self-fulfillment is interiority, and to that we must turn in order to avoid dispersion, for material possession and exterior activism can lead to alienation and nourish a sense of frustration:

> The images that stem from exaltation and volubility do not allow us to see the immutable unity. Space offers us something to love; time removes that which we love, leaving in the soul a vortex of images that foment the passions toward ever new objects. Thus does the soul become unquiet and tormented because it is frustrated in its desire to possess that by which, in fact, it is possessed. Therefore is it called to tranquility, that is, not to love those things

---

51. The Bishop of Hippo analyzes this subject in a truly masterly way. On this topic see, among others, A. Pieretti, *Interiorità e intenzionalità: La dignità del finito*, in L. Alici, R. Piccolomini, and A. Pieretti (eds.), *Ripensare Agostino: Interiorità e intenzionalità* (Rome: Institutum Patristicum Augustinianum, 1993), 99–120; L. Alici, *L'altro nell'io: In dialogo con Agostino*, cit., 73–81, 105–107, 263–289.

52. "So we do not lose heart. Even though our outer nature is wasting away, our inner nature is being renewed day by day" (2 Cor 4:16).

53. Augustine, *De Civitate Dei*, I, 26. On the noncomplete exteriorization of the interior man, see also K. Wojtyła, *The Acting Person*, cit., 7–13.

54. Cf. Augustine, *De Civitate Dei*, XI, 10, 2.

55. *Id, Sermo* 127, 3, 3.

which cannot be loved without torment. And thus, in fact, it will dominate them; it will not be possessed by them but will possess them.[56]

8.3. Self-distancing, Love, and the Giving of Self

The self-transcendence of the person is also expressed in what is known as the capacity for self-distancing, which lies at the basis of the sense of humor and is one of the resources man has in the face of mental and social factors. The psychiatrist Viktor Frankl speaks of "the human capacity for 'self-transcendence' as a condition that makes dereflection possible";[57] dereflection being to cease to concentrate obsessive attention on one's own symptoms, one's own defects, and thinking of others or of the other. The best existential attitude to overcome many forms of neurosis, which Frankl called "noogenic" (i.e., deriving from a problem of meaning or sense), is precisely that of laughing at oneself, distancing oneself from whatever it is that produces fear or anguish and transcending it.[58]

Self-possession and self-control, which characterize the exercise of human freedom, make it possible to give freely of the self, an act of generous self-distancing with which man places himself before and above his own self in order to decide about himself to open himself totally to the other.[59] In Guardini's view, this experience is a guarantee of authenticity:

> Man does not consist of himself but is "open and outstretched," bordering on risk, toward that which is other than him and especially toward another human being. In this he is truly and authentically himself, and he becomes so to an ever greater degree the more he dares to affirm himself not as a closed individuality but open and outstretched toward something that justifies that risk. To express ourselves in everyday language, man becomes himself by "becoming detached" from himself.[60]

---

56. Id, De Vera Religione, XXXV, 65.

57. V.E. Frankl, Alla ricerca di un significato della vita, cit., 34.

58. In logotherapy this clinical approach is called the "therapeutic technique of paradoxical intention": cf. ibid, 57–59; id., Teoria e terapia delle nevrosi (Brescia: Morcelliana, 2001), 69–70, 166. There are, however, certain mental pathologies in which such a method is not applicable. As we said earlier, when pain and suffering afflict an individual, he is called to direct the circumstances in which he finds himself toward a value (that is, to transcend them) and not to close himself within them.

59. Remember what was said on this subject in Chapter 11.

60. R. Guardini, Persona e libertà, cit., 42.

This passage from Guardini, which recalls that of Frankl quoted at the beginning of section 8 in this chapter, is important for an adequate understanding of what we have been trying to explain about self-fulfillment. This cannot be understood as a selfish concern to fulfill ourselves at any cost; if we did we would fail miserably in our attempts because the individual, rather than transcending himself, would close in on himself in an ever narrower horizon and through his actions seek only subjective gratification. Self-fulfillment is, in fact, the consequence of openness to values and of giving to others.[61]

As regards the structure and phenomenology of giving, we will limit ourselves to observing that both love and the donation of self require a perspective that goes beyond time. For, indeed, in the giving of self, we aspire to the possession (never complete) of what we have been, what we are, and what we will be, and, in love, we tend toward a perennial union, which must be reconquered ever and anew with the person we love. In giving and in love, man surpasses himself in a kind of bipolarity that has emerged more than once in these comments on self-transcendence. Self-determination presupposes a particular kind of complexity in the person. Thus, a person is he who possesses himself and, at the same time, he who is possessed solely and exclusively by himself.[62]

If we now recall what we said in Chapter 11 about sexuality, it may be understood why the most profound dynamic of the person is that of love. It is the need to love and to be loved that impregnates our actions. We have continual experience of this and, for this reason, associate happiness and love so closely. To feel oneself to be truly loved means to be happy; to love with all our hearts fills us with happiness. This is why it is important to direct our love correctly, "for a person lives in those things that he loves, which he greatly desires, and in which he believes himself to be blessed."[63]

---

61. Frankl warns that self-fulfillment is, and must remain, the unintentional effect of self-transcendence; it would be harmful and frustrating to make it the object of a precise intention. What holds true for self-fulfillment also holds true for happiness and pleasure. It is precisely the strenuous search for happiness that prevents it from being achieved. The more we make it the direct object of our efforts, the more surely will we miss the target (cf. V. E. Frankl, *Teoria e terapia delle nevrosi*, cit., 42, 201).

62. Cf. K. Wojtyła, *The Acting Person*, cit., 106–107.

63. Augustine, *Letter to Proba*, 130, 3, 7 ("*Agit enim homo in iis quæ diligit, quæ pro magno appetit, quibus beatum se esse credit*").

8.4. Self-transcendence of the Person and Transcendence

We have seen how Blondel considers a person's dissatisfaction with the results of his own actions to be a clear sign of human poverty, of that striving toward the Absolute which underlies every instant of human existence.

The self-transcendent impulse inherent to man requires and denotes an origin and an end that are outside and above him. Only the Absolute, or divine Transcendence, can create such a tension and give it complete fulfillment. Only by bearing in mind the relationship between finiteness and infinity, between temporality and eternity in human life and history, can we radically avoid that reductive conception of man that restricts him to a single dimension and considers him as an object to be programmed and manipulated. In the light of this relationship with the Absolute and our awareness of personal dignity founded upon it, the self-transcendence of the human person appears not only as a capacity we must use but above all as a duty to which we are called.

This idea is well summarized in the following passage from Heschel:

> Prayer is not a need but an *ontological necessity*, an act that constitutes the very essence of man.... The dignity of man consists not in his ability to make tools, machines, guns but primarily in his being endowed with the gift of addressing God. It is this gift that should be a part of the definition of man.[64]

SUMMARY OF CHAPTER 14

The human person is *causa sui*, cause of himself, not in an ontological sense but in a dynamic-existential sense. Each individual has the task of self-fulfillment, i.e., of living an authentically human existence. Conformism, indifference, and emotivity all run counter to living an authentic existence, while intimate coherence and faithfulness are characteristics of authenticity. In our striving after the free fulfillment of self, we come face to face with the possibility of experiencing evil and with the trial of pain. Self-realization means above all self-transcendence; in other words, dynamically forging one's own life, tending toward ever more exalted goals, drawing from one's own inner depths so as not to remain enslaved to the exterior world. The fullest expression of self-transcendence consists

---

64. A.J. Heschel, *Man's Search for God* (New York: Scribner, 1954), 78; emphasis in original.

in love and in giving of self. Only in God, who is Absolute and Transcendent, can the human person's drive to self-transcendence find its ultimate goal.

CHAPTER 15

THE RELATIONALITY
OF THE PERSON

1. ORIGINARINESS OF RELATIONALITY

The human person is a relational being and cannot be understood if this factor is neglected because it is one of his fundamental characteristics. Relationality is an originary quality in the sense that it lies at the origin of the individual, who does not create himself. As we said in Chapter 13, each person is instituted as a novelty in being: The human creature is born in a relation with divine love and with human love and is characterized by the foundational relationship of filiation-paternity-maternity.[1] However, just as personal existence is an ontological reality that involves an existential duty (in the last chapter, we saw how we must fulfill ourselves authentically as persons), so also filiation, paternity, and maternity are basic relationships that contain an ethical responsibility; in other words, they cannot be reduced to a birth certificate or a biological datum but must be lived in an authentically human way.

Therefore, the person is ontologically and physiologically characterized by his openness to relationships to such an extent that no human dynamic, faculty, or inclination escapes this basic tendency.[2] The way in which we live and exist is relational, open to others.[3] Corporeity, and especially the sexuality that characterizes it (in both men and women); the will as capacity to love; and the faculties of knowledge and language are all essentially communicative. Of

---

1. Cf. M. Serretti, *Natura della comunione: Saggio sulla relazione* (Soveria Mannelli: Rubbettino, 1999), 136 ff.

2. Cf. *ibid*, 14, 140. The author of this book rightly believes that the word "communion" better indicates the tripartite relationship that lies at the origin of the human person. However, we feel that the concept of "communion" can be adequately understood only in the light of Christian Revelation, and, since we cannot explain its theological foundations here, we will not use it.

3. Cf. P. Donati, *Pensiero sociale cristiano e società post-moderna* (Rome: A.V.E., 1997), 20. Heidegger observes that in man's existence the presence of others is not merely accidental, something that can be omitted: Even being alone is a way (a defective way) of coexisting with others; indeed, solitude can only be understood on the basis of this inherent predisposition to coexistence: cf. M. Heidegger, *Being and Time* (New York and Evanston: Harper & Row, 1962), § 26, 153–163.

course, the ways in which relationality is put into effect depend
on the individual, but even voluntary isolation and the rejection of
social relationships represent a way, however negative, to translate
sociability into practice. By sociability, we mean the characteristic,
inherent to man, of intentional openness to others (mankind and
God). On the other hand, in speaking of "sociality," we are referring
to the effective realization of that capacity.

2. MAN IS SOCIAL BY NATURE

In the light of what we have just said, the axiom of classical philosophy that holds that man is social by nature emerges in all its validity.
Already in his time Aristotle maintained that sociability is essential
to man. In his reflections on the specifically human characteristic of
living in society, he proceeds by degrees, moving from a historical-
existential type of observation to more metaphysical reasoning. First,
he speaks of living in community because of the necessities of life,
then affirms that the State exists to live well, i.e., in a way worthy
of man. Finally, after having affirmed that sociability is principally
expressed in language, he concludes that man is by nature "political"
(i.e., social). The passage in which this appears most clearly is this:

> When several villages are united in a single complete community
> large enough to be nearly or quite self-sufficing, the state comes
> into existence, originating in the bare needs of life and continuing
> in existence for the sake of a good life. And, therefore, if the earlier
> forms of society are natural, so is the state, for it is the end of them,
> and the nature of a thing is its end. For what each thing is when
> fully developed, we call its nature, whether we are speaking of a
> man, a horse, or a family.... Hence, it is evident that the state is
> a creation of nature and that man is by nature a political animal.
> And he who by nature and not by mere accident is without a
> state is either a bad man or above humanity.... The proof that the
> state is a creation of nature and prior to the individual [4] is that the
> individual, when isolated, is not self-sufficing, and, therefore, he
> is like a part in relation to the whole. But he who is unable to live

---

4. This is affirmed on the basis of the principle according to which the whole is
   prior to its parts. For this reason, Aristotle maintains that "the state is by nature
   clearly prior to the family and to the individual, since the whole is of necessity
   prior to the part" (*Politics*, I, 2, 1253a 18–19). This principle leads Aristotle to
   make ethics subordinate to politics, the good of the individual subordinate
   to that of society: cf. G. Reale, *Introduzione a Aristotele* (Rome and Bari:
   Laterza, 2002), 101–102, 119–120.

in society, or who has no need because he is sufficient for himself, must be either a beast or a god: he is no part of a state.[5]

The conclusion Aristotle reached is shared by many scholars, who see in human beings a specific way of establishing relations with others. The same thing also emerges from various studies in anthropology, paleontology, and neurology. For example, studying the behavior of the higher animals does not reveal any truly altruistic behavior, although the term "altruistic" does get used in animal ethology. According to Eccles,[6] in order to denote true altruism, an action has to be characterized by *intentionality* (i.e., not a form of conduct that is merely instinctive (however habitual it may be) because an animal may, by instinct, live in a group or alone) and by *relationality* (i.e., it must be consciously directed at another individual or individuals and undertaken in the interests of others). These two characteristics are not observable in animal behavior.

The first indications of social behavior, as verified by paleontology and characteristic of individuals of the human species, are the sharing of food, community life, funerary rites such as placing flowers and other objects by the tomb, and caring for others. In 1971 a study was published concerning the skeleton of a Neanderthal man (who lived some 45,000 years ago) who had not only been seriously disabled from birth but also showed signs of subsequent injuries. Nonetheless, this individual was kept alive for around forty years, and this can only have happened if other members of the tribe looked after him.[7]

However, scientific contributions are not of themselves enough to prove definitively and empirically that the way in which man establishes relations with others is specifically different from that which

---

5. *Politics*, I, 2, 1252b 28–1253a 29. Elsewhere, too, he says: "Man by nature is a being who lives in community" (*Nicomachean Ethics*, A, 7, 1097b 11: the Greek adjective used is *politikòn*. This work also contains, among other things, the affirmation that friendship is necessary for individual happiness). The extract quoted here highlights the passage from satisfying material needs, which is what lies at the origin of small human communities, to political life that lies beyond natural spontaneity: It requires the exercise of intelligence and will and a conscious orientation toward certain values. For an interpretation of the Aristotelian concept, see: S. Vergnières, *Éthique et politique chez Aristote: Physis, Éthos, Nomos* (Paris: PUF, 1995), 147–160, and, for useful terminological clarifications, E. Berti, *Profilo di Aristotele* (Rome: Studium, 1979), 281–318.

6. Cf. J. C. Eccles, *Evolution of the Brain: Creation of the Self* (London and New York: Routledge, 1989), 117–120.

7. Discussing these discoveries in the book mentioned in note 6, Eccles refers to studies by J. Goodall, J. Hawkes, and R. S. Solecki.

exists among animals. Such contributions are undoubtedly useful, but they must always be interpreted in the light of philosophical anthropology, which studies man in all his dimensions. The aim, in fact, is not to deny that other living beings have relationships with their surroundings and with their fellows but to show why such relations in man have an exclusive specificity. For example, to go back to what we said in the first paragraph of this chapter, animals also have relationships based upon procreation and birth, but they are experienced only as responses to biological and instinctive factors.

It is important, likewise, to bear in mind the metaphysical analysis of Chapter 13. On the basis of an adequate conception of the person, which is in turn the basis for the concept of freedom, it is possible to gain a better understanding of man's inherent sociability. The intrinsic difference between a herd of animals and human society consists precisely in the fact that, while the former is necessarily governed by instincts that depend on the species, the latter is guided by the freedom of its individuals (one proof of which, among many, is the diversity of institutions and forms of society). Nor should it be forgotten that, from our very beginnings, we are aware of the difference between man and animals and that our conception of the human person is not simply the sum of a series of experimental data. It follows that reflection on human beings and on other living creatures takes place on the basis of prior experience and knowledge.

3. SOCIALIZING TENDENCIES AND SOCIAL VIRTUES

In order to enrich our understanding of the relationality inherent to the human person, we may add that biological, anthropological, and sociological studies all lead us to recognize certain socializing tendencies in man that lie at the basis of his expressions of sociability.[8] These tendencies are also to be found in animals, but, in man, they have a specific orientation and development: They are the foundation for virtues because they are guided and perfected by reason and freedom, and, therefore, they also relate to culture. They are the factors that regulate social dynamics and the underlying rules that

---

8. We will mention nine of these inclinations, which seem to us to be the most important, although others could be added. We will bear in mind and seek to organize our ideas on the basis of the following books: J. Choza, *Manual de antropología filosófica* (Madrid: Rialp, 1988), 451–453; *id., La realización del hombre en la cultura* (Madrid: Rialp, 1990), 143–159; L. Polo, *Quién es el hombre: Un espíritu en el tiempo* (Madrid: Rialp, 1998), 76–77, 127–143.

structure the ordering of society. In other words, they lie at a level more fundamental than politics and even normative ethics, i.e., at an anthropological level.

Let us make it clear that we are saying this while avoiding biological determinism, that is, the theory that explains all human behavior, even ethics and religion, solely on the basis of biological data. It must, indeed, be borne in mind that the terms "inclination" and "virtue" are not synonymous, although we can say that classical thought saw the virtues as the development and enhancement of a natural tendency[9] on the grounds that there is no opposition between a moral life and human nature.

The virtues to which we will refer have been amply studied by classical philosophy.[10] They are called social virtues because they concern the way to live a better life; that is, a life more worthy of man from an individual and a social standpoint. The tendencies upon which these virtues are based can be freely oriented by the individual toward good or deviated toward evil. Thus, we find ourselves in the area of the relationship among freedom, morality, and human nature, which, however, we cannot go into more deeply here.[11]

3.1. Relations with the Origins, Tradition, and Authority

We will begin with *pietas*, i.e., with the virtue based on the inclination to recognize the foundation of one's own being, one's own life, and one's own knowledge, and thus to venerate God, one's parents, and one's homeland or native soil, to feel oneself bound to one's

9. With reference to Aristotle (cf. *Nicomachean Ethics*, II, 1103a 18–26), St. Thomas explains that "aptitude to virtue is in us by nature, but the complement of virtue is in us through habituation or some other cause. Hence, it is evident that virtues perfect us so that we follow in due manner our natural inclinations" ("*aptitudo ad virtutem inest nobis a natura, licet complementum virtutis sit per assuetudinem vel per aliquam causam. Unde patet quod virtutes perficiunt nos ad prosequendum debito modo inclinationes naturales*") *Summa Theologiæ*, II-II, q. 108, a. 2; see also *ibid*, I-II, q. 95, a. 1.

10. They appear, among others, in Aristotle in his *Nicomachean Ethics* (especially in books IV, VIII, and IX); Cicero in *De Officiis* (especially book III), who in turn makes reference to Panætius and Posidonius; and St. Thomas Aquinas in his *Summa Theologiæ* (in particular qq. 101–117 of part II-II).

11. For a study of the virtues with reference to morality and human nature, see the following works: R. García de Haro, *L'agire morale e le virtù* (Milan: Ares, 1988); A. Rodríguez Luño, *La scelta ética: Il rapporto fra libertà e virtù* (Milan: Ares, 1988); M. Rhonheimer, *The Perspective of Morality* (Washington, D.C.: The Catholic University of America Press, 2011), 188–214. The fact that these virtues are traditionally called "social virtues" must not lead us to think there are exclusively individual aspects to a person's existence, i.e., ones that have no influence on society: cf. J. Escrivá, "Human Virtues" in *Friends of God*, 76 (London: Scepter, 1981).

past and one's own history, in other words, to one's origins, to the "place" from which we come and in which we have "implanted" ourselves.[12] As we will see, this is the foundation that helps to give meaning to celebration, the anthropological value of which derives, among other things, from the fact that it highlights the links with one's own roots. This virtue can be called religiosity, filial love, or patriotism; the inclination that lies at its basis is often referred to with such expressions as the "call of the blood" or the "call of the land." Its symptoms are nostalgia and the joy of return.

The ties and dependency inherent to this virtue should not be seen in a negative sense as if they indicated only passivity and closure to the future. The capacity to take initiatives and make plans is always based on the past; for example, a tradition that is not renewed and given new life is destined to become extinct as is a family without children or a country without new citizens. Thus, growth and renewal require some kind of bond or faithfulness to one's own identity. Deviations of this inclination include racism and nationalism and, contrastingly, such risks as disorientation or the loss of one's own roots.

We will now move on to *observantia*, which is the virtue based on the inclination to respect legitimate authority, to submit oneself to a dominant individual who possesses greater dignity. When many individuals are all oriented to a single end, there is always one who leads and guides. This does not contrast with freedom; rather, it is specific to the social nature of man.[13] Indeed, as Plato observes, even "a band of robbers and thieves, or any other gang of evildoers" could not "achieve anything if among themselves they behaved without any principle of justice."[14] A daily proof of this is also to be seen in

---

12. Cf. P. Laín Entralgo, *Sobre la amistad* (Madrid: Espasa and Calpe, 1986), 203–204. On this subject, the author specifically refers to the ideas of X. Zubiri. Lewis describes the implications of love for homeland in the following terms: "First of all there is love of the house, or place, we grew up in or the places, perhaps many, which have been our homes, and of all places fairly near these or fairly like them, love of old acquaintances, of familiar sights, sounds and smells.... With this love for the place there goes a love for the way of life: for the beer and tea and open fires, trains with compartments in them and an unarmed police force, and all the rest of it, for the local dialect and (a shade less) for our native language" (C.S. Lewis, *The Four Loves* [London: G. Bles, 1960]).

13. Cf. St. Thomas Aquinas, *Summa Theologiæ*, I, q. 96, a. 4; Aristotle, *Politics*, I, 119 (1254a 28). The concept of authority from the point of view of analytical philosophy is examined by J.M. Bochenski, *Autorität, Freiheit, Glaube: Sozialphilosophische Studien* (Munich and Vienna: Philosophia, 1988).

14. Plato, *Republic*, I 351 d.

youth groups of various kinds (a school classroom, a sports team, and so on), in which one of the members takes on the function of "head."

Anarchism, which has its theoretical roots in such authors as M.A. Bakunin (1814–1876) and P.-J. Proudhon (1809–1865), on the one hand confirms and on the other denies this inclination: It does, in fact, recognize a natural inclination to social order but also proposes the abolition of all forms of imposed State authority.

Partly associated with this virtue is that of *dulia* (i.e., to honor, to pay due honor), the virtue based on the inclination to recognize the merit of the best, to respect the best, and to be respected, to seek to be the best, and to excel. It is closely connected to *pietas* and is one of the elements that coordinates the ordering of society, the so-called sociogram in which each individual plays a role or takes on a task in accordance with his own merits. One expression of this virtue is the emergence of leaders and heroes,[15] of sports and show business stars, and of saints; another is the election of representatives to institutional bodies. In this latter case, the electors choose (or should choose) people who stand out over other candidates for their possession of certain qualities. This virtue means that each man should enjoy his own degree of fame and has the right to see his reputation respected because it is right to recognize the honor of others. Deviations of this tendency are, on the one hand, vanity and ambition, which are rooted in the desire to deceive or overawe others, and, on the other, pusillanimity, which leads a person to undervalue his own talents and capacities and encourages inertia.

The recognition of the talents of others is not *per se* a sign of passivity or resignation because the capacity to emulate and to form oneself consciously on the model of another person is an important part of personal fulfillment, as we will see later. A morally valid decision to emulate another requires an energetic act of will as well as a certain amount of self-confidence because we look to the actions of our hero in the hope of being worthy to achieve them ourselves.

---

15. There are two important theories in this field. One is that of T. Carlyle (1795–1881) on the cult of heroes as the foundation of social order (especially in his 1841 work *On Heroes and Hero Worship and the Heroic in History*, which reveals an evident influence of Romanticism and of an aristocratic view of history); the other of F. E. Spranger (1882–1963) on the educational power of living models. However, considerable importance is also given to this subject by, among others, M. Scheler (especially in his *Vorbilder und Führer*, in which he develops his theory of "personal models"), and H. Bergson (in the essay *Les deux sources de la morale et de la religion*).

The reaction of a narcissistic or, more generally, individualistic personality is quite different. In this case, the individual is anguished and passive, lacking willpower; his unconscious emulation is not an expression of his search for a role model but of his lack of positive interior images, the fear of mediocrity or defeat.[16]

The last in this group is *obedientia*, which is the virtue based on the inclination to follow commands, to keep to norms. Man, in fact, has an inherent desire for security, a need for social order, and a wish to see his role in society accepted.[17] Moreover, for society to evolve and develop, it is necessary that there be a certain number, however minimal, of stabilizing rules (founded on elementary expressions of merit and demerit, the satisfaction of needs, and the distribution of wealth). One phenomenon that contrasts with this is that of terror, which arises from a complete absence of security and is, indeed, the aim pursued by terrorism, which seeks to overthrow society. Yet it is clear that terrorism is itself a confirmation of this inclination because it shows that, when the inclination is frustrated, a person is unable to order his existence in a worthwhile and harmonious way.

3.2. Relations of Reciprocity and Friendship

Gratitudo is the virtue that perfects the inclination to repay benefit received. It establishes among individuals a series of social relationships that are nonjuridical but nonetheless very important for society.

The opposite of the above is *vindicatio*, which is the virtue that perfects the natural inclination to repay harm received. It is a virtue when the inclination is oriented toward good, i.e., depending on the particular case, ensuring the penitence of one who has committed evil (or at least preventing him from committing any more evil, thus safeguarding the peace of others) or defending social justice and the honor of God. In contrast to these is the vice of cruelty or feroc-

---

16. Cf. C. Lasch, *The Culture of Narcissism: American Life in An Age of Diminishing Expectations* (New York and London: W.W. Norton & Co., 1991), 84–86. Reference is made, among others, to J. Henry, *Culture Against Man* (New York: Knopf, 1963), 223, 226, 228–229. In modern, media-driven society, the process of the psychological formation of the self is strongly influenced by various kinds of "nonreciprocal distance relationships," which give rise to such phenomena as the idea of proximity of a television personality and other forms of experience characteristic of fans: cf. J.B. Thompson, *The Media and Modernity: A Social Theory of the Media* (Stanford, CA: Stanford University Press, 1995), 207–234.

17. Though in different contexts and with different conclusions, this inclination is discussed by, among others, T. Hobbes and C. Lévi-Strauss.

ity and that of compliance or acquiescence.[18] The administration of justice in society represents the institutionalization of these virtues.

Next comes *veritas*, or *veracitas*, that is, the virtue based on the inclination to manifest oneself as one really is (expressing one's subjectivity) or to manifest things as they are (the recognition of reality). This is part of the need for authenticity, which is inherent in every man and is given particular emphasis by existentialist and personalist philosophers; we made partial reference to this in Chapter 14. Distortions of this inclination include falsity, hypocrisy, and arrogance.

A particularly important role is played by *amicitia* (also called *affabilitas*), being the virtue that gives a positive orientation to the inclination to establish and cultivate relations of affinity with others. It finds expression in forms of behavior often described with such words as cordiality, joviality, and affability. These, to be authentic, have to be directed toward the good of others; in other words, they must be born from a benevolent soul that does not exclusively pursue utility or individual pleasure. Among others, M. Scheler made important contributions to the subject in his 1923 book *The Nature of Sympathy*, although Aristotle's words in books 8–9 of his *Nicomachean Ethics* remain fundamental.

Finally, we must mention *liberalitas*, which perfects the inclination to give a part of what we possess. It finds expression in the various cultural traditions concerning the exchange of wealth and gifts [19] and in hospitality. Contrasting forms of behavior include avarice and prodigality.

3.3. The Roots of Society

This brief overview of social virtues and socializing tendencies shows the richness and complexity of sociability in the human person. Because sociability is a characteristic inherent to his nature, man can never eradicate or suppress it completely. For example, however widespread avarice may be, it is impossible for someone to give nothing of their own, even if it is just a piece of information. The same applies to the inclination to express something of oneself: It is

---

18. Cf. St. Thomas Aquinas, *Summa Theologiæ*, II-II, q. 108, aa. 1–2. See also *id.*, *De Malo*, q. 12, a. 1 c., which has a useful reference to the relationship between inclination and virtue.

19. Though from a sociological point of view, in 1924 M. Mauss (1872–1950) dedicated an important ethnological study to this question, entitled *Essai sur le don: Forme et raison de l'échange dans les sociétés archaiques*.

impossible to repress all spontaneous expressions of sympathy. Likewise, it is impossible to lie always and about everything; we can do so only in isolated acts because our natural inclination is to tell the truth,[20] and spontaneously, at the level of the preconscious, individuals tend to express their feelings with gestures, facial expressions, tone of voice, etc. Moreover, if they did not believe one another or tell one another the truth, mankind could not coexist and the fabric of society would decay.[21]

Thus, if the culture of a particular age and society or certain of its manifestations or structures were directed at repressing or corrupting some of these foundations of sociability, it would be acting against its own roots. The inclination to honor, for example, is central to the individual and to society (even though in man it finds complete and authentic fulfillment only in the glory received from God, who does not judge appearances but scrutinizes the heart), and if cynicism and degradation were to predominate, the social community would come apart. In any case, the complete repression of one or more of these inclinations — though it has been pursued by regimes through violence and propaganda — would be impossible because it would mean eradicating humanity from man.

These tendencies and the virtues based upon them are linked to one another in such a way that one cannot be rendered absolute at the expense of the others; if it were, it would no longer be a virtue. Indeed, virtues are *per se* well ordered or, we could say, correlative. Friendship, for example, increases with gratitude, but it cannot contrast with veracity or with respect for justice (*vindicatio*). Vice versa, the inclination to honor and respect cannot be separated from recognition of one's own origins (*pietas*) because we are indebted to others and have ties with them. Finally, it must be said that, as is the case for all the spiritual qualities of the person, the family plays a very important role in the development and consolidation of the social virtues. The relations between father and mother, between parents and children, and between siblings are a model and test bench for these virtues.

---

20. Cf. J. Choza, *La realización del hombre en la cultura*, op. cit., 154.
21. Cf. Thomas Aquinas, *Summa Theologiæ*, II-II, q. 109, a. 3, ad 1.

4. PERSONAL SELF-FULFILLMENT AND SOCIETY

The examination of socializing tendencies and social virtues con-firms the fact that human existence takes place within a network of relationships not only because I need others in order to achieve nearly all my objectives but also because other people are likewise indispensable if I am to achieve adequate self-fulfillment. Even the experience and knowledge I have of myself are strengthened by my relations with my fellows, for I affirm and gain awareness of myself in my dealings with others, who intervene directly or indi-rectly in the formation of my psychological identity. This is evident in the period of childhood as, for example, when children identify or contrast themselves with the father or mother figure or with their teacher, thereby developing a knowledge of themselves. But it is also to be seen in adults, who seek, knowingly or otherwise, the approval, respect, and support of others.

It follows that my possession of my self-fulfillment and my own identity always come about in a context of reciprocal recognition,[22] and thus living an authentic life is not the fruit of an arbitrary or exclusively subjective choice: Comparison with others is an indis-pensable prerequisite for authentically human behavior. If this were not the case, i.e., if my actions had validity only for me, everything would become irrelevant and insignificant. The choices I make are important for me and for others because they refer to an entire structure of values that are universally recognized or recognizable.

Precisely because of this inherent openness to others, the individual manifests spontaneous forms of behavior such as sharing feelings and convictions, dialogue, and even verbal conflicts with others. However, where communication and the adequate development of relations with others are lacking, not only does the human com-munity disintegrate (be it a family, a group of friends, an associa-tion, a firm, or an entire society) but also the individual himself is hindered in his self-fulfillment as a human being, in the formation of his personality.

The interpersonal dimension comes to light in the "me-you" rela-tionship, in which each man is considered in his irreducible onto-

---

22. Cf. R. Spaemann, *Basic Moral Concepts*, cit., 35–36, 60, 63; C. Taylor, *The Ethics of Authenticity*, cit., 43–53. The acceptance and recognition of one's own role in society also contribute to this (what we said about *honor* as a social virtue is applicable here).

logically founded personality. "Me-you" appropriately expresses the idea of reciprocal recognition between people, a recognition that would remain concealed in the terms "him" and "them," in which man is considered from the outside, as an object, and not understood in his personal subjectivity.[23] And yet, for interpersonal relations to favor the authentic maturation and self-transcendence of "me" and "you," it is necessary that both parties be oriented toward a sphere of meanings and values that transcend them. Only in this way will they be able to overcome their respective egoisms and closures.[24]

Interpersonal relations do not come about in a way that is automatic or to be taken for granted. Man must second his inborn capacity to open himself to others responsibly and voluntarily, to welcome them and accept them as "another self": "Each of us has experience of our own humanity only in the measure to which we are capable of participating in the humanity of others, of experiencing them as 'another self.'"[25]

Definitively speaking, then, a person can lead a life worthy of man (Aristotle's "good life," as we mentioned at the beginning of this chapter) and fulfill himself completely only thanks to a network of relationships. However, it must not be forgotten that society can also play a negative role, one of reduction, conditioning, or debasement: Suffice to recall — to mention just one of the more superficial aspects — the standardizing effects of passively following the dictates of fashion. There is even a risk of reaching the level of depersonalization described by Heidegger:

> In utilizing public means of transport and in making use of information services such as the newspaper, every Other is like the next. This Being-with-one-another dissolves one's own Dasein completely into the kind of Being of "the Others," in such a way, indeed, that the Others, as distinguishable and explicit, vanish more and more. In this inconspicuousness and unascertainability, the real dictatorship of the "they" is unfolded. We take pleasure and enjoy ourselves as *they* [*man*] take pleasure; we read, see, and judge about literature and art as *they* see and judge; likewise we

---

23. Cf. K. Wojtyła, *Perché l'uomo: Scritti inediti di antropologia e filosofia* (Milan: Arnoldo Mondadori, 1995), 95–98.

24. Frankl highlights this point with reference to the philosophy of dialogue of M. Buber and F. Ebner: cf. V.E. Frankl, *Una co-esistenza aperta al logos*, "Attualità in logoterapia," 1 (1999), 53–62.

25. K. Wojtyła, *Perché l'uomo: Scritti inediti di antropologia e filosofia*, cit., 131.

shrink back from the "great mass" as they shrink back; we find "shocking" what *they* find shocking.[26]

5. INDIVIDUALIST CONCEPTIONS AND COLLECTIVIST CONCEPTIONS

Thus far, we have seen how man, considered in the fullness of all his dimensions, has an ontologically founded individuality and is constituently in relation with others. And we have come to the conclusion that this is so deeply rooted in him that the completeness of his self-fulfillment also depends on the way in which he lives his relationality.

These two aspects (the value of singularity and that of relationality) must always be considered together. If by any chance they are separated, we run the risk of unilaterally emphasizing either the autonomy of the individual or the role of the society, presenting them as being mutually conflictory. If the former prevails, then other people become a mere restriction on my freedom of initiative; if the latter predominates, then collective interests appear as the overarching goal to which to sacrifice the good of the individual. Thus, would we have, on the one hand, individualism and, on the other, collectivism, in their various possible forms.

Both the individualist and collectivist conceptions, to which we will refer below, give exclusive or exaggerated consideration to one of the fundamental characteristics of the human person we talked about in Chapter 13 (autonomy, completeness, relationality), ignoring the others. The historical-political conclusions to which these conceptions have led should give us food for thought when reflecting on the consequences of any kind of reductionism in our understanding of man.[27]

---

26. M. Heidegger, *Being and Time* (New York and Evanston: Harper & Row, 1962), § 27, 164, emphasis in original.

27. It is useful to recall Pareyson's words: "Respect for the person is the very possibility of society itself because it is the condition of the birth both of the person and of society. Person and society are born together, and it is not possible to imagine the person without society or to imagine society without the person" (L. Pareyson, *Esistenza e persona* [Genoa: Il Melangolo, 1985], 187). In this context, what Buber wrote also remains very true: "If individualism only comprehends a part of man, collectivism does not comprehend man save as a part. Neither the one nor the other leads to the entirety of man, to man as a totality. Individualism considers man only in his condition of relation with himself. Collectivism does not see *man* at all; it sees nothing save '*society*.' In the one, the face of man is deformed; in the other, it is masked" (M. Buber, *Il problema dell'uomo* [Leumann: Elledici, 1990], 119).

5.1. Self-sufficiency and Individualism

Taking a different standpoint from that indicated by Aristotle (which we quoted at the beginning of section 2 of this chapter), some philosophers give greater emphasis to man's self-sufficiency and individuality. This approach often derives from a specific anthropological conception (in many cases a dualistic conception) that holds that associating with other men is merely a requirement imposed by our corporeal state, while the human spirit of itself tends to independence and autonomy.

A number of views characteristic of this approach are to be found in ancient philosophy, for example, those of Epicurus (341–270 BC) and of Plotinus (205–270). According to the former, in order to achieve happiness and peace, man needs only himself; he does not need the State, institutions, or nobility, not even God. He is perfectly autarchic.[28] Consequently, he delivers the following admonition: "Do not fool yourselves, men; do not allow yourselves to be deceived; do not fall into error; there is no natural society of beings who reason with one another"; "each thinks only of himself."[29] Hence the Epicurean commandment to "live secretly" (λάθε βιώσας).[30] Plotinus, too, held that "it is not possible to live happily in society 'with the body.'"[31]

We mention these two authors merely by way of example, but this approach emerges repeatedly over the history of philosophy and takes on various social and cultural forms. On the basis of this view, the fact that man lives in society is seen as an unavoidable necessity that sacrifices the individual's ideal of autonomy or, as the result of an agreement reached between individuals, to avoid contrasts and conflicts of interest. In brief, this view holds that the social community comes into being as a rationalized necessity with utilitarian ends. Capitalism and a certain form of liberalism may be identified with this approach in that they consider solidarity or commitment to

---

28. Cf. G. Reale, *Storia della filosofia antica*, Vol. II, (Milan: Vita e Pensiero, 1991), 174–175. Yet not even Epicurus could avoid admitting the importance of friendship.

29. Phrases attributed to Epicurus by Epictetus and Lactantius, in *ibid*, 258.

30. *Ibid*, 259.

31. Plotinus, *Enneads*, I, 4, 16. And similar affirmations are also to be found in Plato: "But when [*the soul*] returning into herself she reflects; then she passes into the realm of purity, and eternity, and immortality, and unchangeableness, which are her kindred, and with them she ever lives, when she is by herself and is not let or hindered; then she ceases from her erring ways, and being in communion with the unchanging is unchanging" (Plato, *Phaedo, 79* C).

resolve social injustices merely as means to guarantee the increase of wealth and individual well-being.

We could trace the development of the notion of man's autarchy or self-sufficiency from antiquity to modern-day individualism, and, along the way, we would see how the human being is always considered closed in his own subjectivity,[32] his aim being to dominate nature with technology, to dominate his own body with reason, to dominate others with politics or capital, etc. In this way, the human being inexorably closes in on himself, but, as we have seen, there are other aspects inherent to the notion of the person: openness to the natural world respected in its reality, recognition of other men in their dignity, and the integral relationship between the self and the mental-biological dimensions of the body.[33]

This individualistic approach has also been present in the evolution of law as the person has increasingly been seen as an unrepeatable, autonomous, and absolute singularity, standing above relations among nations or among the various sectors of society. This has had positive effects such as the *Declaration of the Rights of Man*, but it has also involved negative aspects, for, if we formulate rights for the individual (i.e., attributed to the single isolated individual), we overlook relationality among men and can provoke conflicts between rights.[34] One particularly evident example, among others, is the increase in sometimes paradoxical claims such as that supposed "right to have a healthy child."

5.2. Forms of Collectivism

Yet the sociability of the person cannot be accentuated to such an extent as to give it absolute priority in our understanding of man. This concept reached its most complete expression in Marxism, in which the collectivistic approach is united to an overarching materialism. According to K. Marx (1818–1883), "The essence of man is no abstraction inherent in each single individual. In reality, it is the ensemble of the social relations";[35] "it is not the consciousness of

32. Cf. J. Ballesteros, *"La costituzione dell'immagine attuale dell'uomo"* in I. Yarza (ed.), *Immagini dell'uomo: Percorsi antropologici nella filosofia moderna* (Rome: Armando, 1997), 23–37.

33. Cf. *ibid*, 32–37. On the subject of these anthropological properties, Ballesteros mentions M. Buber, E. Lévinas, and P. Ricoeur.

34. Cf. F. D'Agostino, *Pluralismo culturale e universalità dei diritti*, "Acta Philosophica," II/2 (1993), 230–231.

35. K. Marx, *"Thesen über Feuerbach"* in *Ausgewählte Schriften in zwei Bänden* (Berlin: Dietz Verlag, 1972), Tape II, 371, n. 6.

men that determines their existence but their social existence that determines their consciousness."[36] L. Feuerbach (1804–1872), who partly inspired the philosophy of Marx, also held that the essence of man is contained only in the community;[37] he took a negative view of things personal and individual and exalted the role of the intellect (or understanding), which he defined as the "true faculty of the genre," i.e., of that which is not specific: "The heart represents particular circumstances, individuals—the understanding, general circumstances, universals; it is the superhuman, i.e., the impersonal power in man."[38]

In the collectivist view the essence and dignity of the human person are subordinated to an earthly reality that is higher than the individual. This can be, depending upon the philosopher, society or one of its classes, a political party, the State, historical progress, the defense of the race, or the evolution of humanity. Thus, the individual is seen as a mere tool useful to attain certain general ends that can be reached by overseeing the working of economic and social mechanisms. Individual freedom is considered with suspicion, and the capacity of initiative is harnessed to structures imposed from above.

A similar approach is to be found in sociologism, in which the scientific study of social phenomena is considered as the key with which to explain—by making them a science—all the spiritual phenomena of man. In its various formulations, what this means is the absolute primacy over the person of the supposed social will of empirical society with its mechanisms of power and organization.

SUMMARY OF CHAPTER 15

The human person is characterized by his relationality. He is relational in terms of his origins (because at the origin of the person is his relationship with God, with his parents, with the social context) and in terms of his constitution (the person constitutes and structures his identity on the basis of relationships). Aristotelian philosophy explains how the human being is "social by nature" not

36. K. Marx, "*Critica dell'economía politica*" in *Le opere* (Rome: Editori Riuniti, 1966), 746–747; cited in C. Tullio-Altan, *Manuale di antropología culturale: Storia e metodo* (Milan: Bompiani, 1998), 206.

37. Cf. L. Feuerbach, *Principles of the Philosophy of the Future* (Indianapolis, IN: Hackett Publishing Company, 1986), 72.

38. L. Feuerbach, *The Essence of Christianity* (New York: Calvin Blanchard, 1854), 58.

only in order to satisfy his material wants but also to "live well," that is, to live an authentically human life. The inherent relationality of the person also finds expression in the possession of socializing inclinations, from which social virtues arise. These inclinations and their associated virtues are the roots of society. Also, it must not be forgotten that social relationships are necessary for self-fulfillment, but they can also become an obstacle to authentic self-fulfillment. In the history of philosophy, some thinkers have given overarching emphasis to the individual's self-sufficiency and autonomy, presenting the relationship between the person and society in individualistic terms. Others have exaggerated the importance of social relations, even going so far as to overlook the value of the individual and to develop collectivist ideas.

CHAPTER 16

CULTURE

1. THE MEANING OF THE WORD "CULTURE"

To introduce our reflections on culture, it might be helpful to give an exact etymology of the word, to which end we will make reference to, among others, certain observations of Gadamer.[1]

1.1. Cultivation, Formation, and Cult

The word "culture" comes from the Latin verb *colere*, in which three meanings are combined.[2]

A first meaning refers to education, or the cultivation of gifts or natural faculties in the physical-technical sense: Thus, we say "to cultivate the earth" or we speak of a "natural formation" to refer to the external appearance of a thing (for example, a formation of mountains, which created itself without artificial interventions, or a neoformation to indicate a benign tumor). What prevails here is the idea of letting things act according to nature, following their own specific processes until reaching an observable and recognizable result.

But culture has also a second meaning, deriving from the fact that the verb *colere* also means to embellish, to adorn, i.e., not just allowing things that already exist to grow but actively intervening in their final configuration. This is the meaning the German word *Bildung* (culture, formation) has assumed from the nineteenth century on, meaning not so much the mere education of natural faculties or talents but the inner process of developing and assimilating what we receive from others, in other words, the inner spiritual conformation to an image (*Bild* in German), which may often be considered as the ideal image of the human person but can also be taken in a mystic sense, that is, as the image of God that man carries with him and that orients his development. The prevalent idea here is that

---

1. Cf. H.G. Gadamer, *Truth and Method* (London and New York: Continuum, 2006), 8–17.

2. Apart from the meanings mentioned above, the verb *colere* also signifies to live or to reside, but we will not dwell on this definition, which may be considered as deriving from the first meaning indicated in the text.

of formation received from educators and of self-formation. In this sense, when we speak of a cultured man, we mean a man formed or conformed to an image or model of the human person (thus, a man may be fully developed from the physical or natural point of view but may be uncultured from the point of view of his spiritual formation).

The verb *colere* also has a third meaning, a religious meaning, whence derives the idea of "cult," that is, the worship and veneration of God. This definition is by no means negligible and, in fact, many writers emphasize the religious component of cultures.

From studying the first two definitions of the term, it is clear that the concept of culture embraces the nature and exercise of man's spiritual faculties (that is, natural gifts and their transformation according to a model),[3] the biological order and the free intervention of man that configures that order, and the transmission of knowledge and its interior assimilation.

1.2. Culture and Human Existence

In the light of what we have just said about the semantic roots of the word, it may be understood that culture cannot be reduced to learning, education, or an academic qualification but has a much broader scope. What culture does, in fact, is establish an intimate relationship between the bodily sphere and the spiritual sphere, between what is shared and what is individual, between what is universal and what is personal. The cultured individual (in the sense indicated above), on the one hand, conforms to universal human traits and, on the other, is individually unique. Culture, understood in this sense, is not achieved by merely applying a technique (didactic, pedagogic, mnemonic) or by transmitting a body of knowledge. The cultured person has creatively and freely assimilated what he has received.

In Guardini's view, "Culture is everything that man creates and exists in his living encounter with the world that surrounds him."[4] This is not an overly generalized statement because man's existence and activities with respect to his surroundings are not limited to the natural dimension but, by virtue of his freedom, always have a cultural dimension. Culture is associated with a person's level of being not with his level of having, the level of being here: *being* understood

---

3. In German the terms *Bild* (image), *Vorbild* (model), *Nachbild* (reproduction) all come from the same root.

4. R. Guardini, *Persona e libertà: Saggi di fondazione della teoría pedagogica* (Brescia: La Scuola, 1990), 50.

in the dynamic-existential sense about which we spoke at length in Chapter 14. The level of having concerns only the attainment of certain abilities and the possession of various forms of knowledge; the level of being, on the other hand, concerns the living of an authentically human existence, in other words, personal self-fulfillment.

Thus, for example, it would be wrong to think that schools must favor an education that focuses on what man possesses and his capacity to use it, limiting their academic aims to supplying knowledge, experience, and abilities. Schools supply education, and education involves what man is and what he is called to be. Remember that, in this context, my being a person is, from an existential standpoint, a task to be undertaken and not a result already achieved. Thus, we must not deceive ourselves into thinking we can allow a boy or girl to grow up with absolute spontaneity, imagining that in this way we do not influence their "natural" disposition or condition the choices they make. There is no "natural uncontaminated state" in man, unrelated to any kind of value. All free choices and all teaching are inspired by a specific model of the human person.

Guardini uses a very effective image: Education, be it at school or in the family, is a road with which the young are presented and down which they start to travel, but, being a road, it always has a particular direction, a destination.[5] There is no such thing as a road that leads nowhere, and to pretend that there is would be a deception, or not a road at all but a car park. It is important, then, to make the goals of education clear, something that can be illustrated with the following example. If, in the course of a lesson, I explain the composition of the human body, I could affirm that human conduct is entirely determined by such and such a neurobiological structure, or I can simply ignore the problem of man's freedom, or I could show that freedom cannot be explained in neurobiological terms. In the first case, I am presenting a materialist vision of man; in the second case, I am presenting a superficial view of existence; in the third case, I am presenting an integral vision of the person.

---

5. Cf. R. Guardini, *Persona e libertà: Saggi di fondazione della teoria pedagogica*, cit., 63. On this subject Lewis observes that, in education, we cannot expect to act like a poultry-keeper with young birds, who are raised for reasons of which they know nothing. It is necessary to reveal the values that inevitably come to be considered important, even if they are just well-being and security (cf. C.S. Lewis, *The Abolition of Man* [London: Fount, 1999], 14–18). We will discuss values in section 2.3 of this chapter and, especially, in Chapter 17.

If this fundamental aspect were overlooked, man would risk becoming the unwitting object of ideological and political manipulation. Referring back to the meanings of the verb *colere*, let us reiterate that there is no culture without a model or without an image of man nor an education without reference values. (This holds true, to give another example, for the supposed neutrality of so-called sex education in schools or of State information campaigns about AIDS: In man there is no exclusively biological or anatomical sexuality independent of choices for which he is responsible.)

Thus, when we say that only man has culture, we mean to indicate that in man natural, individual, and environmental realties are absorbed into the sphere of freedom and there acquire a new kind of potentiality.[6] Man's response to his instincts and his basic needs (nutrition, survival as defense against his surroundings) is, unlike the animals, cultural and historic, i.e., it changes according to circumstance. This lack of rigidity is, in fact, the sign of human freedom.[7] Sometimes, animal ethology also speaks about "cultural behavior," but the sense is ambiguous. It is true that individual animals can learn to resolve certain problems in a new way, for example, using a branch as a club or even learning some kind of rudimental navigation in water, but these "discoveries" do not lead to the birth of a civilization nor any epoch-making change.

2. THREE FUNDAMENTAL ELEMENTS OF CULTURE

2.1. Language and Cultural Traditions

Considered from the point of view of cultural anthropology, culture can be defined as a historically transmitted, structured assemblage of meanings expressed in symbols, a system of hereditary concepts by which men communicate, hand down, and develop their knowledge and their attitudes to life.[8] Integrating this notion into philosophical

---

6. Cf. R. Guardini, *Das Ende der Neuzeit: Ein Versuch zur Orientierung* (Basel: Hess, 1950), 98.

7. Cf. A. Millán-Puelles, *Economía y libertad* (Madrid: Confederación Española de Cajas de Ahorro, 1974), 28–36; A. Malo, "La libertà nell'atto umano: La tendenzialità dell'uomo come espressione di libertà," in F. Russo and J. Villanueva (eds.), *Le dimensioni della libertà nel dibattito scientifico e filosofico* (Rome: Armando, 1995), 75–76.

8. Cf. C. Tullio-Altan, *Manuale di antropología culturale: Storia e metodo* (Milan: Bompiani, 1998), 78–79; L. Formigari, *Il linguaggio: Storia delle teorie* (Rome and Bari: Laterza, 2001), 185.

anthropology, it should be highlighted that these symbols and concepts are interiorized by individuals who find in the cultural system models for perception (which present reality as already organized by experience), models for evaluation (which attribute a positive or negative meaning to specific events and phenomena), and models for action and behavior.

The language spoken by a social community plays a vital role in the transmission of cultural systems, and this is the first element to which we must now turn our attention. To begin with, it may be helpful to recall that, while speech indicates the human capacity to communicate with others and to represent reality (its specific nature was examined in the first part of this book), language (English, Italian, Swahili, and so on) is the communicative system used by a specific group of individuals.

As Wilhelm von Humboldt (1767–1835) explained, the fundamental difference between languages cannot be reduced to sounds or signs; rather, it depends on particular "worldviews" (*Weltansichten*), on the development of the spirit of a particular people, and on the conditions in which they live.[9] Language is not static and definitive; rather, it reflects the incessant activity of the human mind in such a way that "language is, as it were, the outer appearance of the spirit of a people."[10]

Setting his idealistic conceptions aside, von Humboldt very rightly maintains that language expresses the harmony that comes to be established between the world and man. Language, as Coreth observes,[11] carries in itself all the history of a society. It hands down patterns of thought, opinions, and representations of the world; it gathers all the sedimentation of a spiritual-cultural tradition: consider, for example, the richness of proverbs and popular sayings. A social group expresses its own cultural identity both in the pho-

---

9. Cf. W. von Humboldt, *On Language* (Cambridge, MA: Harvard University Press, 1999), 46.

10. *Ibid*, 33. Von Humboldt highlights the relation among language, the culture of a people, and individual creativity: "Whether and to what extent [language] promotes clarity and correct order among concepts or puts difficulties in the way of this? Whether it retains the inherent sensuous perspicuity of the ideas conveyed into the language from the worldview? Whether, through the euphony of its tones, it works harmoniously and soothingly or again energetically and upliftingly upon feeling and sentiment? In these and in many other such determinations of the whole mode of thought and way of feeling lies that which constitutes its true character and determines its influence on spiritual evolution" (*ibid*, 34).

11. Cf. E. Coreth, *Was ist der Mensch? Grundzüge einer philosophischen Anthropologie* (Innsbruck and Vienna: Tyrolia, 1986), 50.

netic (harsh or soft sounds or varieties of tone as in Chinese) and in the semantic aspects of its language.[12] The prevalence of certain sounds or of certain conceptual representations expresses the religious, scientific, humanistic, or technical character of a culture. This is reflected in many ways; for example, numerous expressions reveal clues to a bond with the transcendent such as the German greeting *grüss Gott* or the Italian expression *ogni ben di Dio* to refer to an abundance of something. Moreover, the numerous suffixes of Italian (*-ino, -rello, -uccio, -etto, -tino*, some of which can be combined with one another, increasing the possibilities) may perhaps indicate a propensity for nuance and an accommodating approach to life.[13]

We may gain direct experience of this if, for example, as adults we seek to learn another language: We have the impression of approaching a new world that possesses its own intellectual structure and a well-defined way of looking at life. Moreover, thanks to this experience we become better able to perceive the specific structure and distinctive traits of our own mother tongue.[14]

As Cassirer observes, if speech only had the function of copying or imitating the order of things, then it would be logical to wish to discover which of the current "linguistic copies"—i.e., which of the spoken languages—is the most adequate. Yet language also contains the productive or constructive aspect of speech; that is, its capacity to establish a particular rapport with reality (the world, other people) to enrich it and modify it.[15]

---

12. An etymological study of synonyms in various languages would confirm this. Von Humboldt examined the terms used to indicate the moon in Greek and in Latin; the Greek word (*mên*) indicates the moon's function in measuring time, while the Latin expression (*luna, luc-na*) refers to its luminosity (cf. E. Cassirer, *An Essay on Man: An Introduction to a Philosophy of Human Culture* [Garden City, NY: Doubleday and Co., 1953], 173; in referring to these studies, however, Cassirer reaches questionable conclusions concerning the relationship between the names and the truth of things).

13. Cassirer mentions Hammer-Purgstall's 1855 study on the names used in Arabic to designate the camel, according to which there are no fewer than five or six thousand [*sic!*] words to express specific details about that animal's form, size, color, age, gait, etc. He likewise observes that in different languages there is a great abundance of names for colors, often referring to the hues of plants and animals, and that the languages used by certain American Indian tribes contain a surprising variety of terms to designate particular activities, such as walking or striking (cf. *ibid*, 174–175).

14. Cf. *ibid*, 172.

15. Cf. *ibid*, 168–169.

2.2. Usage and Custom

A second element that characterizes the culture of a people is its uses and customs, which are so numerous as to elude any exhaustive description: They range from food to clothing, from education to furnishing, from religious ceremonies to political life. We become aware of them especially when we travel to a foreign country or when we meet someone of a different nationality or even just from a different city.

Alongside the shared characteristics in the customs of peoples determined by their bio-physiological and environmental heritage, there are also considerable differences that depend upon such factors as demographic growth, historical events, racial or geographical particularities, and even the affections. In this context suffice to mention a number of very obvious examples: The physical gifts of a certain people may facilitate the practice and popularity of a particular sport (think of African long-distance runners); the climate of tropical countries prevents an overly accelerated lifestyle and imposes a precise pattern on daily events; certain peoples have an inborn propensity for rhythm and are naturally gifted for dancing and singing; some populations (be they Genoese, Scots, or Neapolitans) are proverbially famous for certain inveterate characteristics, which have distant roots, although we must avoid generalizations.

This should help us to understand the truth of Guardini's affirmation about culture quoted in section 1.2 of this chapter: "Culture is everything that man creates and exists in his living encounter with the world that surrounds him." This means that the entire existence of man (in his corporeal-spiritual totality) in relation to the surrounding environment lies at the root of his cultural expressions, i.e., of his behavior, which is not exclusively determined by nature.

2.3. Values in Culture

Although we will examine this from a more general standpoint in Chapter 17, we must make brief reference to the values that different cultures seek to safeguard and transmit. This is the third element of culture at which we wish to look. It is evident that the customs and language of a civilization or social group reflect its predominant values, i.e., the things held to be most worthy of respect. History shows that there have been societies that attributed considerable importance to the value of courage in war, respect for the divinity, burial customs, and so on, all the way down to modern societies in which the values of well-being and health seem to predominate (one sign of which, among others, is the proliferation of magazines and television programs dedicated to this subject).

Clearly, the hierarchy of predominant values reflects a specific conception of man and his ultimate end, and it is just such radical questions as these that enable us to evaluate the degree of "civilization" of a historical period. Thus, it is not possible to uphold cultural relativism in any absolute sense, and for this reason we can speak about the values and the "nonvalues" of a particular culture. Certain ideals or forms of behavior can assume the role of a "nonvalue" in a society when they obfuscate or deny the truth about man; for example, exalting one's homeland or race ignores the inherent relationality of the person and can lead to inhumane political actions such as discrimination or deportation. And so it is upon an anthropological foundation — and not just by assessing their literacy levels or economic development — that civilizations can be evaluated.

Intimately associated with the role of values in a culture is the question of the inseparable tie between religion and civilization. It is not possible to study history or culture without taking the religious sentiment of peoples into account; indeed, it could be said that each culture is characterized by the way in which man faces the mystery of God. In Dawson's view, "The great religions are, as it were, great rivers of sacred traditions that flow down through the ages and through changing historical landscapes that they irrigate and fertilize."[16] In fact, by examining historical events we realize that

> [faith] introduces into human life an element of spiritual freedom which may have a creative and transforming influence on man's social culture and historical destiny as well as on his inner personal experience.[17]

In this sense, the role of Christianity has specific characteristics which makes its meeting with culture a unique phenomenon.

---

16. C. Dawson, *Religion and the Rise of Western Culture* (New York: Doubleday, 1991), 12.

17. *Ibid*, 14.

3. Culture and Society

3.1. The Interaction Between Personal Culture and Social Culture

In order to understand the relationship between the culture of individuals and that of the social group to which they belong, it may be helpful to make some brief reference to structuralism, a school of thought that became popular in the twentieth century. According to structuralists,[18] fundamental structures come together in each culture just as common elementary structures (phonemes) do in a language.

The way in which structuralists study society and culture tends to highlight the unvarying structures underpinning institutions, social relationships (even relationships between blood relatives), and customs.[19] Rather than seeking to understand them from within, history and society are dissected from the outside with the same scientific detachment as is used in the natural sciences and linguistics. This approach does have a positive aspect in that it seeks to avoid a historicist and individualist view of culture, a view inherent to some exponents of existentialism and to the thought of J. P. Sartre, which exalted individuality and singularity. On the other hand, however, it can lead to the conclusion that society and culture develop in accordance with an autonomous process of which man is an unconscious product and instrument. In this view, the human individual could only be understood in (and, in the final analysis, reduced to) his social relationships. This approach tends to forget man's transcendence over society and its structures (it is significant that this school of philosophy should be associated with Marxism) because it denies or overlooks his inner freedom.[20]

3.2. The "Three World Theory" of K. R. Popper and J. C. Eccles

In order to give a brief explanation of the interaction between social culture (in other words, a civilization) and personal culture (personality understood in its cultural sense), we feel it may be useful to

---

18. Among the most famous structuralists are C. Lévi-Strauss (1908), L. Althusser (1918–1990), and M. Foucault (1926–1984).

19. According to Lévi-Strauss, "It is necessary and sufficient underlying each institution and each custom, in order to obtain a principle of interpretation valid for other institutions and other customs, provided of course that the analysis is carried far enough." (C. Lévi-Strauss, *Structural Anthropology* [New York: Basic Books, 1974], 21).

20. A useful summary and criticism of structuralist positions is to be found in B. Mondin, *Philosophical Anthropology: Man: An Impossible Project?* (Rome and Bangalore: Urbaniana University Press, 1985), 146–149.

recall the "three world theory" as elaborated by Popper and Eccles.[21] They schematically presented reality, the environment in which man is inserted, as follows:

WORLD 1	WORLD 2	WORLD 3
PHYSICAL OBJECTS AND STATES	STATES OF CONSCIOUSNESS	OBJECTIVE KNOWLEDGE
1. INORGANIC Matter and energy (universe)	Subjective knowledge	
2. BIOLOGY Structure and actions of all living beings – human brains	Experience of: – perception – thought – emotions – intentions – memories – dreams – creativity	Cultural heredity codified in material substrata: – philosophical – theological – scientific – historical – literary – artistic – technological
3. ARTIFACTS material substrata – of human creativity – of tools – of machines – of books – of works of art – of music		Theoretical systems, scientific problems, critical arguments

This is, of course, a schematic and, hence, nonexhaustive representation, as its authors themselves make clear. We use it independently of their overall anthropological theory, which would anyway require separate treatment, especially as concerns Popper. Nevertheless, it is a useful summary not only because it gives a graphic representation of the interaction between social culture and individual culture but also because it will serve as a reference when considering the subject of work in Chapter 18.

---

21. Cf. K.R. Popper and J.C. Eccles, *The Self and Its Brain* (New York: Routledge, 1984), 36–50; J.C. Eccles, *Evolution of the Brain: Creation of the Self* (Abingdon and New York: Routledge, 1991), 73–76, 229–232.

The three columns distinguish three distinct areas of human experience, which, however, interact with one another. The development of World 1 leads to a growth of World 2, which in turn enriches World 3. New knowledge of World 3 awakens richer experiences of World 2, which translate into an expansion of World 1. As we explained in Chapter 14, cultural progress does not take place in man only as a response to material needs or material situations; often it is the person himself who raises problems and creates alternatives. We must not, therefore, interpret the relationship between World 1 and the other two Worlds in a deterministic sense as if they were communicating vessels. Moreover, the schematic representation must not make us forget the role of personal freedom, thanks to which the individual can orient and even overturn the development of his environment or make up for certain material inadequacy.

Nonetheless, it is evident, for example, that the possibility of transmitting cultural traditions and ideas (World 3) through paper and ink (World 1) enables a greater development of the subjective resources of World 2. The critical and mature relationship with which a person interacts with these areas of reality is an important part of the growth process of individual personality. Bear in mind the fact that the role of a person's biological gifts, which can be developed or inhibited, also comes into the relationship between the three "worlds"; this is why in the "World 1" column mention is also made of human brains. This theory can be associated with what we have said concerning the language of a people as spoken by individuals in which phonetic, semantic, affective, and spiritual aspects unite: Mastery of linguistic resources enables greater communicative and receptive capacity, and hence better interaction between personal and social culture.

In order to underline the importance of interaction between the individual, his fellow man, and the surrounding world, we will cite just three of many possible examples. The first is the case, mentioned by Eccles, of a young girl called Genie who was kept closed in isolation in a loft by her psychotic father: Until the age of eight months, no one addressed a word to her, and, from the age of twenty months to thirteen years, she received only indispensable care. The absence of contact with World 3 and the meager resources of World 1 caused considerable damage to her personality. The doctor who cared for her noted how her lack of exposure to dialogue had caused considerable damage to the left side of her brain even though the right side compensated for this deficit with some very limited speech. Happily, the girl gradually managed to make up for her educational deficiency.[22]

Guardini cites another example not so precise in scientific terms but equally significant. Salimbene writes that a thirteenth-century Holy Roman emperor, Frederick II of Hohenstaufen (who had a marked interest in the natural sciences and philosophy), wished to discover whether the primordial language of man was Latin, Greek, or Hebrew. To this end he had three orphans taken to an isolated house with orders for them to be treated well but for no one to speak to them. The result was that all three presently died.[23]

Finally, there is the famous story of the boy found abandoned in the woods of Aveyron, in France, at the end of the 1700s. The doctors who examined him deduced that he had been abandoned in the early years of life and had survived without human contact almost until adolescence. The brain damage due to his isolation proved an insurmountable obstacle to teaching him verbal language and the normal development of his intelligence, although it was not possible to establish whether the boy had been affected by mental problems before his abandonment.[24] The story was made into an excellent film entitled *L'enfant sauvage* by F. Truffaut.

These three examples emphasize the interaction between the culture in which a person lives and his individual existence. They are also further proof of what we explained about relationality in Chapter 15: Relationships and comparison with others are an integral part of the development of human personality.

SUMMARY OF CHAPTER 16

In order to understand the meaning of the term culture it is helpful to recall its etymological roots in the Latin verb *colere*, which brings together three meanings: cultivating natural gifts and faculties, favoring development in accordance with an ideal model, and worshiping God. Due to his freedom the human being's existence

22. Cf. J.C. Eccles, *Evolution of the Brain: Creation of the Self*, cit., 231–232. This case was studied in 1977, but more recent news reports have also highlighted similar cases.

23. Cf. R. Guardini, *Persona e libertà: Saggi di fondazione della teoria pedagogica*, cit., 197.

24. See the account of this story in the book by J.M. Itard, *The Wild Boy of Aveyron* (Norwalk, CT: Appleton & Lange, 1962).

in the world is never merely spontaneous or natural but always cultural: He freely orients his existence with reference to specific values and not just as a univocal response to his vital instincts. The fundamental elements that constitute and transmit culture include language, customs, and values. These elements act at the level of the culture of the individual and at that of the culture of a people. These two levels also influence one another as has been underlined by structuralism which, however, does not take due account of the freedom of the individual. The "three world theory" of K. R. Popper and J. Eccles helps us understand how individual and social culture interact. It highlights how the culture of the individual and of an entire civilization are influenced not only by ideas but also by geographical, climatic, and physiological factors.

CHAPTER 17

VALUES

1. PERSONAL EXISTENCE ORIENTED TOWARD VALUES

Man always acts with a view to an end, which guides his actions and his choices. Generally speaking, that end is the attainment of truth and goodness, toward which our human nature is oriented, but this basic orientation is specifically determined in practice by each individual. Thus we can say, by way of a first approximation, that values are truth and goodness seen not in an abstract sense (in theory or in general) but in practice,[1] i.e., as referred to my own existence. In fact, either consciously or unconsciously, we always act on the basis of a prior perception of what we believe to be a value. Health, success, money, and so on are some of the most common motives behind our daily activity.

It is not possible, then, to speak superficially about an "absence of values" in a society or in a person's life because the problem actually consists in discovering what basic motives orient social transformations and individual behavior.

1.1. The Hierarchy and Experience of Values

The values to which we refer and on the basis of which we act derive partly from the culture in which we live, a culture transmitted though tradition and education, but each man, drawing on his own personal experience, also builds his own hierarchically structured system of values; in other words, he identifies and establishes what he considers to be important in his life, with respect to which he is ready to accept various degrees of compromise.[2] For example, we may be flexible as concerns the pastime we have chosen for a weekend but not ready to yield so easily in matters concerning friendship or work; or again, some people are very fussy concerning the quality

---

1. Cf. R. Yepes, *Fundamentos de antropología: Un ideal de la excelencia humana* (Pamplona: Eunsa, 1996), 136–151. These pages contain a clear and effective analysis of the relationship between practical truth, values, and human conduct.

2. Cf. C. Taylor, *The Ethics of Authenticity* (Cambridge, MA, and London: Harvard University Press, 1992), 37–39.

and presentation of food, while others will make do with a hurried meal in order to have time to practice a sport. These things depend on the importance we attribute to one value with respect to another.

Yet this hierarchy of values has a certain objectivity that becomes clear through experience and comparison with reality. It is on this basis that we establish our preferences and are able to judge them. We will seek to explain this with a reference to artistic experience.[3] I may prefer the Gothic style or the Romantic, but this does not prevent me from admiring the beauty of Baroque architecture. The preference for one style or another is a question of taste, which nonetheless does not (or should not) blind me in my judgment of other artistic expressions. On a more mundane level, the success of a summer pop song may cause me to listen to it with pleasure on a number of occasions, but I know well that within a few years it will lose its savor and be forgotten. On the other hand, a Beethoven symphony or the work of a talented singer-songwriter will always stand the comparison with seasonal fashions.

These two examples, of the many we could have used, imply two consequences. Firstly, the scale of values is not completely arbitrary but refers to a known reality; secondly, it is possible to cultivate and develop one's sensibility toward the value contents of reality, learning to recognize them and arrange them into a hierarchy. Let us seek to explain this more clearly.

1.2. The Transmission and Recognition of Values

Rather than being a form of theoretical baggage, values are passed on from one generation to the next through everyday attitudes and behavior such as the ways in which the problems of life are faced, especially in the family environment, where intergenerational ties and the complementarity of the roles of father and mother play an important role. This creates a continuity between young people and adults that is deeper than it may seem.[4] Yet, although values are transmitted and taught, each man has to recognize and appreciate them for what they are because values are not something cold or neutral but involve — in varying degrees and depending upon their importance — the entire person, his will, and his feelings. This means

---

3. Similar effective arguments are to be found in R. Spaemann, *Basic Moral Concepts*, cit., 26–27; cf. C.S. Lewis, *The Abolition of Man*, cit., 12–18.

4. Various sociological studies confirm this: cf. P. Donati and I. Colozzi, *Giovani e generazioni: Quando si cresce in una società eticamente neutra* (Bologna: Il Mulino, 1997), 16–17, 166–171.

that there must be personal involvement in them and, hence, free adherence to them; otherwise, we remain in the sphere of indifference.

For example, it is not enough to hear people talk about the importance of solidarity or of study because, if we show no openness and interest in these or other values, we are unable to recognize them. Something similar happens if, in an official ceremony, I am introduced to many people. If I show no interest or openness toward the other guests, theirs is little more than a walk-on role in my life, and I will immediately forget their faces and names. It is vital, then that a person's affectivity be brought into play. For example, we can approach certain values with passion, which is an advantage because it makes us attentive to a particular quality. However, it should be remembered that "all passion can ever do is to bring us into a new relationship with a value, but it cannot tell us what an appropriate, free response to it should be,"[5] and that, in order to exercise freedom, judgment and evaluation are also necessary.

Because values act as guideline-criteria for personal existence, man's self-fulfillment will be greater in the degree to which it is oriented toward more exalted values, i.e., values that are less relative and less fleeting. If I assume wealth, well-being, or pleasure as my guideline-criteria, my life will be exposed to the variability and instability inherent to these sense objects. If, on the other hand, I concern myself with stable and universal values, an increase of freedom comes about in the sense that my spiritual potentials tend toward objects that do not expire: Friendship, solidarity, and love for God do not have preset limits and are not contingent.

1.3 Stability of Values and Personal Self-fulfillment

Today, there exists a widespread and dangerous separation between theoretical and practical truth, between what an individual recognizes and considers as true (and hence a value) and the reflection of that truth or value in his personal behavior. If this coherence, which

---

5. R. Spaemann, *Basic Moral Concepts*, cit., 32.

is part of authenticity, is lacking,[6] values end up losing their significance and force because they become a "notion" known only in theory. This is one of the reasons that leads to the so-called relativism of values, according to which there is no such thing as universal values and that their choice is purely an individual and subjective matter, dependent on whim. When there is no coherence between what we hold to be true and our personal behavior, we end up losing the capacity of correct judgment.

There is another factor that tends to reinforce this unstable approach. As we saw when we discussed culture, values are always transmitted by living models and examples, which are offered to us in our daily life or our social-cultural context: heroes and saints but also "celebrities," famous people, sports champions, and singers.[7] Now, in a society as information-based as our own, the excess of reference "types" can lead to inconstancy and superficiality because the models presented are often contradictory or idealized.

In order to avoid this danger, we must reconsider what we have already said concerning the experience of values. In Spaemann's view,[8] we apprehend the value contents of reality in an act of pleasure or of regret, of respect, of contempt, of hatred, of fear, or of hope; consequently, we can talk of a kind of "feeling of values" because knowledge of values implies affectivity. But the value contents are revealed to us little by little and in the degree to which we learn to make our interests objective. For example, we have to learn to listen to and understand good music if we are to enjoy it; we have to learn to read a text attentively in order to appreciate a literary style; we have to learn to distinguish between various wines in order to appreciate them; and we have to learn to understand other men in order to value their gifts.

This means that a formative process is necessary through which each man objectifies and diversifies his interests or desires and, hence,

---

6. Remember what we said about authenticity and self-fulfillment in Chapter 14. St. Augustine attributes such incoherence to love for a false image of the truth: "Truth is loved in such a way that those who love something else besides her wish that to be the truth which they love. Since they are unwilling to be deceived, they are unwilling to be convinced that they have been deceived. Therefore, they hate the truth for the sake of whatever it is that they love in place of the truth. They love truth when she shines on them and hate her when she rebukes them" (Augustine, *Confessions*, 10, 23, 34).

7. See what we said in Chapter 15 concerning the social virtue of *dulia* and the philosophical theories that emphasize its importance.

8. Cf. R. Spaemann, *Basic Moral Concepts*, cit., 24–32.

increases his capacity to suffer and be happy. Although we may be obtuse or blind to certain values, "the formation of a sense of values, of a sense for the hierarchy of values, of the capacity to distinguish what is important from what is not important is necessary for the success of each individual's life and is also a prerequisite of his ability to communicate with others."[9] Indeed, stable reference to objective values gives continuity to our life project and enables us to achieve happiness, understood also as inner harmony. If our behavior is only a function of casual external stimuli or of moods and is not based on an objective order of values, then we lack the conditions to achieve harmony with ourselves and even agreement with others. If we did not have the capacity to organize and relativize our desires in accordance with an objective viewpoint, then no agreement would be possible and the conflict between various claims of personal satisfaction would predominate.

1.4 The Contribution of Max Scheler's Axiology

In the history of philosophy as it regards values, Max Scheler (1874–1928) has a particularly important place.[10] In 1916 he wrote the essay *Formalism in Ethics and Nonformal Ethics of Values: A New Attempt Toward the Foundation of an Ethical Personalism*[11] in which he undertakes a phenomenological analysis of moral experience, assuming, among other things, an axiological perspective[12] in which the conclusions we reached earlier are present. This is why we make brief mention of it now.

Scheler believed that the human person is capable of intuiting axiological values and, therefore, that "there are *authentic* and *true* value-qualities, and they constitute a special domain of objectivities; have their own *distinct* relations and correlations; and, as value-qualities, can be, for example, higher or lower. This being the case, there can be among these value-qualities an *order* and an *order of ranks*, both of which are independent of the presence of a *realm of goods* in which they appear, entirely independent of the movement

---

9. *Ibid*, 49.
10. Scheler was the son of a Jewish mother and Lutheran father. He converted to Catholicism but later abandoned it, turning to what could be defined as a kind of historicist pantheism.
11. *Der Formalismus in der Ethik und die materiale Wertethik: Neuer Versuch der Grundlegung eines ethischen Personalismus.* The first part of this work was published in 1913; the third edition appeared in 1927.
12. The word axiology comes from the Greek word *axía* (and from its corresponding adjective *axios*), which means value or worth.

and changes of these goods in history, and '*a priori*' to the experience of this realm of goods."[13]

Pointing to the hierarchical structure of values, Scheler distinguishes the following categories, among others: values of the agreeable and the disagreeable (which concern the sphere of sensibility); vital values (those correlated to vital feeling, whence arise, for example, joy or sadness, courage or anguish, the impulse of revenge or anger); spiritual values (which cannot be reduced to a mere biological law and concern beauty and ugliness, justice and injustice, truth); and values of the sacred (which are apprehended with a specific act of love, before which we respond with faith or with lack of faith, with veneration and adoration, experiencing blissfulness or despair).[14]

As Lambertino makes clear,[15] in Scheler's view, values have an autonomy that is at once ontological and cognitive in the sense that they do not depend on the experience of the subject or on his affective states. Axiological qualities possess "a determinate order of ranks with respect to 'higher' and 'lower.' This order is independent of the form of being into which values enter."[16] Scheler's reflections are important because they rigorously uphold the objectivity and universality of values. In contrast to the tendency to make them subjective and relative, he holds that value is imposed in itself and of itself, while people tend to grant validity only on the basis of what is accepted by the majority, what others think. However, Scheler does not give a satisfying explanation of a person's dominion over his acts, as the individual seems almost passively drawn toward the world of values.[17] There are also some problematic aspects in his conception of the person.

---

13. M. Scheler, *Formalism in Ethics and Nonformal Ethics of Values* (Evanston, IL: Northwestern University Press, 1973), 15; emphasis in original.

14. Cf. *ibid*. A few pages earlier, explaining the superiority and inferiority of values, he writes: "It appears that values are 'higher' the *more* they *endure* and the *less* they partake in '*extension*' and *divisibility*. They are higher the *less they are* 'founded' through other values and the *deeper* the '*satisfaction*' connected with feeling them. Moreover, they are higher the *less* the feeling of them is *relative* to the *positing* of a specific bearer of 'feeling' and 'preferring'" (*ibid*, 90; emphasis in original).

15. Cf. A. Lambertino, *Max Scheler: Fondazione fenomenologica dell'ética dei valori* (Florence: La Nuova Italia, 1996), 98.

16. M. Scheler, *Formalism in Ethics and Nonformal Ethics of Values*, cit., 17.

17. Cf. A. Rodríguez Luño, *Etica* (Florence: Le Monnier, 1992), 132. For a more specific examination, see K. Wojtyła, *Valutazioni sulla possibilità di costruire l'ética cristiana sulle basi del sistema di Max Scheler* (Rome: Logos, 1980).

2. Metaphysical Analysis of Value

Thus far, our reflections on values have been directed from a phe-nomenological-existential perspective, referring to different realities (among them well-being, success, happiness, goodness, truth, and the love of God) that have in common the fact of being suitable for the person, i.e., an intentional relationship of appreciation and evaluation with the human subject. Now, as we did earlier when we reflected upon the person, we will seek to undertake a metaphysical analysis in order to understand the ontological foundation of this common characteristic.

2.1. Value and Being

Let us begin with a statement by Guardini, according to whom "'value' is what makes a being worthy to exist and an action worth performing."[18] This is evidently not a technical definition; rather, it indicates that value is a quality inherent to reality, implicating an intentional reference to the person who perceives reality. If, as we have said, value works as a guide, or reference, for human activity, this is because the person is capable of apprehending it in the various sectors of reality. Thus, in order to gain a deeper understanding of the notion of value, we must consider it from a metaphysical perspective, placing it in relation to existence.

It can be stated that the human person knows the value of every-thing that exists, that he discovers value as a property inherent to reality. Therefore, value does not belong to the area known in metaphysics as "predicamental"[19] (which concerns particular ways of being such as dimension, weight, color, and so on), and it would seem more appropriate to focus our analysis of value on the so-called transcendental field, which, transcending particularities, concerns everything that exists. Transcendental properties, in fact, inhere in everything that exists by virtue of the simple fact that it exists. For example, while I cannot say that everything I see is red, I can affirm that everything I see has its own goodness or perfection.

---

18. R. Guardini, *Freedom, Grace, and Destiny: Three Chapters in the Interpretation of Existence* (Chicago: Henry Regnery Company, 1965), 88.

19. "Predicament" is the not-entirely-accurate Latin translation of the Greek term "category" used by Aristotle.

Among the various transcendentals recognized by metaphysics,[20] three refer to the relationship between reality and the human person. They are *verum, bonum,* and *pulchrum* (truth, goodness, and beauty), which indicate the relationship of reality with the intellect and will of man who apprehends, respectively, the intelligibility, goodness, and beauty of that reality. We may, then, as various authors in fact do, propound the thesis that value is associated with these three transcendentals in the sense that, just as we discover a varying degree of goodness, truth, or beauty in each single object (that is, in everything that exists), so do we understand and appraise its value and dignity, i.e., its axiological aspect. This also means that, like the transcendentals, value has its foundation in being and does not depend exclusively upon the subject who perceives it.

Although it may seem easier to demonstrate that value is an aspect of goodness, it is also possible to consider truth in an axiological sense and, hence, to establish a relationship between value and truth. They are, in any case, inseparable, i.e., our experience of values is a cognitive experience because we know the truth of a particular object as something good for us.[21]

2.2. Value, Beauty, and Truth

If we do not lose sight of the metaphysical perspective we outlined in the preceding section, we understand that values cannot be justified only in historical and sociological terms but also require a metaphysical reflection that reaches back to their ultimate causes. Bearing in mind what we said about their association with truth, goodness, and beauty, it should be clear that values need to be examined with a metahistorical and metasociological analysis. With the aim of outlining such an analysis, we can adopt the arguments used by Plato and by St. Augustine to show the absoluteness and transcendence of,

---

20. On the subject of the transcendentals, consult the second half of T. Alvira, L. Clavell, and T. Melendo, *Metaphysics* (Manila: Sinag-Tala, 1991), which also makes brief mention of the value-goodness relationship with reference to M. Scheler.

21. Cf. K. Wojtyła, "The Acting Person," in *The Yearbook of Phenomenological Research 10*, 139–143 (Dordrecht: D. Reidel, 1979). There is a "dynamic and inclusive synthesis" between the transcendentals in the sense that we cannot divide them from one another: Beauty is, as such, goodness and truth (the goodness and truth of beauty, of what is beautiful inasmuch as it is beautiful) just as goodness is beautiful and true and, in its turn, truth is good and beautiful. (cf. M.F. Sciacca, *L'uomo questo "squilibrato"* [Palermo: L'Epos, 2000], 18–19).

respectively, beauty and truth.[22] We will quote these two authors at some length so as not to deprive their reasoning of any of its force.

In his *Symposium*, Plato uses these words to describe the most exalted degree of love for beauty that may be reached through knowledge:

> When a man has been thus far tutored in the lore of love, passing from view to view of beautiful things in the right and regular ascent, suddenly he will have revealed to him, as he draws to the close of his dealings in love, a wondrous vision, beautiful in its nature.... First of all, it is ever-existent and neither comes to be nor perishes, neither waxes nor wanes; next, it is not beautiful in part and in part ugly, nor is it such at such a time and other at another, nor in one respect beautiful and in another ugly, nor so affected by position as to seem beautiful to some and ugly to others. Nor again will our initiate find the beautiful presented to him in the guise of a face or of hands or any other portion of the body, nor as a particular description or piece of knowledge, nor as existing somewhere in another substance, such as an animal or the earth or sky or any other thing but existing ever in singularity of form independent by itself while all the multitude of beautiful things partake of it in such wise that, though all of them are coming to be and perishing, it grows neither greater nor less, and is affected by nothing.[23]

This passage should not induce us into supporting the idea of a kind of Platonism of values, i.e., attributing to them a separate existence in a world by themselves. Rather, we have drawn on the Platonic argument in order to underline the fact that, although values are attributed to particular realities, this does not mean that they are entirely variable and subjective. Just as happens with beauty, we recognize the value of a thing precisely because it is not we who arbitrarily decide that value, and we learn to show greater appreciation for more exalted values with respect to less durable ones.

In order to corroborate this conclusion further, St. Augustine's views on truth are also helpful:

> We have, therefore, in the truth a possession which we can all enjoy equally and in common; there is nothing wanting or defective in it.... All cling to it; all touch it at the same time. It is a food

---

22. This argument has been suggested by, among others, B. Mondin, *Philosophical Anthropology: Man: An Impossible Project?* cit., 197–199. A very profound analysis of value with respect to *bonum*, *bonitas*, and *natura boni* is to be found in J. de Finance, *Essai sur l'agir humain* (Rome: Presses de l'Université Grégorienne, 1962), 79–92.

23. Plato, *Symposium*, 210E–211B.

that is never divided; you drink nothing from it that I cannot drink. When you share in it, you make nothing your private possession; what you take from it still remains whole for me, too.... No one ever takes any part of it for his private use, but it is wholly common to all at the same time.... No thronging crowd of hearers keeps others from approaching the beauty of truth and wisdom, provided only there is a constant will to enjoy them. Their beauty does not pass with time nor move from place to place. Night does not interrupt it nor darkness hide it, and it is not subject to bodily sense.... It changes all its beholders for the better; it is itself never changed for the worse. No one is its judge; without it no one judges rightly. Clearly, therefore, and undoubtedly it is more excellent than our minds, for it is one and yet makes each separate mind wise and the judge of other things, never of the truth.[24]

From the arguments of Plato and St. Augustine, it follows that we do not apprehend beauty and truth in an absolute sense; rather, it is by virtue of the beauty and truth that things, and we ourselves, share that we can judge something as being beautiful or true. Thus, it follows that beauty and truth are not a product of the human mind but transcend it and are universal. In the same way, the foundation of values transcends personal subjectivity and positions itself in the ontological sphere, to which man opens himself with his intelligence and his will.

It is, of course, possible to follow other routes in order to achieve an adequate understanding of value. We could, for example, examine values from a more directly personalistic perspective, focusing on the good specific to man, toward which each person tends. Yet we feel that what we have said has a certain validity also because it underlines the fact that reflection on this subject must not be superficial. Indeed, it must not be forgotten that discussion about values has, in many ways, become misleading in the end because the concept of value is often characterized by subjectivism, intimist spirituality, or psychologism. When considering this subject in the nonphilosophical sphere, it is all too easy to fall into platitude.

SUMMARY OF CHAPTER 17

People always act with a view to an end and orient their behavior toward certain values, which may be success, well-being, or wealth. We establish a hierarchy among the values that guide our activ-

---

24. Augustine, *De Libero Arbitrio*, 2, 14.

ity — that is, we consider certain values as more important than others — and this hierarchy is never completely arbitrary but has objective foundations. Values are transmitted to us by culture and education, and we learn to understand their importance thanks to personal experience. Coherence between what we hold to be important and our own personal behavior enables us to achieve complete self-fulfillment as human beings. Phenomenological arguments such as those of Max Scheler help to explain that values have objective roots, although he does not give sufficient weight to the role of freedom in an individual's orientation toward values. From a meta-physical standpoint, on the other hand, the ontological foundations of values can be demonstrated by referring to the doctrine of the transcendentals of existence, i.e., those metaphysical properties that belong to each being simply by virtue of the fact that it exists. Two of these transcendentals are truth and goodness, and value may be considered an aspect of the truth and goodness of that which exists. In order to understand that values are transcendent, in the sense that they are not subjectively created by the individual, some useful reflections are to be found in Plato on beauty and in St. Augustine on truth.

CHAPTER 18

WORK, FEAST, PLAY

1. THE WORK OF MAN IN THE WORLD

In Chapter 16 we explained that culture is a way of existence specific to man, one which characterizes his relationship with the surrounding world: He is part of that world and dependent upon it, but his response to stimuli and situations is mediated by freedom. This particular way of being part of the world is reflected in work, by which the person provides for his own needs and transforms the natural environment.

In fact, the most obvious dimension of work is precisely the relationship that has come to be established over the centuries between man and his habitat. There have been a number of decisive stages in the evolution of this relationship such as the use of fire and the fusion of metals, which reveal the essential difference between man and animals. The human person is not completely subject to the needs of the species but seeks and discovers new opportunities, and the great discoveries cannot be explained if we consider them merely as a response to elemental needs; think, for example, of the use of fire to cook food, the invention of the arrow, or agriculture. In a certain sense, we can say that it is man himself who invents new needs then resolves them.[1] Moreover, it is the human body itself, which at first sight may seem less well adapted than that of many other animals, that characterizes man's work and his relationship with the environment. For example, the erect posture and the mobility of the hands enable man to make extremely versatile use of natural objects. The human body is the worthy correlative of man's free activity.

In contrast to the way in which animals use natural resources for their own survival, the specificity of human work does not derive from some somatic trait but from the person himself. An animal tends by nature toward goodness as determined by its own needs to the good *for itself* and for its species. Man, on the other hand, self-consciously tends toward the good *in itself*, and he can, therefore, renounce an immediate good with a view to a higher good, or he can

---

1. Cf. L. Polo, *Quién es el hombre: Un espíritu en el tiempo* (Madrid: Rialp, 1998), 68–69.

consciously seek good for others.[2] The specialized and technically perfect activity of an ant, a bee, or a beaver is an insurmountable limit for those animals, but this is not true of man who freely orients himself toward an end and can change his activities or lifestyle.[3] Referring back to the etymological roots of the word "culture," we can say that man inhabits the world while cultivating it; in continuity with nature he causes new possibilities to emerge.[4]

2. THE NOTION OF WORK

Only in recent times have considerations on work begun to find space in philosophy, especially in philosophical anthropology. Studies on the subject have to take account of an unquestionable evolution in the way work is seen in the existence of the human person. Biblical Revelation throws a fundamental light on these reflections even though the relationship between Christianity and the view of work does present some problematic aspects.

Over the course of history, in fact, work has been considered as an unavoidable necessity, if not as a curse. This view has been influenced not only by a certain reading of the biblical narrative of Original Sin but also by the fact that Greek and Latin culture took a negative view of work as evinced by the words they use to describe it (πόνος and *labor*), which have an original meaning of weariness and suffering that has been transmitted into many modern languages.[5] One small sign of how persistent this viewpoint has been may be found in the words written in 1964 by J. Pieper, a philosopher who died in the late twentieth century and who made some very interesting observations on this subject: "In fact, as is well known, the

---

2. Another example is almost limitless dedication to work, as described by Isaac B. Singer in his moving short story entitled "The Washwoman": "On one of those freezing winter days the washwoman, who must have been nearly eighty, came to visit us.... My mother offered her a teapot full of tea to warm herself and gave her some bread. The old woman sat on a chair in the kitchen; she was trembling and wracked with shudders. She warmed her hands against the teapot. Her fingers were gnarled from work and perhaps from arthritis, too. Her fingernails were strangely white. These hands spoke of the stubbornness of mankind, of the will to work not within the limits of one's strength and possibilities but beyond them" (I. B. Singer, *A Day of Pleasure: Stories of a Boy Growing Up In Warsaw* [New York: Farrar, Straus, and Giroux, 1986], 80).

3. Cf. T. Melendo, *La dignidad del trabajo* (Madrid: Rialp, 1992), 220.

4. Cf. L. Polo, *Quién es el hombre: Un espíritu en el tiempo*, cit., 167.

5. However, it is important to avoid generalizations because there are variations between different periods and different authors: cf. A. Negri, *Filosofía del lavoro: Storia antologica*, Vol. I: *Dalle civiltà orientali al pensiero cristiano* (Milan: Marzorati, 1980), 147–152.

sacred texts of Christianity designate work—and, indeed, death—as a punishment."[6]

However, to an attentive reader, the Bible speaks of work as an original vocation of the human person, who was created by God to cultivate and protect the earth.[7] What emerges from Christian Revelation, then, is a fundamental equality of the dignity of work though differentiating the various professions and tasks. This truth was reaffirmed beginning in the 1930s by St. Josemaría Escrivá[8] and has been reiterated in recent magisterial teaching, particularly in St. John Paul II's encyclical *Laborem Exercens* (dated September, 14, 1981). Work is a fundamental dimension of human existence in the world, and so it remains, though characterized by fatigue, even after Original Sin.[9]

In order to arrive at an adequate notion of work, we must seek to remain equidistant between two extremes: On the one hand, an overly restricted definition that fails to include all areas of work (such as, for example, academic research, domestic work, and so on), and, on the other, defining it in such general terms that it is not then possible to distinguish its specificity with respect to other areas of human activity. Bearing in mind the views of various philosophers, Melendo gives the following definition: Work is any specifically human activity, undertaken with effort, necessary as a means and technically definable, that contributes to promoting the common good and enhances the person who performs it.[10] This, we feel, is a sufficiently ample notion, even though, as the author himself acknowledges, it does not fully resolve all the questions that arise on the subject in a changing society such as our own. Among the elements it includes, two are of more fundamental importance: the usefulness of work for an ulterior aim and the effort it involves. These two characteristics enable us to distinguish, say, a profes-

6. J. Pieper, *Zustimmung zur Welt: Eine Theorie des Festes* (Munich: Kösel-Verlag, 1964), 19. We quote this remark because we find it striking and because it is relatively recent; it would have been much easier to find similar assertions in texts and authors from earlier years.

7. Cf. Gn 2:15.

8. For an evaluation of the influence of St. Josemaría Escrivá's teachings see, among others, studies by J.L. Illanes, *The Sanctification of Work* (New York: Scepter, 2003); "*Lavoro, carità, giustizia,*" in *Santità e mondo* (Vatican City: Libreria Editrice Vaticana, 1994), 167–196; G. Faro, *Il lavoro nell'insegnamento del beato Josemaría Escrivá* (Rome: Agrilavoro Edizioni, 2000).

9. Cf. John Paul II, encyclical letter *Laborem Exercens*, 4, 9.

10. Cf. T. Melendo, *La Dignidad del Trabajo*, cit., 127–128. A broad analysis of changes in the notion of work is to be found in M.P. Chirinos, *Un'antropologia del lavoro: Il "domestico" come categoria* (Rome: Edizioni Università della Santa Croce, 2005).

sional sportsman from an amateur or a journalist from someone who keeps a diary.[11]

3. Subjective and Objective Meanings of Work

The definition of work given above alludes to one of its particularly important characteristics: that of contributing to the enhancement of the person who performs it. This means that, in order for it to be a specifically human activity that accords with the dignity of the human person, it must not only seek to achieve some external objective but must also contribute to the self-fulfillment of the individual.

It is evident that work has an objective significance as regards its tangible outcomes, i.e., the transformation of nature or of reality in general. This may be seen in agricultural work or in the crafts that produce new objects and tools but also in intellectual work, which increases that area of reality that we, with Popper and Eccles, have called "World 3" and which includes cultural heritage and theoretical and scientific systems.[12] But an activity is human when it is undertaken voluntarily with an understanding of the end in view and of the means necessary to achieve that end. And so, being a human activity, work also has a subjective significance as regards the self-fulfillment of the person who performs it; i.e., it is not just the individual procuring the means to maintain life but also his self-expression. Work, then, has an inescapable existential and ethical dimension due to the fact that "the one who carries it out is a person, a conscious and free subject, that is to say a subject that decides about himself."[13]

This explains what we said above about the fundamental equality of people who work, which is placed in a new light by Christian Rev-

---

11. This is convincingly explained in Aristotle's story of "the person who made promises to a lyre-player, promising him the more the better he sang, but in the morning, when the other demanded the fulfillment of his promises, said that he had given pleasure for pleasure" (Aristotle, *Nicomachean Ethics*, IX, 1).

12. Cf. Chapter 16, section 3.2.

13. John Paul II, encyclical letter *Laborem Exercens*, 6. Bear in mind also what we said in Chapter 14 about the self-fulfillment of the person, who forges his personality though his own activities. On the basis of the classical distinction between what is transitive and what is immanent in human acts, Wojtyła writes that "whatever man does in his actions, whatever their effect or 'product,' at the same time he is always—so to say—producing himself, expressing himself, forming himself, in some way 'creating himself'" (K. Wojtyła, *Perché l'uomo: Scritti inediti di antropologia e filosofia* [Milan: Mondadori, 1995], 182).

elation. The dignity of work does not depend exclusively on external results or on the objects produced nor on belonging to a certain social group but is associated with the dignity and enhancement of the person who performs it. Hence, *"the primary basis of the value of work is man himself."*[14] And even if a profession has less economic or social relevance, from a subjective point of view it does not lose the value it possesses for the person who performs it. It is on this basis that it becomes morally necessary to overcome situations of injustice or discrimination in the world of work because they are contrary to the dignity of the human person.

We can, then, conclude that the subjective significance of work has a preeminence with respect to the objective significance, but this does not mean that the result to be achieved through work is entirely unimportant; on the contrary, precisely because carrying out a profession is a personal act, it is always intentionally aimed at an object or goal, the adequate realization of which is a condition for the self-fulfillment of the subject.[15] Mere generic "good will" is not enough if not accompanied by the commitment to bring what we are doing to a positive conclusion. Moreover, it would be wrong and alienating to carry out a profession exclusively as a means to achieve economic gain and a higher level of well-being. These motivations, which are part of the subjective aspect, must not cause us to overlook completely the value of professionalism and the service we give thereby to society.

4. RELATIONAL SIGNIFICANCE AND ECOLOGICAL SIGNIFICANCE OF WORK

What we have just said about the service offered to society through work may be better understood if we bear in mind the inherent relationality of the person, something we discussed in Chapter 15. The complete self-fulfillment of the individual requires the development of relations with others, of a consciously experienced network

---

14. *Ibid.*, emphasis in original. In a text written in 1963, St. Josemaría Escrivá says: "In itself work is not a penalty or a curse or a punishment: those who speak of it that way have not understood Sacred Scripture properly. It is time for us Christians to shout from the rooftops that work is a gift from God and that it makes no sense to classify men differently, according to their occupation" (J. Escrivá, *Christ Is Passing By* [New York: Scepter, 1974], 47).

15. The person can, however, overcome the objective conditioning of work if he experiences it as part of the vocation and task entrusted to him by God. On this subject, see J.J. Sanguineti, *L'umanesimo del lavoro nel Beato Josemaría Escrivá: Riflessioni filosofiche, "Acta Philosophica,"* II/1 (1992), 264–278.

of social ties. Therefore, even if we have affirmed the preeminence of the subjective significance of work, this cannot lead us to consider professional activity exclusively as a source of self-satisfaction and self-affirmation. If we did we would, perhaps, obtain considerable external results, but we would fail in the task of our own inner maturation and, not infrequently, leave ourselves open to various kinds of neurosis.

It is not just a question of realizing that each of us can only carry out our own work thanks to the work of others (for example, that of the person who supplies me with electricity, raw materials, financial resources, or channels of communication); rather, understanding the relational significance of work means, above all, taking account of the fact that I can achieve my personal good only by contributing to the common good and that in all professional activities there must be an implicit attitude of service to others. Unfortunately, the individualistic mentality to which we referred in Chapters 14 and 15 makes it difficult to recognize the importance of this dimension of work, and this may also explain why, to mention just one example, many people in Italy and other wealthy nations avoid going into the nursing profession, which is so manifestly oriented toward serving others.

Furthermore, the preeminence of the subjective significance of work must not mean that, in order to achieve the aims I have set myself, I have the right to ignore the consequences my actions have on the world and the environment. There is, in fact, what we could call an "ecological" significance of work, which concerns respect for, and improvement of, the habitat in which we live. What is more, an irresponsible attitude to nature would end up turning against man himself in his present and, above all, in his immediate future.

5. Technology and the Relationship with Nature

The importance of the ecological and environmental significance of work brings us to another question, which has particular relevance today: the problem of technology, which we will mention briefly without entering into strictly ethical questions.

It is true that through work man humanizes the world and renders it habitable; makes it an environment fit for himself by building roads, bridges, and houses or planting trees and protecting forests;

but his relationship with nature (and hence also with his own body) cannot be seen only in terms of absolute dominion or exclusively as a struggle. The occurrence of natural catastrophes and the outbreak of diseases should make it clear that there are limits that must be respected and a harmony that needs to be continually regained and conserved.

Technological progress and the creation of increasingly efficient tools are signs of man's freedom, of his continuous surpassing of himself. Nonetheless, as many authors have pointed out, today we are exposed to the dangers of technocracy, i.e., of a society in which man is dominated by the technology that he himself has created. We can no longer do without this technology, and we spend a large part of our energies in maintaining and augmenting it; our lives are largely conditioned by it (think, for example, of the difficulties that arise when the electricity or water supply is interrupted or when the telephone lines break down). The problem must not be considered in isolation; rather, we must ask ourselves if current technological progress, with all its implications, facilitates or hinders the self-fulfillment and authentic existence of the human person. Or, to put it another way: The objective significance of technologically specialized work (that is, its results and the goals it sets itself) must remain in harmony with its subjective significance (i.e., with the existential and ethical dimensions) and with its relational and ecological significance.

Uncontrolled dependency on technology could lead to the destruction of the environment in which we live and, in the final analysis, to the alienation of human beings themselves. We must not forget that, from an anthropological and ethical standpoint, it may be necessary to avoid certain actions that are, in fact, technically possible. Therefore, although it is important to avoid catastrophism or purely negative views of technology, the growing interest in ecology is fully understandable.

Contrary to what is often believed, it is precisely a creationist view of the world (not completely to be identified with what is today known as "creationism" in the U.S.) that provides an adequate foundation for ecological arguments: the creation calls for respect, recognition, and protection; we can share in the divine work of creation and in a certain sense continue it, but not tyrannically appropriate it for ourselves. Hence, it is important that man does not lose his capacity to contemplate, i.e., to look at reality in itself and for itself, appreciating and enjoying its beauty, without the utilitarian or practical vision imposed by technology and by a disproportionate desire for his own well-being; otherwise, what will prevail will always be the desire to modify the world, to manipulate it, and to possess it for his own exclusive benefit.[16]

Many philosophers have examined the negative consequences that arise when technology achieves indiscriminate domination. Among them we will mention the views expressed in the works of Martin Buber, according to whom the expansion of the material world with its products, machines, and manufacturing processes causes a diminishing of interpersonal relations. The spread of selfish and utilitarian attitudes makes us less capable of establishing dialogical relationships. Indeed, one of the causes of inner solitude in man is the technology of machines which, "invented in order to serve men in their work, impressed him into their service."[17]

One final observation must be made. Today, developments in technology and in the virtual world seem to open prospects that exceed human nature itself. In some people this has consolidated the idea that it is not possible to achieve a unitary understanding of man because he seems to be in a state of continuous metamorphosis marked by a plasticity of tendencies in which each person is or could become what he himself wants to be. But this means renouncing personal identity and unconsciously placing oneself at the mercy of the people who administer and govern technology.[18]

6. Feast

It is on the basis of an adequate understanding of work, seen as a fundamental dimension of man's life on earth, that we can comprehend the meaning of feast in human existence. Just as work is a specifically human activity with which man establishes a special relationship with nature, so feast characterizes the temporal rhythm of the human person and enables him to maintain a living bond

---

16. In Pieper's view, this disinterested approach, free from any desire to dominate and subdue, can only be fully achieved if the world is considered as God's creation: cf. J. Pieper, *Was heißt philosophieren?* (Olten: Hegner, 1948), 31–32. Other very useful observations on the subject are to be found in J. Ratzinger, *In the Beginning… A Catholic Understanding of Creation and the Fall* (Edinburgh: T. & T. Clark, 1995).

17. M. Buber, *Between Man and Man* (London and New York: Routledge, 2002), 187.

18. Some examples of these attitudes are to be found in G. Deleuze, *Tecnofilosofia: Per una nuova antropologia filosofica* (Milan: Mimesis, 2000).

with his own roots and with his ultimate foundation, i.e., with transcendence.

The importance celebratory rituals have in our existence is a sign that man is a "situated" being, as so many existentialist and personalist philosophers have pointed out. This means, in the first place, that the individual is strongly rooted in his past, his history, and his circumstances. Secondly, it follows that in order for a feast to be authentic it must have an appropriate relationship with surrounding reality, a consensus regarding the world [19] without which it would only be the superficial clamor of spectacle. This is why reflections on this subject must also be related to what we will say in the next chapter concerning the temporality of the person, who is inserted in time but outstretched toward eternity.

To understand why feast enables us to keep the bond with transcendence alive, we must not limit ourselves to the most superficial and everyday meaning of the word; rather, we must think of the tendency to "celebrate" that is inherent to every culture. People celebrate what they consider to be important, and more solemnly the more exalted the values involved are. People rejoice for a birth or a marriage, for the harvest in the fields or the beginning of the year, for coming of age or the arrival of spring. Feast is related to the origins of man, to the fundamental truths of his existence, to what defines and transcends his life, to his desire for happiness. Hence, feast has particular importance and solemnity when it involves religious values, and it is closely connected to what we said in Chapter 15 about the virtue of *pietas*, through which we honor God, family, and homeland.

It becomes clear just how important feasts are in maintaining the bond with our roots alive if we consider what happened at the time of the French Revolution and in Nazi Germany and the Soviet Union during the twentieth century: The newly established regimes immediately instituted new feasts in order to transform popular culture rapidly and deeply, uprooting it from its past.[20]

Finally, mention must be made of two other important anthropological elements that are present in feast though not directly associated with our reflections on work. Firstly, human feast reveals the inher-

---

19. This is one of the principal theories supported in J. Pieper, *Zustimmung zur Welt: Eine Theorie des Festes* (Munich: Kösel-Verlag, 1964).

20. See the interesting historical references contained in J. Pieper, *Zustimmung zur Welt: Eine Theorie des Festes*, cit., 97–104, 111–119.

ent relationality of the person because we celebrate in communion, at least spiritual communion, with others. Secondly, the propensity to celebrate is a sign of the unquenchable desire for happiness that is inherent to the human individual, a desire never fully satisfied in the course of his personal history.

7. PLAY

It is likewise on the basis of an adequate understanding of work that we are able to comprehend the particularity of play and to consider it as a dimension of existence associated with the self-fulfillment and self-expression of the human person, though its role changes from infancy to adulthood. Play is often part of feast; it is not just an expression of the need for physical repose, distraction, or entertainment (understood as the interruption of physical or mental effort and the performance of a pleasurable activity) but also involves the human person's creativity, his capacity to detach himself from, and laugh at, reality. Both feast and play have the essential characteristic of being an end unto themselves, i.e., of not referring to some external utilitarian goal of self-interest or material need.[21] Nonetheless, feast and play are not equivalents: In the act of feast, the reason for which we celebrate is important; it is what fills the feast with meaning: "In fact, human activity receives its meaning above all from its content, through its own object, not through the 'how' but through the 'what.'"[22]

Taking human recreational activity as an interpretative model, it is possible to create a philosophy or theory of play, in various fields, and it is in this context that this subject has importance today. Consider how, in a game, the effect of a move contains an element of imponderability because what we do always depends on what others do; there is a close interdependence because we win or lose not only through our own capacities but also as a consequence of the capacities or incapacities of others. Moreover, players can agree

---

21. Analogously, it can be said that animals (especially baby animals) play and that play is also to be found in natural phenomena (thus we speak of the "play of the waves," the "play of colors," the "play of the light," and so on). All these phenomena share the characteristic of being ends unto themselves, yet, when we move into the sphere of human existence, we must take into account the awareness and freedom with which man acts, by virtue of which he knows he is playing and wants to play.

22. J. Pieper, *Zustimmung zur Welt: Eine Theorie des Festes*, cit., 26; this book contains detailed reflections on the meaning of feast, also with reference to play.

among themselves, and such an agreement may be respected or disregarded.

This perspective can be applied, for example, in the field of sociology: Just as each player has his own role in a game, so each individual has a role in society (this is the so-called "role theory" propounded by, among others G. H. Mead, R. Linton, and T. Parsons); the activities of social interaction can be seen and explained as a game in which participants win and help others to win.[23] The same perspective can be applied in the field of economics: In 1994 the Nobel Prize in Economics was won by three academics (J. C. Harsanyi, J. F. Nash, and R. Selten) who, examining the world of finance (especially macroeconomics and the management of industry), observed the importance of what are known as "noncooperative games" to predict the results of strategic economic interactions, to analyze the influence of presumptions of error in the decision-making process, and to study the behavior of financiers who do not have all the necessary information. The perspective can also be used in the field of biology where, in fact, we speak of the strategy (game) living organisms use to survive. This interpretive model is also used to an even greater extent in hermeneutics and in psychology.

To summarize, the living being may be considered as a player and his activity of self-organization and self-development as the game in which he participates, observing its rules (this also enters everyday language with such phrases as "I'm playing for my life"). Play, in fact, fulfills all the conditions of an "open system"; that is, a system that is not absolutely and rigidly predetermined but depends upon the creativity and freedom of individuals.[24]

Nonetheless, we must avoid unduly expanding the scope of play because not only would it lose its specificity but also we would run the risk taking the wrong approach to real life. Either everything would become a game, with the consequent lack of commitment and reflection, or everything would become serious, and we would lose our capacity to detach ourselves from the burdens of everyday life.[25] Furthermore, from a psychological and sociological standpoint, many scholars warn against the dangers inherent to the age of electronic

23. Cf. L. Polo, *Quién es el hombre: Un espíritu en el tiempo*, cit., 143–144.

24. Cf. *ibid*, 32–33, 70–71.

25. Cf. R. Yepes, "*La región de lo lúdico: Reflexión sobre el fin y la forma del juego*," in *Cuadernos de Anuario Filosófico 30*, 9 (Pamplona: Serie Universitaria, 1996). The book also contains a useful bibliography on the subject of play.

communication, video games, and so-called "virtual reality": Often we risk losing an authentic perception of our relations with others, of the foundations of reality, and even of our own personality.

SUMMARY OF CHAPTER 18

Work may be considered as a human activity: an activity that requires exertion that is necessary as a means to reach a further goal, needs technical skill, and is oriented to the common good and the enhancement of the person who performs it. From an anthropological viewpoint, work may be seen as having a fourfold significance: subjective (the personal fulfillment of the worker), objective (the result produced), relational (the service to others and to the common good), and ecological (respect for and improvement of the natural environment). Reflecting on these four aspects also helps to highlight the risks of technocracy, that is, of technical and scientific development that does not respect the dignity of the human person or ecology. Feast and play are related to work. Feast marks the temporal rhythm of the human person and enables him to maintain a living bond with his own roots and with his ultimate foundation, i.e., with transcendence. Play does not arise just from the need for physical repose, distraction, or entertainment but is associated with the self-fulfillment and self-expression of the person.

CHAPTER 19
TIME AND HISTORY

1. HISTORY AND FREEDOM

In order to know a person, we generally seek to learn where and when he was born, what he has done, from what family he comes; to put it briefly, we seek to learn his history, his historical circumstances. It is, of course, obvious that each man has his own history, but in considering this fundamental anthropological characteristic, we must avoid falling into two opposing extremes.

On the one hand we must avoid the various kinds of historicism that hold man is his history, that historicity is the essential and defining characteristic of man, an unsurpassable horizon that entirely comprehends the meaning of human life. According to this view there can be no truth about man because all knowledge would be the product of a particular age; everything would depend on the current historical moment.[1] On the other hand, it is important not to succumb to a static vision of the person, i.e., to a kind of substantialism that considers historicity as an accident without importance for the human person, when, in fact, it is a property that cannot be separated from his situation in the world.

History is closely associated with the freedom of man, who is not impelled by his nature in a single direction but freely impels himself toward certain of the possibilities that are offered to him, opening new ones and precluding others. Attitudes taken and decisions made affect each of us as human beings, but they are not a burden imposed upon us because they could have been different from how in fact they are. It is precisely this free initiative of the person that makes history of what would otherwise be only measurable temporality. By giving responses that are not unequivocally imposed

---

1. For this reason, proponents of historicism—among them W. Dilthey, B. Croce, and A. Gramsci—reject any metaphysical perspective capable of abstracting universal and suprahistorical values from changing reality.

by the stimulus, man opens himself to nonnecessary possibilities.[2]
Therefore, we can say, with Heidegger, that while objects (especially
inanimate objects but also plants and animals) are like things already
taken as given, only man exists in the proper sense; i.e., he is in a
conscious relationship with the possibilities of his own existence.[3]
A rock may bear the marks of passing time, but that is something
quite different from the events of my life, which I can narrate.

However, the self-determination of the individual considered in this
way must not make us think of a contrast between human nature,
seen as a stable foundation, and freedom, seen as the progressive
historical fulfillment of the individual. Freedom is not in contrast
with human nature; rather, it is a specific property of human nature.
Historicity, therefore, is rooted in the dynamism and potential of our
being: The individual is not mere mobility, pure occurrence, but has
a permanent ontological unity, which, as we have seen, has its own
orientation and suprahistorical dimension.

2. Cyclical and Linear Nature of History

Before examining certain aspects of the temporality of the individual
more closely, let us briefly mention two interpretive paradigms of
history. Temporal succession, or the succession of historical events,
can be interpreted using a cyclical or a linear model. According to
some scholars the oldest interpretations of history, among both
Greeks and Romans, followed a cyclical conception of time. Plato,
for example, held that any cosmic or social event reflects its own
paradigm in the eternal world of ideas; time passes in accordance
with a cyclical process based on a perfect numerical proportion.[4]
Aristotle was also of the opinion that the rotational movement of the
heavens indicated the cyclical eternity of time.[5] Greek history held
that what effectively exists is the *perihodos*, the "period" of rotation

---

2. Cf. J. Cruz Cruz, *Filosofía de la historia* (Pamplona: Eunsa, 1995), 22–23, 123. As
   Pieper says: "An event becomes historical when what is specifically human comes
   into play in it: freedom, responsibility, decision, and therefore also the possibility
   of willful blunder and guilt" (J. Pieper, *Hope and History: Five Salzburg Lectures*,
   tr. D. Kipp [San Francisco: Ignatius Press, 1994], 34).

3. Cf. M. Heidegger, *Being and Time*, cit., §§9, 72. In this sense, we can also affirm,
   as we did in section 2 of Chapter 13, that only man dies in the true sense because
   only he is conscious of death, whereas other living beings perish and decay:
   cf. M.F. Sciacca, *Morte e immortalità* (Palermo: L'Epos, 1990), 134.

4. Cf. Plato, *Timaeus*, 33A–38E.

5. Cf. Aristotle, *Physics*, 223 b 19.

(always the same) of the heavens,[6] and the Stoics also believed that the world was subject to an infinite cycle of birth and death, which followed precise intervals.[7]

Christian Revelation, on the other hand, introduced and established a linear conception of history: Man and the cosmos were created by God from nothing, and their temporal trajectory consists in establishing the Kingdom of God until man comes to participate in divine eternity. With the unique and unrepeatable event of the Incarnation, history and time acquire a positive connotation; they are not the pallid reflection of a preexisting ideal world but derive from the impulse of the creative act in which human freedom has a share. St. Augustine explains how, in the cyclical conception of time and the doctrine of reincarnation, the immortal soul endlessly tends toward false happiness and endlessly returns to true unhappiness.[8] And Löwith notes that the cyclical theory, which is of pagan origin, is without hope because hope and faith are by their essence linked to the future, and there can be no true future if time past and time to come are seen as equivalent phases within a constant cycle of recurrence that has neither beginning nor end.[9]

Nonetheless, however well founded it may be, we must not overstate the dichotomy between cyclical and linear time;[10] rather, they should be seen as two dimensions that work at different levels or that constitute a spiral, or helicoid, process. Moreover, even from a historiographical perspective, cyclical periodization has not completely disappeared. Suffice it to mention the doctrine of the stages of nations, or the *corsi* and *ricorsi* of history, as elaborated by Giambattista Vico (1668–1744). It is also true that individual temporality, as we will see, develops following precise rhythms and a series of alternations that tend to harmonize with cosmic time and nature: day and night; sleep and waking; tiredness and rest; enjoyment and hope; birth and death.[11]

6. Cf. H.G. Gadamer, *"Die Kontinuität der Geschichte und der Augenblick der Existenz"* in *Gesammelte Werke*, cit.,Vol. II, 154.

7. On the subject of the circular or cyclical periodization of antiquity, see J. Cruz Cruz, *Filosofía de la historia*, cit., 75–79, 91–108; M. Castagnino and J.J. Sanguineti, *Tempo e universo: Un approccio filosófico e scientifico* (Rome: Armando, 2000), 67–74.

8. Cf. Augustine, *De Civitate Dei*, XII, 20, 2–3.

9. Cf. K. Löwith, *Meaning in History* (Chicago: University of Chicago Press, 1949), 163–164.

10. Cf. J.J. Sanguineti, *Scienza aristotelica e scienza moderna* (Rome: Armando, 1992), 88.

11. Cf. R.Yepes, *Fundamentos de antropología* (Pamplona: Eunsa, 1996), 404–405.

The prevalence of the linear paradigm in the interpretation of history, precisely because of its Christian roots, induces us to see the course of history as a progression toward a transcendent future. It is a typically Christian attitude to feel oneself to be heir to earlier conquests while at the same time avoiding closure or overly rigid schematism. Think of the constructive approach of scholastic philosophers toward both Greek and Muslim thinkers. Over the centuries humanity has had an internal finality, by virtue of which the succession of generations and of individual events acquires unity and intelligibility. This is why St. Bonaventure could liken the history of the world to a poem, the beauty of which can only be appreciated by a broad vision not limited to the individual words. In the same way, St. Augustine was able to consider the spread of the Roman Empire and its culture as providential (though the source of cruel persecutions) because it eventually became the foundation for the propagation of Christianity.[12]

This historical view has had considerable influence on later attempts to explain universal history, although the tension toward God is often replaced by the action of some immanent force or by the definitive attainment of some earthly outcome. This secularization of the Christian idea of providence has given rise to totalitarian concepts, that is, concepts that seek to accomplish the complete development of progress or to reach an insurmountable pinnacle of history. However, although a teleology of history and society does exist, an insuperable and static situation of development will never be achieved because it is an impossible goal at all levels: individual, social, or historical. The dynamic nature of freedom makes progress an open-ended series of events. In a utopia this series is artificially closed, but an idea, however perfect it may be, can never fully cover every aspect of concrete reality.[13] It would be a utopian idea to chase after the myth of progress in itself, imagining a perfect mechanism of constant growth toward an epoch of definitive and timeless perfection. Human action, precisely because it is ethical, implies the need to decide in the face of various alternatives and is *per se* open to enhancement or failure.[14]

---

12. Cf. É. Gilson, *The Spirit of Mediæval Philosophy* (New York: Charles Scribner's Sons, 1940), 383–402.

13. Cf. J. Choza, *La realización del hombre en la cultura* (Madrid: Rialp, 1990), 127.

14. Cf. L. Polo, *Quién es el hombre: Un espíritu en el tiempo* (Madrid: Rialp, 1998), 107, 119.

3. BIOGRAPHICAL TEMPORALITY

We will now turn our attention to the temporality of the individual. This is something of which we have constant experience: We are aware of successive changes in ourselves and in those around us; we are aware that time passes or that we lack time; we abandon ourselves to memories of the past and elaborate projects for the future.

Considered objectively, i.e., from the standpoint of one who studies the human person, human temporality has three aspects: One concerns the corporeal state understood as an organism whose activity (including conception, birth, growth, and aging) constitutes life in the biological sense; another concerns human existence as a conscious continuum of lived experiences, choices made and insertion into a historical epoch, which is life in a biographical sense; and the final one concerns the aspect of man's spiritual tension toward eternity, which is expressed in his religiosity and his constant projection toward the future (something we have already mentioned when discussing self-transcendence in Chapter 14 and to which we will return at the end of this chapter).

If, on the other hand, we examine human temporality subjectively, i.e., from the standpoint of the person himself, we find that the three aforementioned aspects are closely melded together: The organic processes have an effect on our consciousness, which in turn has an influence on them, while the spiritual tension involves the body and orients the choices we make. This is why, in order to reach a full understanding of an individual, we have to take his past, present, and future into account; in other words, we have to consider his entire personal universe also from a temporal perspective because he possesses a profound unity.

The reference to subjectivity is very important for our study because, if spiritual consciousness did not exist, then time (which is formally a measure of movement) would not exist in any real sense either. Thus, as we said in the first section of this chapter, animals are not, properly speaking, historical because their awareness is completely immersed in the flux of their existence —"only a consciousness that is not itself entirely temporal can have a measure of movement; i.e., of time"[15]— and only in human consciousness does time pres-

---

15. J. Cruz Cruz, *Filosofía de la historia*, cit., 121. On this subject see also M. Castagnino and J.J. Sanguineti, *Tempo e universo: Un approccio filosofico e scientifico*, cit., 47–48.

ent itself as a simultaneous totality in which past and future inhere in the present of our lifespan.

3.1. Past, Present, and Future

As regards the way that man, with his subjectivity, experiences time and lives in time, we can speak of three "stages": the past, which we experience with memory; the present, which we experience with attention; and the future, which we experience with hope and expectation.[16]

Heidegger speaks of the three "ecstasies" of time, using that word in its etymological meaning of "outside the self": The future is the meaning of existence, man's projection toward a possibility; the past is what has been, which never fully disappears; the present is his proximity to things.[17]

As regards the first of the "stages," it must be said that it is precisely with memory and tradition that history is born. Cicero, in fact, called it *vita memoriæ* ("life of memory").[18] Obviously, history cannot be reduced to a simple act of recollection but comes into being through man's self-interrogation about his own origins and past because it is a fundamental question in his understanding of himself.[19]

There is, in fact, a close bond between past and present in man. According to St. Augustine, memory is the connective tissue of the life of the spirit because "one who works ought to have respect to both [beginning and end]. For he who in every forthputting of activity does not look back on the beginning does not look forward to the end."[20] A man without a past would be unsettled and disoriented.[21] Augustine's observations find confirmation in neurology: From a

16. Cf. L. Pareyson, *Essere e libertà: Il principio e la dialettica*, in "Annuario filosofico" 10, 22 (1994); the direct source is St. Augustine, according to whom these three "times" exist and are present only in the human soul; thus does he speak of "*præsens de præteritis memoria, præsens de præsentibus contuitus, præsens de futuris exspectatio*" ("a present of things past, a present of things present, and a present of things future": *Confessions*, 11, 20, 26).

17. Cf. M. Heidegger, *Being and Time*, cit., §§ 68–69, 79; S. Vanni Rovighi, *Uomo e natura: Appunti per una antropología filosófica* (Milan: Vita e Pensiero, 1980), 161.

18. Marcus Tullius Cicero, *De Oratore*, II, 9, 36.

19. J. Cruz Cruz, *Filosofía de la historia*, cit., 13–14, 23.

20. Augustine, *De Civitate Dei*, VII, 7.

21. It is on individual memory that collective memory is founded, as is evident in the history of peoples who defend and hand down their past and customs. A heritage of memories represents an indispensable mental resource in maturity, a resource from which we also draw in order to innovate: cf. C. Lasch, *The Culture of Narcissism* (London and New York: W.W. Norton, 1991), XVI–XVIII.

psychological and neurological perspective, the temporal organization of human consciousness is based on a chronological paradigm of past-present-future. Conscious awareness of the present includes not only recollection of episodes from the past but also prevision of future events. Such anticipation involves a complex series of mental processes, including the recollection of previous anticipations of the future.

D. H. Ingvar and J. Eccles speak, respectively, of *memory of the future* and of *memorized anticipations*, alluding to our recollection of the anticipations that arise when we think about future actions with all their possible consequences. An excellent model of this process is to be found in the game of chess: Each player makes his own move while remembering the moves thus far made and seeking to forecast the possible countermoves of his adversary. These ideas have been corroborated in scientific experiments that measure the increased blood flow to the prefrontal cortex of the brain during so-called "daydreams," i.e., those situations in which the subject contemplates what could happen or what he would like to happen in the future. Moreover, it has been shown that damage to that area of the brain can provoke the syndrome of "loss of the future," the symptoms of which include apathy, lack of ambition, and scant capacity to plan ahead.[22]

In any case, the way in which the human person approaches the future is highly specific because it is always accompanied by an awareness of his own mortality not in the sense that we are constantly thinking of the certainty that we must die but in the sense that we seek to foresee a future that we know not to be indefinite and that we perceive as being an opportunity to be seized, a one-off adventure. If this were not so, we would fall prey to indecision and inertia, a situation well described in Borges's short story entitled *El inmortal* in which he portrays a city inhabited by people who are not subject to death and in whose lives — past, present, and future — become confused to such a degree as to lead them to a state of inertia and indifference.[23]

---

22. Cf. J. C. Eccles, *Evolution of the Brain: Creation of the Self*, cit., 240. Lersch notes that "mental life is thus entirely filled with impulses that induce us to reach states that we do not yet possess and that constitute, so to say, guidelines in the directives and designs of life. Each moment of mental life thus contains an anticipation of the future, an impulse to tend toward something that may not even be in the subject's consciousness" (P. Lersch, *Der Aufbau des Charakters*, cit., 134).

23. Cf. J. L. Borges, "*El inmortal*," in *El Aleph* (Madrid: Alianza, 2000), 7–31.

3.2. Haste, Preoccupation, and the Life Project

The way in which we experience the present can give rise to haste, a typically human phenomenon that is often the result of acceleration, the increase in pace that technology enables and provokes. However, such behavior can generate anxiety and other pathological symptoms that derive from the interruption of natural rhythms.[24] Here, too, the specificity of man emerges: Animals are never in a hurry and remain subject to natural rhythms; man, on the other hand, since he eludes mere materiality, seeks to surpass temporal limits and to dominate them in order to reach a goal (think, for example, of the use we make of clocks). As Heidegger says, man would not be preoccupied if he were completely predetermined, if his path were already laid down, if he were completely constrained by a *de facto* situation, if he did not have the possibility almost of being ahead of himself (*Sich-vorweg-sein*), of forerunning and choosing from various possibilities. Thus, preoccupation is the way of being of one who is, at one and the same time, constrained and free.[25]

We have already remarked — when discussing authenticity and the personal life project — on the need to coordinate past, present, and future in individual existence:[26] Man can authentically fulfill himself only by assuming a correct approach toward these temporal factors. Unbalanced attention on the part of the individual toward just one of these dimensions of temporality would lead him into inauthentic and immature behavior.

Quoting the conclusions reached by a psychiatrist, we can say:

> A mature man is one whose temporal equation may be described as follows: he lives situated in a present in which the past is digested and everything is impregnated with the future. He has overcome his traumas and has no need to go over and over his past because he has been able to absorb it; he looks ahead and prepares to achieve his goals.[27]

---

24. Cf. R. Yepes, *Fundamentos de antropología*, cit., 406.

25. Cf. M. Heidegger, *Being and Time*, cit., § 40; S. Vanni Rovighi, *Uomo e natura: Appunti per una antropología filosófica*, cit., 156.

26. Cf. also the explanations of C. Taylor concerning the identity of the self and the so-called "punctual," or "neutral," self in *Sources of the Self* (Cambridge, MA: Harvard University Press, 1994), 27–30, 159–176.

27. E. Rojas, *Una teoria della felicità* (Cinisello Balsamo: Paoline, 1989), 225. Just how important continuity among past, present, and future is for the success of individual life is also highlighted by R. Spaemann, *Basic Moral Concepts*, cit., 27.

This may be better understood if we reflect upon the fact that, for example, an excessive dependence on present circumstances would mean an incapacity to channel those circumstances toward an end, toward a project we seek to achieve by knowing ourselves and our past;[28] we would end up by merely conforming ourselves to our environment.

It must also be pointed out that man has a tendency to evade his own historical time and that this tendency, partly inherent by virtue of his self-transcendence, is reinforced by the modern world of technology and communications in which newer and more appetizing possibilities and models are constantly being presented to us. This can lead people to experience their own present with a sense of mediocrity and frustration with respect to what they would like to obtain. It follows that there is an increasing production of myths toward which to project and identify ourselves, and by means of which we evade our own real history. Think, to mention only the most superficial aspects, of the phenomenon of celebrities, escapist literature, or so-called "status symbols," which become objects of desire.[29]

3.3. Hope and the Desire for Eternity

Over and above these typical characteristics of modern civilization, the tendency of the human person to project himself beyond time is more profoundly expressed in hope and in the desire for happiness that characterize human existence.

With reference to the ideas of Gabriel Marcel, we can say that hope is not simply desire, which is circumscribed to particular objects;[30] nor is it mere optimism, which is superficially to await a happy outcome; nor is it pure vitality.[31] Rather, when we feel a hope, even with respect to a well-defined object or a precise goal, that objective is always part of a wider project and a further request. Hence, we can say that we hope at one and the same time for "something" and

---

28. Cf. A. Polaino-Lorente, *Amore coniugale e maturità personale: Fattori psicologici e psicopatologici* (Cinisello Balsamo: Paoline, 1994), 16–17.

29. Cf. J. Cruz Cruz, *Filosofía de la historia*, cit., 123–126, which makes reference, among other things, to the ideas of M. Eliade on the value of myth, and of U. Eco on the devaluation of time.

30. Cf. G. Marcel, *Homo Viator: Introduction to the Metaphysic of Hope* (Gloucester, MA: Peter Smith, 1978), 33–34.

31. Cf. *ibid*, 36–39.

for "everything"[32] because that result is always associated with the whole of our life. Human hope, in its awareness and authenticity, implies recognition of one's own finiteness and openness to a transcendent dimension, the experience of limitation, and the tendency to surpass it. Hope is not the simple projection of a human need but the gratuitous and fulfilling response to the search of a man who does not content himself with finite and transient goods but is orientated toward goodness in its entirety.

For this reason, authentic hope is a sign of the human condition as *ens religatum*,[33] which owes the possibility of its complete fulfillment to God, who is transcendent and perfect good. In this sense, the thought of our own death not only does not prevent us from hoping but is, or can be, an important element reinforcing our intimate perception of the fact that what we hope eludes tangible images of a life in the world, goes beyond any calculations we can perform, and lies outside our control.

Man's condition on earth is that of seeking, tending beyond, awaiting, planning, hoping: "The condition of being on a journey represents the most intimate constitution of a creature's being. It is the intrinsic and entitative 'not yet' of created things."[34] Human hope contains traces of something not yet definitively accomplished but for which we long, the imprint of eternity to which we aspire in history.[35] And clearly hope is intertwined with the desire for happiness, which is characteristic of human beings and which is given such importance by classical philosophy;[36] desire for happiness, in the final analysis, is desire for eternity.[37]

32. Cf. P. Laín Entralgo, *La espera y la esperanza: Historia y teoría del esperar humano* (Madrid: Alianza, 1984), 581. On the anthropology of hope of the doctor-philosopher Laín Entralgo, consult M.T. Russo, *La ferita di Chirone: Itinerari di antropología ed ética in medicina* (Milan: Vita e Pensiero, 2006), 251–266.

33. Cf. P. Laín Entralgo, *La espera y la esperanza: Historia y teoría del esperar humano*, cit., 583–584. Here there is explicit reference to the terminology of X. Zubiri.

34. J. Pieper, *Über die Hoffnung* (Leipzig: Jakob Hegner, 1935), 15.

35. This is why G. Marcel speaks of hope as a "spring" or a "leap" over time toward transcendence: cf. *Être et avoir* (Paris: Aubier-Montaigne, 1935), 115.

36. See the comments of Thomas Aquinas on this subject in book III of his *Summa Contra Gentiles*, in which he draws on the arguments of ancient philosophers, particularly Aristotle.

37. Do not forget what Plato said concerning the fact that men not only desire the good to be theirs "but theirs always.... Love loves the good to be one's own for ever"(Plato, *Symposium*, 206A).

SUMMARY OF CHAPTER 19

The human person is a historical being thanks to his freedom. Precisely because he is free, the person can act in a way that is not determined exclusively by nature, for while the traces of passing time are to be found in everything that exists, only the human person can narrate the story of his life. The individual lives his temporality with reference to the past, the present, and the future, experiencing the past with memory, the present with attention, and the future with expectation. In order to fulfill himself, the person must maintain a correct relationship with these three "stages" of time: He cannot seek refuge only in memories of the past, he cannot be concerned only with the present instant, and he cannot live dreaming only about the future. However, the human person is constantly oriented toward the future, and this is a sign of his inherent desire for eternity, of his hope for a fuller and more lasting happiness.

BIBLIOGRAPHY

Agostino, *La speranza*. Rome: Città Nuova, 2002.

Albanese, B., *"Persona (storia),"* in *Enciclopedia del Diritto*, 169–181. Milan: Giuffrè, 1983.

Alici, L., *L'altro nell'io: In dialogo con Agostino*. Rome: Città Nuova, 1999.

Alici, L., R. Piccolomini, and A. Pieretti, *Il mistero del male e la libertà possibile*, vol II: *Linee di antropología agostiniana*. Rome: Institutum Patristicum Augustinianum, 1995.

Alvira, T., L. Clavell, and T. Melendo, *Metaphysics*. Manila: Sinag-Tala, 1991.

Arendt, H., *The Human Condition*. Chicago: The University of Chicago Press, 1958.

Aristotle, *Metaphysics*. London — Cambridge, MA: Harvard University Press, 1993.

———, *Nicomachean Ethics*. London — Cambridge, MA: Harvard University Press, 1962.

———, *On the Soul*. London — Cambridge, MA: Harvard University Press, 1975.

———, *Parts of Animals*. London — Cambridge, MA: Harvard University Press, 1998.

———, *Politics*. London — Cambridge, MA: Harvard University Press, 1990.

Arnold, W., H.J. Eysenck, and R. Meili, *Encyclopedia of Psychology*. New York: The Seabury Press, 1972.

Artigas, M., *Le frontiere dell'evoluzionismo*. Milan: Ares, 1993.

Artigas, M., and J.J. Sanguineti, *Filosofia della natura*. Florence: Le Monnier, 1989.

Augustine, *Confessions*. Oxford: Clarndon Press, 1992.

———, *Letters*. Hyde Park, NY: New City Press, 2003.

———, *Of True Religion*. London: Regnery / Gateway, 1991.

———, *Sermons*. Hyde Park, NY: New City Press, 1990.

———, *The City of God*. Washington, D.C.: Catholic University of America Press, 1981.

———, *The Teacher: The Free Choice of the Will; Grace and Free Will*. Washington, D.C.: The Catholic University of America Press, 1990.

———, *The Trinity*. Washington, D.C.: The Catholic University of America Press, 1992.

———, *Tractates on the Gospel of John*. Washington, D.C.: The Catholic University of America Press, 1988–1995.

Ballesteros, J., *"La costituzione dell'immagine attuale dell'uomo,"* in I. Yarza, *Immagini dell'uomo: Percorsi antropologici nella filosofía moderna*, 23–37. Rome: Armando, 1997.

Basti, G., *"Dall'informazione allo spirito: abbozzo di una nuova antropologia,"* in *L'anima*, 48. Milan: Mondadori, 2004.

Berdyaev, N., *Slavery and Freedom*. London: G. Bles, 1943.

Bergson, H., *Essai sur les données immediates de la conscience*. Paris: PUF, 1970.

———, *Il riso: Saggio sul significato del comico*. Rome and Bari: Laterza, 1994.

Berti, E., *Profilo di Aristotele*. Rome: Studium, 1979.

Blondel, M., *Action (1893)*. Notre Dame, IN: University of Notre Dame Press, 2007.

Bochenski, J.M., *Autorität, Freiheit, Glaube: Sozialphilosophische Studien*. Munich and Vienna: Philosophia, 1988.

Boethius, S., *The Theological Tractates*. London — Cambridge, MA: W. Heineman / Harvard University Press, 1953.

Borges, J.L., *"El inmortal,"* in *El Aleph*, 7–31. Madrid: Alianza, 2000.

Borghi, L., *L'antropologia tomista e il* body-mind problem *(alla ricerca di un contributo mancante)*, "Acta Philosophica," II/1, 279–292. 1992.

Brock, S.L., *"Tommaso d'Aquino e lo statuto fisico dell'anima spirituale,"* in *L'anima*, 69–72. Milan: Mondadori, 2004.

————, *Action and Conduct: Thomas Aquinas and the Theory of Action*. Edinburgh: T&T Clark, 1998.

Brown, H., *Brain and Behavior: A Textbook of Physiological Psychology*. Oxford: Oxford University Press, 1976.

Buber, M., *Between Man and Man*. London and NewYork: Routledge, 2002.

————, *Il problema dell'uomo*. Leumann: Elledici, 1990.

Campodonico, A., *Etica della ragione: La filosofia dell'uomo tra nichilismo e confronto interculturale*. Milan: Jaca Book, 2000.

Cardona, C., *Metafisica del bene e del male*. Milan: Ares, 1991.

Cassirer, E., *An Essay on Man: An Introduction to a Philosophy of Human Culture*. Garden City, NY: Doubleday and Co., 1953.

Castagnino, M., and J.J. Sanguineti, *Tempo e universo: Un approccio filosófico e scientifico*. Rome: Armando, 2000.

Cazzullo, C.L., "*La libertà nell'interpretazione della struttura e della dinamica della personalità*," in F. Russo and J.Villanueva (eds.), *Le dimensioni della libertà nel dibattito scientifico e filosófico*, 44–45. Rome: Armando, 1995.

Cervós-Navarro, J.,"*Libertà umana e neurofisiologia*," in F. Russo and J.Villanueva (eds.), *Le dimensioni della libertà nel dibattito scientifico e filosófico*, 25–34. Rome: Armando, 1995.

Chirinos, M.P., *Un'antropologia del lavoro: Il "domestico" come categoria*. Rome: Edizioni Università della Santa Croce, 2005.

Choza, J., *La realización del hombre en la cultura*. Madrid: Rialp, 1990.

————, *Manual de antropología filosófica*. Madrid: Rialp, 1988.

Cicero, Marcus Tullius, *De Officiis*.

————, *De Oratore*.

Colom, E., and A. Rodríguez Luño, *Scelti in Cristo per essere santi: Elementi di Teologia morale fondamentale*. Rome: Edizioni Università della Santa Croce, 2003.

Conti, E., "*Antropologia filosofica in Italia*," "*La Scuola Cattolica*," 31–74. 2004.

Coreth, E., *Antropología filosófica*. Brescia: Morcelliana, 1991.

————, *Was ist der Mensch? Grundzüge einer philosophischen Anthropologie*. Innsbruck and Vienna: Tyrolia, 1986.

Cotta, S., "*Persona (filosofia del diritto)*," in *Enciclopedia del diritto*,Vol. XXXIII, 162–167. Milan: Giuffrè, 1983.

Crosby, J.F., *The Selfhood of the Human Person*. Washington, D.C.: The Catholic University of America Press, 1996.

Cruz Cruz, J., *Filosofía de la historia*. Pamplona: Eunsa, 1995.

D'Agostino, F., "*Pluralismo culturale e universalità dei diritti*," "*Acta Philosophica*," II/2, 230–231. 1993.

Dawson, C., *Religion and the Rise of Western Culture*. NewYork: Doubleday, 1991.

De Finance, J., *Essai sur l'agir humain*. Rome: Presses de l'Université Grégorienne, 1962.

De Leo, G., "*Vuoto esistenziale e devianza minorile: Elementi per una lettura psico-sociologica*," in E. Fizzotti and A. Gismondi (eds.), *Giovani, vuoto esistenziale e ricerca di senso: La sfida della logoterapia*. Rome: Las, 1998.

Deleuze, G., *Tecnofilosofia: Per una nuova antropologia filosofica*. Milan: Mimesis, 2000.

Descartes, R., *I principi della filosofia*, Pars Prima.Torino: Bollati Boringhieri, 1992.

Donati, P., *Pensiero sociale cristiano e società post-moderna*. Rome: A.V.E., 1997.

Donati, P., and I. Colozzi, *Giovani e generazioni: Quando si cresce in una società eticamente neutra*. Bologna: Il Mulino, 1997.

Eccles, J.C., *Evolution of the Brain: Creation of the Self*. London and NewYork: Routledge, 1989.

Echarte, L. E., *Limiti e classificazione del nuovo campo della Neuroeticà: Identità, responsabilità, informazione e manipolazione del cervello, "Medic. Metodologia didattica e innovazione clinica: Nuova Serie,"* 2 / 12, 19–20. 2004.

Esclanda, R., and F. Russo, *Homo patiens: prospettive sulla sofferenza umana.* Rome: Armando, 2003.

Escrivá, J., "Human Virtues," in *Friends of God.* London: Scepter, 1981.

———, *Christ Is Passing By.* New York: Scepter, 1974.

———, *Conversations with Monsignor Escrivá de Balaguer.* Sydney: Little Hills & Scepter, 1993.

Fabro, C., *Il personalismo.* Rome: A.V. E., 1974.

———, *L'Anima: Introduzione al problema dell'uomo.* Segni: Edivi, 2005.

———, *Percezione e pensiero.* Brescia: Morcelliana, 1962.

———, *Riflessioni sulla libertà.* Segni: Edivi, 2004.

Facchini, F., *Origini dell'uomo ed evoluzione culturale: Profili scientifici, filosofici, religiosi.* Milan: Jaca Book, 2002.

Faro, G., *Il lavoro nell'insegnamento del beato Josemaría Escrivá.* Rome: Agrilavoro Edizioni, 2000.

Feuerbach, L., *Principles of the Philosophy of the Future.* Indianapolis, IN: Hackett Publishing Company, 1986.

———, *The Essence of Christianity.* New York: Calvin Blanchard, 1854.

Formigari, L., *Il linguaggio: Storia delle teorie.* Rome and Bari: Laterza, 2001.

Frankl, V. E., *Alla ricerca di un significato nella vita.* Milan: Mursia, 1990.

———, *Homo patiens.* Brezzo di Bedero: Salcom, 1979.

———, *Man's Search for Meaning.* Boston: Beacon Press, 2006.

———, *Teoría e terapia delle nevrosi.* Brescia: Morcelliana, 2001.

———, *Una co-esistenza aperta al logos, "Attualità in logoterapia,"* 1, 53–62. 1999.

Gadamer, H. G., *"Die Kontinuität der Geschichte und der Augenblick der Existenz,"* in *Gesammelte Werke,* Vol. II, 154. Tübingen: J. C. B. Mohr, 1987–1995.

———, *"Kausalität in der Geschichte?"* in *Gesammelte Werke,* Vol. IV, 113. Tübingen: J. C. B. Mohr, 1987–1995.

———, *Truth and Method.* London and New York: Continuum, 2006.

García Cuadrado, J. A., *Antropología filosófica: Una introducción a la Filosofía del Hombre.* Pamplona: Eunsa, 2001.

García de Haro, R., *L'agire morale e le virtù.* Milan: Ares, 1988.

Gehlen, A., *Man: His Nature and Place in the World.* New York: Columbia University Press, 1988.

Gevaert, J., *Il problema dell'uomo: Introduzione all'antropología filosófica.* Torino and Leumann: Elle Di Ci, 1989.

Gilson, É., *The Spirit of Mediæval Philosophy.* New York: Charles Scribner's Sons, 1940.

Gray, P., *Psicologia.* Bologna: Zanichelli, 1997.

Gregory of Nyssa, *The Life of Moses.* New York—Mahwah, NJ / Paulist Press, 1978.

———, *Homilies on Ecclesiastes.* Berlin—New York: W. de Gruyter, 1993.

Guardini, R., *"Conosce l'uomo chi ha conoscenza di Dio,"* in *Accettare se stessi,* 35–72. Brescia: Morcelliana, 1992.

———, *La fine dell'epoca moderna: Il potere.* Brescia: Morcelliana, 1984.

———, *Freedom, Grace, and Destiny: Three Chapters in the Interpretation of Existence.* Chicago: Henry Regnery Company, 1965.

———, *Persona e libertà: Saggi di fondazione della teoria pedagogica.* Brescia: La Scuola, 1987.

Hegel, G. W. F., "Philosophy of Mind," in *Encyclopedia of the Philosophical Sciences.* Oxford: Clarendon Press, 1894.

Heidegger, M., "The Thing," in *Poetry, Language, Thought*, 176. New York: HarperCollins, 2001.

————, *Being and Time*. New York and Evanston, IL: Harper & Row, 1962.

————, *On the Way to Language*. London and New York: Harper & Row, 1971.

————, "What Is Metaphysics?" in *Basic Writings*, 100–106. San Francisco: Harper One, 1993.

Henry, J., *Culture Against Man*. New York: Knopf, 1963.

Heschel, A. J., *Man's Search for God*. New York: Scribner, 1954.

Husserl, E., *Cartesian Meditations: An Introduction to Phenomenology*. New York: Springer, 1977.

————, *Ideas Pertaining to a Pure Phenomenology and to a Phenomenological Philosophy*. The Hague and Boston: Kluwer Academic Publishers, 1989.

Illanes, J. L., "Lavoro, carità, giustizia," in *Santità e mondo*. Vatican City: Libreria Editrice Vaticana, 1994.

————, *The Sanctification of Work*. New York: Scepter, 2003.

Itard, J. M., *The Wild Boy of Aveyron*. Norwalk, CT: Appleton & Lange, 1962.

Jiménez Vargas, J., and A. Polaino-Llorente, *Neurofisiología psicológica fundamental*. Barcelona: Editorial Científico-Médica, 1983.

John Damascene, *Writings*. Washington, D.C.: The Catholic University of America Press, 1970.

John Paul II, encyclical letter *Fides et Ratio*. Vatican City: Libreria Editrice Vaticana, 1998.

————, encyclical letter *Laborem Exercens*. Vatican City: Libreria Editrice Vaticana, 1981.

————, *Insegnamenti*, Vol. VIII. Vatican City: Libreria Editrice Vaticana, 1986.

————, *Man and Woman He Created Them: A Theology of the Body*. Boston, MA: Pauline Books and Media, 2006.

Jolivet, R., *Trattato di filosofia*, Vol. II: *Psicologia*. Brescia: Morcelliana, 1958.

Kant, I., *Critique of Practical Reason*. Mineola, NY: Dover Publications, 2004.

————, *Fondazione della metafisica dei costumi*. Milan: Rusconi, 1994.

Kierkegaard, S., *Diario (1847–1848)*. Brescia: Morcelliana, 1980.

————, *Diario (1850)*. Brescia: Morcelliana, 1981.

————, *Postilla conclusiva non scientifica alle "Briciole di filosofia."* Bologna: Zanichelli, 1962.

Kirk, G. S., J. E. Raven, and M. Schofield, *The Presocratic Philosophers: A Critical History with a Selection of Texts*. Cambridge, MA: Harvard University Press, 1983.

Laín Entralgo, P., *La espera y la esperanza: Historia y teoría del esperar humano*. Madrid: Alianza, 1984.

————, *Sobre la amistad*. Madrid: Espasa and Calpe, 1986.

Lambertino, A., "Aspetti della teoria freudiana dell'uomo," in I. Yarza (ed.), *Immagini dell'uomo: Percorsi antropologici nella filosofia moderna*, 63–76. Rome: Armando, 1997.

————, *Max Scheler: Fondazione fenomenologica dell'ética dei valori*. Florence: La Nuova Italia, 1996.

Lasch, C., *The Culture of Narcissism: American Life in An Age of Diminishing Expectations*. New York and London: W.W. Norton & Co., 1991.

Lersch, P., *Der Aufbau des Charakters*. Leipzig: J.A. Barth, 1938.

Lévinas, E., *Humanism of the Other*. Chicago: University of Illinois Press, 2003.

Lévi-Strauss, C., *Structural Anthropology*. New York: Basic Books, 1974.

Lewis, C. S., *The Abolition of Man*. London: Fount, 1999.

————, *The Four Loves*. London: G. Bles, 1960.

Lombo, J. A., *La persona humana en Tomás de Aquino: Un estudio histórico y sistemático*. Rome: Apollinare Studi, 2001.

Löwith, K., *Meaning in History*. Chicago: University of Chicago Press, 1949.

Malo, A., *Antropologia dell'affettività*. Rome: Armando, 1999.

———, *Il senso antropologico dell'azione: Paradigmi e prospettive*. Rome: Armando, 2004.

———, *"La libertà nell'atto umano: La tendenzialità dell'uomo come espressione di libertà,"* in I. Yarza (ed.), *Le dimensioni della libertà nel dibattito scientifico e filosofico*, 75–76. Rome: Armando, 1995.

Marcel, G., *Être et avoir*. Paris: Aubier-Montaigne, 1935.

———, *Homo Viator: Introduction to the Metaphysic of Hope*. Gloucester, MA: Peter Smith, 1978.

Marx, K., *"Critica dell'economia politica,"* in *Le opere*. Rome: Editori Riuniti, 1966.

———, *"Thesen über Feuerbach,"* in *Ausgewählte Schriften in zwei Bänden*. Berlin: Dietz Verlag, 1972.

———, *Economic and Philosophic Manuscripts of 1844*. Moscow: Progress Publishers, 1959.

Melendo, T., *La dignidad del trabajo*. Madrid: Rialp, 1992.

Metz, J. B., *"Tra la memoria e l'oblio: La Shoah nell'epoca dell'amnesia culturale,"* in E. Boccarini and L. Thorson (eds.), *Il bene e il male dopo Auschwitz: Implicazioni etico-teologiche per l'oggi*, 53–55. Milan: Paoline, 1998.

Milano, A., *"La Trinità dei teologi e dei filosofi: L'intelligenza della persona in Dio,"* in *Persona e personalismi*, 56–61. Naples: Dehoniane, 1987.

Millán-Puelles, A., *Economía y libertad*. Madrid: Confederación Española de Cajas de Ahorro, 1974.

———, *La libre afirmación de nuestro ser: Una fundamentación de la ética realista*. Madrid: Rialp, 1994.

Mondin, B., *L'uomo: chi è: Elementi di antropologia filosofica*. Milan: Massimo, 1989.

———, *Philosophical Anthropology: Man: An Impossible Project?* Rome and Bangalore: Urbaniana University Press, 1985.

Mounier, E., *Personalism*. New York: Routledge & Paul, 1970.

Movia, G., *"Introduction"* to Aristotle, *L'anima*, 21. Milan: Bompiani, 2001.

Nannini, S., *"Mente e corpo nel dibattito contemporaneo,"* in *L'anima*, 36–37. Milan: Mondadori, 2004.

Negri, A., *Filosofia del lavoro: Storia antologica*, Vol. I: *Dalle civiltà orientali al pensiero cristiano*. Milan: Marzorati, 1980.

Nicolosi, J., and L. A. Nicolosi, *A Parent's Guide to Preventing Homosexuality*. Downers Grove, IL: InterVarsity Press, 2002.

Ovid, *Metamorphoses*, Books 6–10. Norman, OK: University of Oklahoma Press, 1972.

Palumbieri, S., *L'uomo, questa meraviglia: Antropologia filosofica I: Trattato sulla costituzione antropologica*. Rome: Urbaniana University Press, 1999.

———, *L'uomo, questo paradosso: Antropologia filosofica II: Trattato sulla con-centrazione e condizione antropologica*. Rome: Urbaniana University Press, 2000.

Papousek, M., H. Papousek, and M. Bornstein, *"The Naturalistic Vocal Environment of Young Infants: On the Significance of Homogeneity and Variability in Parental Speech,"* in T. Field and N. Fox (eds.), *Social Perception in Infants*, 269–297. Norwood, NJ: Allen Publishing Corp., 1985.

Pareyson, L., *Dostoevskij: Filosofia, romanzo ed esperienza religiosa*. Torino: Einaudi, 1993.

———, *Esistenza e persona*. Genoa: Il Melangolo, 1985.

———, *Essere e libertà: Il principio e la dialettica*, *"Annuario filosófico,"* 10. 1994.

———, *Estetica: Teoria della formatività*. Florence: Sansoni, 1974.

———, *Kierkegaard e Pascal*. Milan: Mursia, 1998.

Pascal, B., *Pensées*. Paris: Cerf, 1982.

Pieper, J., *Hope and History: Five Salzburg Lectures*. San Francisco: Ignatius Press, 1994.

————, *Über die Hoffnung*. Leipzig: Jakob Hegner, 1935.

————, *Was heißt philosophieren?* Olten: Hegner, 1948.

————, *Zustimmung zur Welt: Eine Theorie des Festes*. Munich: Kösel-Verlag, 1964.

Pieretti, A., "*Interiorità e intenzionalità: La dignità del finito*," in *Ripensare Agostino: Interiorità e intenzionalità*, 99–120. Rome: Institutum Patristicum Augustinianum, 1993.

Pinillos, J.L., *Principios de psicología*. Madrid: Alianza, 1988.

Plato, *Laws*. London—Cambridge, MA: Harvard University Press/W. Heinemann, 1961.

————, *Phaedo*. Oxford: Clarendon Press, 1983.

————, *Republic*. London: Oxford University Press, 1970.

————, *Lysis; Symposium; Gorgias*. London—Cambridge, MA: W. Heinemann, 1961.

————, *Timaeus*. Rockville, MD: Serenity Publishers, 2009.

Plotinus, *Enneads*. Cambridge, MA: Harvard University Press, 1995.

Pohlenz, M., *Freedom in Greek Life and Thought: The History of an Ideal*. Dordrecht: Kluwer Academic Publishers, 1966.

Polaino-Lorente, A., *Amore coniugale e maturità personale: Fattori psicologici e psicopatologici*. Cinisello Balsamo: Paoline, 1994.

Polo, L., *Quién es el hombre: Un espíritu en el tiempo*. Madrid: Rialp, 1998.

Popper, K.R., *The Open Universe: An Argument for Indeterminism*. London: Hutchinson, 1982.

Popper, K.R., and J.C. Eccles, *The Self and Its Brain*. New York: Routledge, 1984.

Poltawska, W., "*Il celibato sacerdotale alla luce della medicina e della psicologia*," in *Solo per amore: Riflessioni sul celibato sacerdotale*. Cinisello Balsamo: Paoline, 1993.

Ratzinger, J., *In the Beginning… A Catholic Understanding of Creation and the Fall*. Edinburgh: T. & T. Clark, 1995.

Reale, G., *Introduzione a Aristotele*. Rome and Bari: Laterza, 2002.

————, "*Libertà*," in *Storia della filosofia antica*, Vol. V, 152–155. Milan: Vita e Pensiero, 1980.

————, *Storia della filosofia antica*, Vol. II. Milan: Vita e Pensiero, 1991.

Reale, G., and D. Antiseri, *Il pensiero occidentale dalle origini ad oggi*, Vol. I. Brescia: La Scuola, 1985.

Rhonheimer, M., *La prospettiva della morale: Fondamenti dell'ética filosofica*. Rome: Armando, 2006.

————, *The Perspective of Morality: Philosophical Foundations of Thomistic Virtue Ethics*. Washington, D.C.: The Catholic University of America Press, 2011.

Riccobono, S., *Lineamenti della storia delle fonti e del diritto romano*. Milan: Giuffrè, 1949.

Richard of Saint Victor, *On the Trinity*. Eugene, OR: Wipf & Stock Publishers, 2011.

————, *Selected Writings on Contemplation*. London: Faber & Faber, 1957.

Ricoeur, P., *Lectures 2: La contrée des philosophes*. Paris: Seuil, 1992.

Rigobello, A., *L'estraneità interiore*. Rome: Studium, 2001.

Rodríguez Luño, A., *Etica*. Florence: Le Monnier, 1992.

————, *La scelta etica: Il rapporto fra libertà e virtù*. Milan: Ares, 1988.

Rodríguez Quiroga, F., *La dimensión afectiva de la vida*. Pamplona: Cuadernos de Anuario Filosófico, 2001.

Rojas, E., *Una teoria della felicità*. Cinisello Balsamo: Paoline, 1989.

Russo, M.T., *Corpo, salute, cura: Linee di antropologia biomedica*. Soveria Mannelli: Rubbettino, 2004.

————, *La ferita di Chirone: Itinerari di antropologia ed etica in medicina*. Milan: Vita e Pensiero, 2006.

Sabuy Sabangu, P., *La question du dualisme anthropologique: Une analyse d'après Robert Spaemann, "Acta Philosophica,"* II / 9, 241–265. 2000.

———, *Persona, natura e ragione: Robert Spaemann e la dialettica del naturalismo e dello spiritualismo.* Rome: Armando, 2005.

Sanguineti, J.J., *Filosofia della mente e scienza cognitiva, "Acta Philosophica,"* II / 14, 343–348. 2005.

———, *Filosofia della mente: Una prospettiva ontologica e antropologica.* Rome: Edizioni Università della Santa Croce, 2007.

———, *Introduzione alla gnoseologia.* Florence: Le Monnier, 2003.

———, *L'umanesimo del lavoro nel Beato Josemaría Escrivá: Riflessioni filosofiche, "Acta Philosophica,"* II / 1, 264–278. 1992.

———, *Operazioni cognitive: un approccio ontologico al problema mente-cervello, "Acta Philosophica,"* II / 14, 233–258. 2005.

———, *Scienza aristotelica e scienza moderna.* Rome: Armando, 1992.

Scheler, M., *"Die Stellung des Menschen in Kosmos,"* in *Gesammelte Werke,* 44. Bern: A. Francke, 1976.

———, *Formalism in Ethics and Nonformal Ethics of Values.* Evanston, IL: Northwestern University Press, 1973.

Sciacca, M.F., *L'uomo questo "squilibrato."* Palermo: L'Epos, 2000.

———, *Morte e immortalità.* Palermo: L'Epos, 1990.

Searle, J.R., *"L'irriducibilità della coscienza: Intervista a cura di E. Carli,"* in *L'anima,* 105–120. Milan: Mondadori, 2004.

Serretti, M., *Natura della comunione: Saggio sulla relazione.* Soveria Mannelli: Rubbettino, 1999.

Singer, I.B., *A Day of Pleasure: Stories of a Boy Growing Up In Warsaw.* New York: Farrar, Straus, and Giroux, 1986.

Spaemann, R., *"Essere ed essere divenuto: Che cosa spiega la teoria dell'evoluzione?"* in *Natura e ragione: Saggi di antropología,* 41–65. Rome: Edizioni Università della Santa Croce, 2006.

———, *Basic Moral Concepts.* London and New York: Routledge, 1989.

———, *Persons: The Difference Between "Someone" and "Something."* Oxford: Oxford University Press, 2006.

Talamanca, M., *Lineamenti di storia del diritto romano.* Milan: Giuffrè, 1989.

Taylor, C., *Sources of the Self.* Cambridge, MA: Harvard University Press, 1994.

———, *The Ethics of Authenticity.* Cambridge, MA: Harvard University Press, 1992.

Thomas Aquinas, *Commentary on Aristotle's* De Anima. Notre Dame, IN: Dumb Ox Books, 1994

———, *On Evil.* Notre Dame, IN: University of Notre Dame Press, 1995.

———, *On Spiritual Creatures.* Milwaukee: Marquette University Press, 1949.

———, *Questions on the Soul.* Milwaukee: Marquette University Press, 1984.

———, *Scriptum super libros Sententiarum.* Paris: P. Lethielleux, 1929.

———, *Summa Contra Gentiles.* Notre Dame, IN—London: University of Notre Dame Press, 1975.

———, *Summa Theologiæ.* London—New York: Blackfriars Publications / Eyre and Spottiswoode / McGraw-Hill Book Company, 1964.

———, *The Power of God.* New York—Oxford: Oxford University Press, 2012.

———, *Truth.* Eugene, OR: Wipf & Stock Publishers, 2008.

Thompson, J.B., *The Media and Modernity: A Social Theory of the Media.* Stanford, CA: Stanford University Press, 1995.

Tolstoy, L., *The Death of Ivan Ilych and Other Stories.* New York: Barnes & Noble, 2004.

Trapè, A., *"Introduzione: Teologia,"* in Augustine, *La Trinità.*
	Vol. IV, XXXVI–XXXVII, LXII–LXIII. Rome: Città Nuova, 1987.

Tullio-Altan, C., *Manuale di antropologia culturale: Storia e metodo.* Milan: Bompiani, 1998.

Valverde, C., *Antropología filosófica.* Valencia: Edicep C.B., 2000.

Van den Aardweg, G.J.M., *Homosexuality and Hope: A Psychologist Talks About Treatment and Change.* Ann Arbor, MI: Servant Books, 1985.

————, *The Battle for Normality: A Guide for (Self-) Therapy for Homosexuality.* San Francisco: Ignatius Press, 1997.

Vanni Rovighi, S., *Uomo e natura: Appunti per una antropologia filosofica.* Milan: Vita e Pensiero, 1980.

Vergnières, S., *Éthique et politique chez Aristote: Physis, Éthos, Nomos.* Paris: PUF, 1995.

Vernaux, R., *Psicologia: Filosofia dell'uomo.* Brescia: Paideia, 1966.

Vicente Arregui, J., and J. Choza, *Filosofía del hombre: Una antropología de la intimidad.* Madrid: Rialp, 1991.

Villanueva, J., *Le spiegazioni scientifiche dell'evoluzione, "Acta Philosophica,"* 1/8, 135–149. 1999.

————, *Intorno al* body-mind problem, *"Acta Philosophica,"* 1/3, 135–143. 1994.

Von Humboldt, W., *On Language.* Cambridge, MA: Harvard University Press, 1999.

Wojtyła, K., *"The Acting Person,"* in *The Yearbook of Phenomenological Research 10.* Dordrecht: D. Reidel, 1979.

————, *Love and Responsibility.* San Francisco: Ignatius Press, 1993.

————, *Perché l'uomo: Scritti inediti di antropologia e filosofia.* Milan: Arnoldo Mondadori, 1995.

————, *The Acting Person.* Dordrecht: D. Reidel Publishing Company, 1979.

————, *Valutazioni sulla possibilità di costruire l'etica cristiana sulle basi del sistema di Max Scheler.* Rome: Logos, 1980.

Yepes, R., *"La región de lo lúdico: Reflexión sobre el fin y la forma del juego,"* in *Cuadernos de Anuario Filosófico 30,* 9. Pamplona: Serie Universitaria, 1996.

————, *Fundamentos de antropología: Un ideal de la excelencia humana.* Pamplona: Eunsa, 1996.

————, *La persona come fuente de autenticidad, "Acta Philosophica,"* 1/6, 83–100. 1997.

INDEX OF AUTHORS

SUBJECT INDEX